Aruna Asaf Ali

The Dynamic Secular Leader

Aruna Asaf Ali

The Dynamic Secular Leader

Dr. Shiv Gajrani
Dr. S. Ram

Commonwealth

Aruna Asaf Ali

Edition : 2027

ISBN 978-81-311-0363-0

Published by :
COMMONWEALTH PUBLISHERS (P) LTD.
4831/24, Govind Lane,
Ansari Road, Darya Ganj,
New Delhi - 110002
Ph. : 23272541, 23242541
e-mail : commonwealthpublishers2016@gmail.com

Distributed by :
ARJUN PUBLISHING HOUSE
4831/24, Govind Lane,
Ansari Road, Darya Ganj,
New Delhi - 110002
Ph. : 23272541, 23242541
e-mail : arjunbooks2001@gmail.com

Laser Typesetting by :
Dimple Computers
Delhi

Printed at :
Milan Enterprises
Delhi

Preface

Aruna Asaf Ali was born as Aruna Ganguly on July 16, 1908 at Kalka (Haryana) in an orthodox Hindu Bengali family. She played a leading role during Quit India Movement; elected as Delhi's first Mayor; awarded the Lenin Prize for peace in 1975 and the Jawahar Lal Nehru award for International understanding for 1991; honoured with Bharat Ratna in 1998.

She married Asaf Ali in 1928 who was deeply involved with freedom struggle, after marriage Aruna Asaf Ali too plunged into it. Her first major political action was during the Salt Satyagraha in 1930, when she addressed public meetings and led processions. British Government charged her for being a "vagrant" and sentenced her to one year's imprisonment. She was arrested again in 1932 and put in Tihar Jail. In Tihar Jail she went on a hunger strike against the treatment meted out to political prisoners.

In 1942, she attended the Bombay Congress Session with her husband, where the historic Quit India resolution was passed on 8th August. When the Congress leaders were arrested on the day after this resolution was passed, Aruna presided over the flag-hoisting ceremony at Gowalia Tank Maidan in Bombay.

At the time of independence Aruna Asaf Ali was a member of the Congress Socialist Party, which until then had been part of the Congress framework. In 1948, however, the socialists, including Aruna, formed a socialist party of their own. In 1955, this group merged with Communist Party of India and she became a member of its Central committee and a Vice President of the All India Trade Union Congress. In 1958, she left the Communist Party of India and was elected Delhi's first Mayor. She rejoined the Congress party in 1964 but ceased to play any active part in politics.

Authors

Contents

1

Early Career

Aruna was born a Bramahcharya family of Bengal. Her father Mr. Ganguli was a very intelligent man but he being a rolling stone failed to gather any moss. Her mother, the daughter of a Missionary was also a Bramahcharyist. She was a very quiet, affectionate and a homely woman. After marriage Mr. and Mrs. Ganguli did not remain for long in Bengal. They spent most of the years at Kalka where Mr. Ganguli was in charge of the Kalka refreshment room. Aruna the eldest child of the family of two girls and three boys was unassuming though obstinate as a child. Even in her childhood she loved to command. Her religious interest was aroused when at seven she went to visit some of her friends. To her, the offering of prayers to some Mysterious and Invisible Being called God was quite a novel experience. It was her first introduction to this Mysterious Being and she was eager to know more about Him.

Aruna and her younger sister, Purnima, received their early education in the Convent of the Sacred Heart at Lahore where their father was at that time working as a journalist. She almost always topped the list in her class. "Irene" as she was known in school soon became quite a favourite of the Mother Superior. Young Aruna was so much taken up by the Roman Catholic religion and the secluded life of the nuns that she herself began to think seriously of renouncing the world and adopting the black veil and the cross, taking the severe vows of celibacy, obedience and poverty and spending the rest of her life behind the formidable Convent walls.

She spent many a sleepless night not knowing what decision to make. Finally, she made up her mind to become a nun but when she broke the news to her parents they were shocked and scandalized. After giving her a sound scolding they had her removed from the Catholic atmosphere which in her parents, opinion had filled Aruna's little head with unbecoming and impractical ideas, and sent her to a Protestant school at Nainital where Mr. Ganguli had by that time opened a hotel. Aruna thus finished her education at Nainital.

Aruna grew up into a charming young woman. She was small and delicate with an olive complexion, small, black, deep-set eyes, and black, wavy, dishevelled hair which unlike other Bengalee girls was short and which to this day she has never been able to keep tidy. She even finds it difficult to keep the pulla of her saree on her head. Wearing pretty clothes was her weakness. Her taste in choice of her clothes was most unique.

'In spite of her wearing pretty clothes and her sense of cleanliness she is inclined to be careless about the way she dresses. Her carelessness indress, however, gives her a charming neglige appearance which only adds to her attraction and her exquisite personality. Being of a quiet temperament, she likes to be left alone. Like all solitude loving people she is a great lover of books. Books have always been her companions. Her collection includes classics, poetry, fiction, philosophy and politics. Her fine and convincing manner of speech is enough to captivate anyone. Even those who may differ in their opinion or disagree with her point of view like to listen to her attentively. Strong socialistminded Aruna talks to any and everybody in her usual pleasant style.'

The growing Aruna was a growing anxiety to her parents. Like all old fashioned Indian parents, they thought that it was high time they found a husband for their daughter. But Aruna, the born rebel was not going to take things lying down. Her English education had filled her receptive mind with Western ideas and she was not the one to accept the husband chosen by her parents with philosophic resignation to fate, natural to her Eastern sisters. She left her home to earn her own living. She went to Calcutta and started teaching at the Gokhale Memorial School for Girls.

A great change in her life came when she went to spend a part of her Summer vocation at Allahabad with her sister Purnima who had been married to a Bengalee gentleman called Banerjee. It was here that she met Asaf Ali. This young barrister with a flourishing practice in Delhi had then returned from Calcutta after attending a meeting of the Muslim League. At Allahabad, he intended staying for a short time with his very old friends the Benerjees. Asaf Ali was quite a well-known figure even in those days. He had courted imprisonment in the days of non-co-operation in 1920 and was respected by all. His slow manner of speech, his Oscanian accent and his smart suit tailored by Asquith and Lord attracted Aruna. Besides, he like her was interested in English Literature. Both had many a drawing room discussion on poets and authors. Little did Aruna guess at that time that she was slowly drifting into the arms of matrimony. These literary discussions brought the two young people close together and the result was a proposal of marriage from Asaf Ali and the acceptance by Aruna. As expected, Aruna's parents did not approve of this match. First of all there was the most important point—religion. He was a follower of Muhammad while she was a Hindu. Then there was a vast difference in their ages.

He was forty-one while she only eighteen. Once again Aruna had to stand up against her parents and once again she succeeded in having her way. In spite of all obstructions the couple who found love, agreement and perfect harmony in their hearts was joined in matrimony. They had a quiet wedding only two relatives of Aruna and a few common friends being present at the marriage ceremony. This inter-provincial and inter-communal marriage proved a great success. Aruna had made a wise choice indeed. She found the ideal man of Asaf Ali, as she herself tells us, "no husband could be more generous and liberal than Asaf Ali".

After marriage Mr. and Mrs. Asaf Ali shifted to Delhi. Aruna took a great interest in her new home and decorated it most tastefully. Asaf Ali who was a very popular figure in the society proudly introduced his Anglicised wife to his wide circle of friends. Aruna proved an excellent hostess and always appeared happy and blooming with life. She liked the social life she led.

Asaf Ali in his spare time used to write poetry in Urdu on his charming wife. He felt rather disappointed because Aruna, who had only a limited knowledge of Urdu couldn't appreciate her husband's poetry. Dr. Farid Ansari often teased her by saying "Bhabhi, when will you learn to speak Urdu? Asaf Ali is writing so many poems on you that there is every likelihood of an ink famine. You, however, cannot understand his master-pieces". After being teased constantly thus, Aruna at last made up her mind to learn Urdu and she did with the help of her affectionate mother-in-law.

In the early days of her married life, Aruna was not at all interested in Indian politics. In fact, she had no sympathy whatsoever, with Indian aspirations. Her attitude towards Khaddarites was a mixture of ridicule and sneer But when Gandhiji launched his salt tax campaign Aruna naturally drifted into the world of politics. Asaf Ali who had taken an active part in the Satyagraha was arrested. His arrest aroused the political instinct latent in her and she started her political career by making a fiery speech about the origin and significance of the rebellion of 1857. The Chief Commissioner of Delhi thought that he would scare this new comer in politics away by prosecuting her for being a vagrant, having no place of residence and ostensible means of livelihood and by ordering her to furnish a security for good behaviour. As the young revolutionary refused to grant a security she was arrested and sent to Lahore Jail for a year's imprisonment. After a few months when under the Gandhi-Irvin Pact all the political prisoners were released the government decided to detain Aruna. When Aruna's prison mates heard this, they refused to leave the jail, until Aruna was set free. The Superintendent of the prison was in a dilemma. He tried to argue with the ladies for about fourteen hours but all in vain.

The women remained in their resolve. It was only when Mahatma Gandhi and Dr. Ansari intervened and sent telegrams asking them not to insist that they left the jail. Aruna's detention caused an agitation all over India. Finally the Government had to give in to the public. On being released, Aruna was given an enthusiastic reception by a large number of her friends including Khan Abdul Gaffar Khan outside the jail premises. One thing that amused and puzzled Aruna was the name of the jail. It was called Lahore Female Jail. Aruna remarked "why is this jail called a female jail? Why should it not be called a women's jail? Surely jail has no gender." In 1932 movement Aruna was again imprisoned and was ordered to pay a fine of Rs. 200. She refused to pay the fine and the police instead of getting the money from her husband walked away with some of her most expensive sarees which had been gifts from Asaf Ali. In those days political prisoners in Delhi District jail had received a rough and a callous treatment. As a protest, bold Aruna went on hunger strike. Although she fell ill she kept up her fast until the jail authorities agreed to the demands of the political detenus.

When the term of her imprisonment expired Aruna returned to Delhi and for the next ten years took no part in politics. She contented herself by leading a busy social life once again.

Asaf Ali who devoted most of his time to politics often had a number of friends visiting him while Aruna acted the charming hostess. But it was not very long before Aruna's dynamic personality compelled her to do something for her country. Although she had courted imprisonment twice mainly with the intention of keeping pace with her husband and her sense of loyalty to the Congress, she was by no means a political worker. Merely taking part in the annual session of the All India Women's Conference did not satisfy her desire, but she did not know in what way she could help the Indians to win their freedom.

Indian politics in those days were very confusing. It was not an easy matter for her to decide whether to follow Gandhism or Socialism. She spent some of her leisure time in making a deep study of politics and tried to form her own ideas about setting India free. Somehow, Socialistic ideas began to enter her head, she often said "There are a lot of things we have got to break. A lot of things that were taken for granted." By her entry into a Muslim family, she understood Muslim problems thoroughly well. She felt that the Congress many a time irritated the Muslims without being conscious of the fact. The Vidya Mandir Scheme she thought was the case of adding fuel to the fire. The very name was objectionable and irritating. Her idea was that the Mogul period was an ideal period and those sentiments ought to be reawakened and revived with great intensity. She was of the opinion that not Ram Raj but the reign of Akbar and the Mogul period should be our guides. Urdu script, she thought should have an equal place with the Hindi script. "The trouble is," she would say, "nationalism is such a holy concept to Indians that they instinctively express their feelings towards it in religious symbolism being the highest thing they know. Women go to jail as they would go to the temple. Inevitable, the mode of thought is Hindu. They call on the name of God in their songs and so on.

If we are to appeal to the Muslim masses, they must be approached in the idiom they will understand and we shall alienate them if we thoughtlessly go on like this. I know no offence is meant, but the point is that offence is taken." Thus she taxed her little brain trying to find a way out. It was only when she came in contact with the people like Jai Prakash Narayan, Achyut Patwardhan and Ram Manohar Lohia that could she make up her mind and say "towards Socialism I shall march."

In 1940 Gandhiji launched his Civil Disobedience Movement as a protest against the way India had been dragged into the war. The Mahatma was so keen to keep this Satyagraha pure and undefiled by the touch of those who believe in violence that only those who believed cent per cent in the Gandhian Constructive programme of the Congress were chosen. Mr. Gandhi himself selected the Satyagrahis. Mrs. Asaf Ali's name was also on the list. Little did Gandhiji guess at that time that this young follower of his would one day defy his non-violent creed and lead the British Government to a pretty dance. By the end of the year Aruna was arrested in Delhi and sent to Lahore Jail. To her surprise it was still called the Lahore Female jail! The Jail is now placated "Lahore Women's Jail"—thanks to Aruna.

She tried to make them happy by giving them small things such as a comb or a skein of embroidery silk. But she was very tactful about the way she gave these presents. She did not let her generosity be mistaken for charity. Whenever there was trouble in the jail, either with the authorities or among the prisoners, Aruna was always ready to take the matter into her own hands and always succeeded in settling whatever the dispute. She held weekly meetings in which she related the news of the week to all the women. She wanted to educate the women who had come to jail. She tried to explain politics to them. This proved quite a difficult task as even some of those Satyagrahis who had a devotion for Mahatmaji, knew hardly anything of politics and nothing at all of the world outside India.

In August 1942 Asaf Ali took his charming wife to Bombay in order to attend the forty-fifth session of the All India Congress Committee. Asaf Ali had by then become a very prominent Congress leader. Aruna was her usual self-pleasant, graceful and social as ever. She was in fact one of the most prominent figures in the pandal that day. On August 9, early in the morning all the important Congress leaders were arrested. When Aruna heard this she rushed to Bori Bunder where a special train was waiting to carry the leaders to an unknown destination. Aruna tried to enter the station but she was stopped by a Police Inspector with "we have no warrants for you." But she insisted upon entering the station in order to see things for herself. The police inspector warned her, "You might be insulted," but Aruna turned a deaf ear to his warning and boldly made her way to the station. There she saw, "every carriage window framed a face known, respected and loved by millions." Gandhiji appeared grim and stern, Jawahar Lal angry—a lost-in-thought look in his eyes.

After the train steamed out of the plâtform Aruna drove back home. Her blood was boiling at the sight she had seen. "Pearl Harbour methods," she said "are anathemic when practised by yellow-skinned Japs. When employed to crush a revolt they signify fore-thought, courageousness and rulership. Entrenched authority—an usurper authority had decided not to allow freedom of movement, speech or action to natives demanding its withdrawal." As for herself she could not decide as to what action she should take. Since the Congress had not chalked out a definite programme she did not know how to implement the Quit India resolution of the Congress. "What should I do?" was what she kept repeating.

Finally she decided to go to the Gwalia Tank Maidan where Maulana Azad was to have performed the flag hoisting ceremony. But Azad was absent. She heard a Police Sergeant giving orders to hail down the flag which was still unfurled. While the volunteers hesitated Aruna, who had been asked to preside over the flag hoisting ceremony declared that the Flag hoisting ceremony would take place as scheduled. As soon as Aruna had hoisted the flag the police released gas so as to scatter the crowd. But the crowd instead formed a procession and marched to the Congress House, mad with rage.

"It was one of the many processions," says Aruna, that defined police lawlessness that day." What pained Aruna was when looking back at the Gwalia Tank Maidan she says, she saw "the white sergeat treatment on the flag that I had unfurled ten minutes, ago." After seeing this humiliating treatment Aruna says "I vowed that I would help to tear up the British rule."

She spent a few days in Bombay, Her dislike for the British rule turned to hatred when she saw the police impliciting a lathi charge on some of the poor innocent people and opening fire on the angry mob. Her feelings of non-violence were changed to the spirit of retaliation.

Aruna went to Delhi knowing fully well that she would be arrested any day. She also realised that her arrest would mean the end of her work with which she had planned to implement the Quit India resolution. Besides, the people who were now deprived of their leaders needed guidance, so she decided to go underground. During her short stay in Delhi she tried to organise a powerful resistance movement among the Congress workers who were still out of jail. She delivered a message of hope and put new life in the students of Delhi.

2

As a Leader

Aruna gave the following message to the people of Delhi. "Freedom is a misunderstood term today. While I feel overwhelmed by the warmth with which the people of Delhi have greeted me I wish them to know that for those who took part in the August rebellion, freedom from the police interference does not mean the return of civil liberties. So long as the leaders of the underground movement are not free the feeling of elation at the removal of restrictions on one individual would be a delusion." With an air of determination she added : "I have returned as a humble solidier of India's freedom. I shall continue to work for the liberation of my country with the same vigour with which I have so far been doing."

On being requested by the public to address a meeting, Aruna once again spoke to vast gathering. Aruna dressed in a blue Khaddar saree started her speech by saying, "before I relate my story I want to tell you that since I set my foot on the soil of Delhi my eyes have been searching for Satyawati. She is not in our midst today. Before you hear my report, you must think of Satyawati, the story of whose bravery, heroism and sacrifice is engraved in the mind of everyone of us." She asked the crowd to shout "Shrimati Satyawati Zindabad." For a moment Aruna could not speak, she felt chocked with tears. "Satyawati, you all must remember", she said, "had no other interest in life but the service of her countrymen." She worked and worked so hard during her life that the strain told on her health, and she became a total wreck. And when she lay on her death-bed her last words and thoughts were concentrated on the freedom of her country.

Though physically she is no more with us, yet her deeds will always be a source of inspiration to us all in our work . . . .her bravely will sustain us in our moments of hesitation and her unquestionable sincerity will serve as a beckoning light on our arduous journey—the journey that will lead us to freedom. About her own story of her underground life she said, "It is a long tale which cannot be told at a public meeting. In a way you know that story, as you have taken a hand in writing it. It is a story that has been written by the people of India. The people of Delhi have played their part in the drama of August, 1942. You know how the people of Delhi reacted to the arrest of our leaders. Nobody who has seen people being shot in the streets of Delhi during those days can forget the scenes when people were fired at in a most cruel and shameless manner. But with great pride I declare, that the people of Delhi gave a good account of themselves and our English rulers got so frightened that they did not stir out in the streets for three weeks. Standing here before you I salute these soldiers, and in a most respectful manner I pay my homage to those martyrs who for the honour of their motherland sacrificed their lives."

Raising her voice Aruna asked "For whom did these brave sons and daughters of India lay their lives? For you and me is the obvious answer. They died so that we may live. And how are we going to honour those who fell in the battle of 1942? Are we just going to be content by raising slogans and putting flowers around their graves? No." Said Aruna in the most emphatic way. "The best way to honour them is to continue the struggle in which they lost their lives."

Referring to her part in the August upheaval Aruna said "In obedience to Gandhiji's command, we raised the banner of open revolt in Delhi. Today, I stand before you as the symbol of those fearless men and women who generated in speed in the giant wheels of Indian Revolution." Continuing Aruna said, "leaders are necessary but leaders are the creation of the people. They cease to be leaders if they cut themselves from the people. The year 1942 has brought about an unprecedented psychological revolution."

Aruna then explained the meaning and purpose of the part played by her. "It was not a game of hide and seek that I played for 40 months." The British Government, she continued, "had made an attack on the great national organisation which could be compared to the happenings at Pearl Harbour. The Government, however, did not correctly assess the strength of the people. They thought an unbridled wave of repression would frighten them, and damp their spirits. But the people of India stood upright and refused to bend the knee before the John Bull who had literally run amuck. As the top leaders of the Congress had been clapped into prison, the people became their own leaders."

"It was in these circumstances," said Aruna "that we took a resolve that as long as there is breath in us, we shall not get ourselves shut up in the prisons of the enemy. It was a grim decision which should not be compared to a game of hide and seek."

The agents of the Government, said Aruna, hunted for them but if the doors of one house were shut against them, the doors of a thousand others were opened to them. Aruna denied the story that she had been going about in a burqa. "How can," she asked, "a soldier do her work in a burqa?"

Aruna paid glowing tributes to those who had given her comrades shelter while putting their own lives in danger. She declared that the people of Bhagalpur, Midnapur, Satara and Assam hills had been very kind to them.

A women's organization in Delhi had arranged a tea party in Aruna's honour but she refused the invitation saying that it was not the time for tea parties. She wanted the women-folk to think of her colleagues who were still underground and help by collecting funds for them.

It might be recalled that in September 1945 when Wavell returned to India after having talks with the Cabinet members in connection with the political situation in India, every one felt optimistic about India's future. Even Maulana Azad in a speech had said that freedom was fast approaching. Aruna who did not even agree with her husband where politics were concerned, criticised Maulana's views saying, "Maulana Sahib who is our respected leader said at this very place that freedom for which they had been aspiring was about to fall in their jholis.

It pains me to enter into an argument with Maulana Sahib, but I respectfully want to say, it is not freedom that falls into a beggar's jholi. We are not prepared to stand before the British Government like beggars. We must think of the martyrs of 1942 and not think in terms of compromise". Aruna even disagreed with the Viceroy's plan that the Executive Council during the period of transit would be so reconstituted as to command the support of the major political parties in India. She expressed her dissatisfaction in the following words. "If this was our objective we could have got it when Cripps came to India in 1942. We need not have kindled the first of 1942 and raised the mighty slogan of Quit India. After raising our life-giving slogan we were not going to our rulers with a bowl in our hands. We will win freedom by our sacrifices."

She did not even agree with Pandit Nehru who had, in some of his latest speeches, said that he wanted to see the tri-coloured flag flying on the Red Fort. She said that she had the greatest respect for Jawahar Lal Nehru but the speeches he had made had pained her. "This Red Fort," said Aruna, "is a constant reminder of our national humiliation. Every stone of this evil and monstrous structure serves us with a daily reminder of humiliation of Bahadur Shah. It was in this building that the last of our independent rulers was presented with the heads of his sons. Could there be a worse and a more heinous example of butchery?"

"Such being the ugly memories of this Red Fort, how can we tolerate even for a second the sight of this murder house where hundreds of our patriots have been done to death?"

Aruna declared that the National Flag should be hoisted, not on the Red Fort but on the Imperial Secretariat where ordinances after ordinances were manufactured in 1942 to suppress the rising of the people of India when their leaders were in Ahmednagar jail.

Concluding she said, "the path we have chosen in a difficult one. It is not a bed of roses all along the road. There are pitfalls whose jealous jaws greedily gape to swallow people alive. Then there are sharp thorns laid by the bureaucracy to prick our naked feet. Then the journey which we have chalked out for ourselves will be a long and an arduous one. It is beset with nerve shaking difficulties. Many of our comrades will get tried and will not be able to keep pace with us. But we should not indulge in recrimination. We should be tolerant to those who in spite of their best efforts, drop out on the way. Everyone will not be in the firing line. But let those who want to kiss the bullets, kiss them. Let those who want to carry the hangman's rope around their necks, as a garland of flowers, have the privilege of wearing it.

We should not drag down those who want to serve India by embracing the ugly shadows of death. It is their right to do it and it is our duty to stand by them. . . . to lighten the burden of their work . . . . to clear them on their way to self immolation. Such are the people who are the pride of India . . . . the truest sons and daughters of their mothers . . . . the joy of this life and the glorious heritage of our ancient civilization."

The villagers of Mehroli, Gheasa and Bhawana in Delhi province had the proud privilege of seeing Aruna during her short visit to these villages. Every man, women and child flocked to greet her. She knew most of them personally because during the Civil Disobedience Movement of 1940, she had often toured these villages. Much as she wanted to spend a few days with them she could not, as she had some important work hanging on her shoulders as Delhi.

Aruna addressed a large gathering of women in Delhi. She related to them how badly the womenfolk were treated by the British Government during the days of August rebellion. Not only the women who took part in the movement, but also the relations of the underground workers were tortured. She paid glowing tributes to those who had stood firm against all odds. Women, she said, must work side by side with men. Women in every land have played the rightful part in the progress of their country. In Russia, thousands of women fought in the front-line trenches and in China they enrolled themselves as guerrillas. "Why should in India, my sisters keep on darning their husbands' socks, or while away their precious time in idle gossip?"

Aruna laid the following four-fold programme before her attentive listeners :

(i) Every woman should enlist as a four anna member of the Congress and organise herself under one flag.

(ii) Every woman should volunteer her full time services to the Congress.

(iii) Every woman should do constructive work as outlined by Mahatma Gandhi.

(iv) Every woman should boycott foreign goods and launch intensive campaign to popularise Swadeshi goods.

Aruna said she wanted them to remember Satyawati, who was the first woman to go to jail for the sake of her country. She said that she regretted that she and her co-workers had failed to collect one lakh of rupees required for the Satyawati Memorial Fund. She reminded the collectors that not a penny from the capitalists was to be accepted for this fund. Satyawati, said Aruna, had worked for the people so the people should contribute towards the building up of the Memorial. "This Memorial will keep her memory green, it will be a source of inspiration to us all and the tale of her sufferings, which this Memorial will always be relating, will sustain us in our exacting struggle to drive away the British from the soil of India—the chaste soil which their guilty feet have long enough desecrated."

Aruna has always been popular with students. When she addressed the students of Delhi they were so much impressed by her speech that after the meeting they not only took a pledge to boycott foreign goods but about five hundred students decided to launch a campaign in every street of Delhi to popularise Indian goods.

She expressed her appreciation on the part the students had played in the August movement. They had, she said, left their schools and colleges and had plunged into the struggle whole-heartedly. She defined the students' role in 1942 as defiant and protesting and not revolutionary. Now was the time for them to organise on a sound revolutionary basis. The organisation of the students would enable them to develop "resisting element" for the next struggle, therefore, absolute efficiency in organisation was essential. The country, she said, wanted a body of trained and disciplined soldiers and not vague agitators.

It may be recalled that when Arun was declared an absconder, her house was attached by the Government and her Baby Austin had been auctioned. It was now announced that her house would be restored and the sale proceeds of the car would be handed over to her.

While addressing a meeting of the mill workers at Delhi Aruna asked them to unite and to stand by the Congress. She paid a tribute to the workers who had played a great part in India's struggle for freedom. She did not blame those workers who had not helped because she knew fully well that the Communists had set them on the wrong tract. "Whenever we called upon the workers to strike, those agents of British Imperialism came forward with their slogans of 'People's war' and tried to break the strikers. It was an unmanly thing on their part to do as we were working from behind the scene and those betrayers of the great national cause were working in the open and could approach you individually. They succeeded in many places to persuade you to resume your work. I, for one, do not blame you but these henchmen of the foreign Government."

3

Gandhiji's Influence

In response to Aruna's telegram Gandhi asked her to see him at Wardha. She left Delhi on February 7, and according to the wishes of the Secretary of Nagpur Congress Committee stopped for some time at Nagpur. She received a hearty welcome at the railway station. Later, she addressed a public meeting where about 30,000 people were present and told them that they should be prepared for the final struggle for freedom and see that their country was free within one year. "The Congress workers must penetrate into the villages to build up unit formations of Indian Naitonal Army. An Azad Hind Government should be established in the villages, on the basis of this constitutional structure. The veterans of Indian National Army should form the nucleus of an Azad Hind Army, establishing contacts with the masses of the people. In India we have to form a real and effective Azad Hind Government to shape our destiny and all those who praised Subhas Chandra Bose ought to work for this purpose zealously."

She added, Gandhiji's constructive programme had not been faithfully and earnestly carried out. If it had, it would have hastened the achievement of their objective of freedom. But people only raised slogans and shirked the responsibility of working. Instead of being ready to make sacrifices they passed their lives in comfort. Referring to the British Government's attitude towards the acts of violence which were being committed against the Britishers she said the Indians would not yield to British threats. She said that Mahatma Gandhi alone could ask for an explanation from those who had diverted from the path of non-violence but no Britisher had the right to talk of non-violence to Indian people.

Concluding Aruna said, "I am going to meet our leader Mahatma Gandhi at Sewagram and discuss with him all the doings of August 1942 movement. We shall also discuss preparation for the next final struggle for India's freedom."

It was after the evening prayers that Aruna met Gandhiji. The scene reminded one of the return of the prodigal son. For more than one hour she related to him all that she had been doing during her underground life. As Gandhiji wanted to have further talks with her he asked her to prolong her stay by two days.

On the following day Aruna addressed a meeting at Wardha. Wardha, it might be mentioned, was the home town of Seth Jamna Lal Bajaj and he had offered the village of Sewagram to Mahatma Gandhi for building his Ashram. Aruna paid growing tributes to the memory of the Seth who had given Gandhiji a chian of his bungalows for Congress work such as, Indian Village Industries, the All India Spinners Association and a host of others. Not only had he given money, said Aruna, but he had even sacrificed his life for the Congress. Many a time he had courted imprisonment and during his last imprisonment he had fallen so ill that even after his release he could not recover. "This princely hearted Seth was a true soldier in the fight for freedom and a was a faithful follower of Mahatma Gandhi who regarded him as one of his trusted colleagues. He was not only the maker of Wardha, but also of modern India."

Turning to Mahatma Gandhi Aruna said : "He is the man who has made women fearless and bold. It is he who has given the women of India an opportunity to play their part in liberating India. He is truly the father of the Indian nation and it is the duty of one and all to march under his banner."

Before leaving Wardha Aruna addressed a large gathering. She spoke to them about the famine which was fast approaching and suggested that the Congress should organise "grain bands" in every village. Continuing she said, "the Quit India demand becomes a live issue again. The impending threat of mass deaths due to food shortage is the result of callous indifference on the part of the ruling power. The Bengal famine taught it nothing. "The stimulated concern of Lord Wavell during the Bengal famine notwithstanding security on a vaste scale looms ahead. Let us not await death with folded hands. Let us tell every peasant that he is the master of his grain and that this alien Government has no right to snatch away his produce."

"We must here and now organize ourselves and create the requisite authority for challenging the right of Lord Wavell's administration to save India." She said "the Congress could, if it wanted; set itself as a parallel authority in the country. By co-opeation with the British Government in such moment of national crisis we merely strengthen its hold."

"Remember the slogan of 1942. 'Fight for food is the fight for freedom.' Not a grain to feed the rulers, not a pie for the British goods."

Cryptically said Aruna, "without food one cannot live to fight, hence people should fight to live."

Aruna, who had become very weak in health instead of taking rest and spending some quiet time with her husband whose health was also deteriorating, felt it her duty to devote whatever time she could spare to her country. She knew the spectre of famine was looming over the face of India, there was unrest among the labourers, then the election campaign on behalf of the Congress had to be conducted. So Aruna, after considering all these points decided to tour the whole of India. Wherever Aruna went she attracted big crowds.

Aruna had a special fascination for the people of Bombay. When on the day of her arrival in the town she was requested for an address she readily agreed. A reception was accorded to her by the Bombay Provincial Congress Committee. She spoke to the crowd for more than one hour. Recalling her underground life Aruna said that they had resolved on the day the Congress Committee adopted the Quit India resolution to continue the struggle for the freedom of the country.

She declared, "even though the Congress might not have officially sponsored the Quit India movement we believed that the Congress had given the call and we readily responded to it." Continuing she said, "we might have faltered on the path and we might have been caught by the police and locked up behind the bars, but the battle for freedom continued. Forty crores of Indians who had risen in revolt were determined to free our country from the fetters of British Imperialism. If our leaders who could guide us in our freedom movement were taken away from the people and locked up inside the calls, the only possible means of continuing the struggle was by some of us going underground. Our only aim was to see the country liberated and the British rule in our country completely liquidated."

Referring to the British Government's move in making an offer of a National Government and a Constituent Assembly, Aruna warned the people that the British Government was preparing a new trap to keep their hold on India in tact. She said that the British Government had realised that they had to change their tactics in dealing with the people of India. It therefore held out this bait to our leaders to bypass the main demand of freedom to this country, "Our leaders think," she said, "that freedom for our country is soon soon coming and the British Government is earnest in granting freedom to our country." Aruna stated that she, however, had no faith in the bonafides of the British Government.

While in Bombay, Aruna was a very busy person. She had to meet her old acquaintances, discuss the future plans of work and the problems facing India with her co-workers, and address various organisations who pressed her for a message. Aruna told the students of Bombay that it was the duty of those who had that political education to impart it to the kisans and workers and thereby make them fit and ready for the contry's fight for freedom. Referring to Pandit Nehru's declaration that preparations of a psychological nature were necessary, she said that even though she agreed with him, she felt that something more in the nature of a positive action was essential. Emphatically she declared, "we have no place today for mere intellectuals. We want practical people who can carry the message of independence throughout the whole length and breadth of the country."

Some students asked Aruna to address them in English because their knowledge of Hindustani was very meagre. Expressing her inability to do so, Aruna said : "Hindustani being our national language is the language which can give weight to our ideal of independence and I have promised Gandhiji that in Hindustani alone shall I address gathering."

The respect the people of India had for Aruna was revealed when the Indian naval ratings went on strike. Their demands which they had placed before their authorities having been refused they stood up in revolt and challenged the British authority to shoot them if they dared. This was the first time that the Indian seamen had revolted against the discriminatory treatment meted out to the Indians in comparison to that of the white-skinned seamen.

The strikers after three days of looting shops, smashing offices and setting fire to military trucks and trains placed their faith and trust in the hands of the Indian leaders, so that something might he done for them. Aruna who was also approached gave them her advice in the following words :

"Almost 15,000 naval ratings of the R.I.N. have struck work and refused to eat canteen food since Sunday evening. Their demands are essentially legitimate. They have insisted that the inequalities in the scale of pay, allowances and food between the R.I.N. and R.N. should cease.

"They have protested against the appointment of British officers and their insulting and unsufferable behaviour towards the Indian personnel in the navy. These service conditions and economic demands are quite naturally unaffected by the high tension political climate of today. At least young Indians in the services are no longer prepared to submit sheepishly to the hectoring and swearing of their British rulers.

"Be that as it may, I earnestly hope that the strikers will not permit unco-ordinated and spontaneous action to mar the otherwise disciplined move they have made for the removal of their grievances. Solidarity and discipline are the first essentials of success in all collective action of this nature. They must formulate their demands precisely and conduct their struggle with dignity. Care should be taken to eschew injury to person or property in this action. The naval ratings must conduct negotiations through their respective ship committees viz., their Central Naval Strike Committee.

"The naval authorities should note that at the instance of the representatives of the strikers I am giving this advise. I am sure that the Congress, and Labour and the Student Organisation of Bombay will extend their moral support to their legitimate demands.

"It is the first occasion when such an overwhelming number of the Indian seamen have undertaken collective action with such effects. Firmness, discipline and unity on the part of the strikers and the pressure of public opinion should result in a successful conclusion of this spontaneous strike."

The strike situation however, worsened. A complete hartal was observed in Bombay and the mill hands of Bombay struck work as a mark of sympathy with the naval ratings. The Bombay police and military had to resort to firing to disperse the violent mobs that paraded the streets. In fact, the whole city of Bombay presented an ugly picture.

Realising that the situation was out of control, Aruna sent a telegram to Pandit Nehru asking him to visit Bombay and thus save the naval strike from heading towards a climax. The telegram ran—"Naval strike tense. Situation serious climaxing to grim close. You alone can control and avoid tragedy. Request your immediate presence in Bombay."

Pandit Nehru at that time was in Garhwal conducting the election campaign and was completely cut off from the newspaper world. It was only when he returned to Allahabad that he learnt about the serious developments in Bombay. He immediately cancelled his election engagements and went straight to Bombay. Aruna in the meantime went to Poona to meet Gandhiji. She had a ninty-minute talk with him about the R. I.N. ratings.

Clement Attlee, the British Prime Minister, broadcast a stern warning to the mutineers to surrender unconditionally. He had further ordered the British warships to proceed to Bombay and bombard the ships under the control of the mutineers if they refused to surrender. But the arrival of the British warships changed the complexion of the situation. So far as the mutineers were concerned they were prepared to die fighting. But knowing too well that the repercussions of this open fight will be terrible and far-reaching in the Indo-British relations they approached Sardar Patel and he gave them the following advice.

"In the present unfortunate circumstances that have developed the advice of the Congress to the R.I.N. ratings is to lay down arms and to go through the formality of a surrender which has been asked for.

"The Congress will do its level best to see that there is no victimisation and the legitimate demands of the naval ratings are accepted as soon as possible. There is considerable tension all over the city and there has been loss of life and property.

"There is also considerable strain, both on the naval ratings as well as on the authorities. While fully appreciating their spirit and courage and also having full sympathy in their present difficulties, the best advice that, Congress can give them, in the present circumstances, is to end the tension immediately. This advice is in the interests of all concerned."

The R.I.N. ratings listened to the advice of the Congress leaders and surrendered unconditionally.

The terrible anarchy that had prevailed in Bombay pained Mahatma Gandhi. For thirty years he had been preaching in non-violence and now he found there were violent tendencies that the minds of people. He expressed his feelings in the following statement.

"I have followed the events now happening in India with painful interest. This mutiny in the navy and what is following is not, in any sense of the term non-violent action.

"Inasmuch a single person is compelled to short Jai Hind or any popular slogan, a nail is driven into the coffin of Swaraj in terms of the dumb millions of India. Destruction of churches and the like is not the way to Swaraj as defined by the Congress. Looting and burning of tramcars and other property, insulting and injuring Europeans, is not non-violence of the Congress type, much less mine, if and in so far as it may be different from the Congress.

"Let the known and unknown leaders of this thoughtless orgy of violence know what they are doing and then follow their bent. Let it not be said that India of the Congress spoke to the world of winning. Swaraj through non-violent action and belied her world in action and that too at the most critical period in her life. "I have deliberately used the adjective thoughtless, for there is such a thing as thoughtful violent action. What I see happening now is not thoughtful. "If the Indian members of the navy know and appreciate the way of non-violent resistance it can be dignified, mainly and wholly effective, if it is corporate. For the individual it always is. Why should they continue to serve if service is humiliating for them or India? Action like this I have called non-violent non-co-operation. As it is, they are setting a bad and unbecoming example for India.

"A combination between Hindus and Muslims and others for the purpose of violent action is unholy and will lead to and probably is a preparation for mutual violence, bad for India and the world.

"The rulers had declared to quite in favour of Indian rule. Let the action be not delayed by a moment because of the exhibition of distressful unrest which has been lying hidden in the breast. Their might is unquestioned. Its use beyond the bare requirements will be unworthy and even wicked if it is made to suppress the people or a portion of them. The latter have been far too long under the foreign rule."

Aruna after reading this, issued a rejoinder refuting Gandhiji's statement and the Mahatma gave the following reply.

"I congratulate Shrimati Aruna Asaf Ali on her courageous refutation of my statement on the happening of Bombay. Except for the fact that she represents not only herself but also a fairly large body of underground workers. I would not have noticed her reputation only because she is a daughter of mine—not less so because not born to me or because she is a rebel.

"I had the pleasure of meeting her on several occasions while she was underground. I admired her bravery, resourcefulness and burning love of the country. But my admiration stopped there. I did not like her being underground. I do not appreciate any underground activity. I know that millions cannot go underground. Millions need not.

"A select few may have the fancy that they will bring Swaraj to millions by secretly direction their activity. Will this not be spon feeding? Only open challenge and open activity is for all to follow. Real Swaraj must be felt by all, man, woman and child. Lobour for that consummation is true revolution. India has become a pattern for all exploited races of the earth because India's has been an open unarmed effort which demands sacrifice from all without inflicting injury on the usurper.

"The Millions in India would not have awakened but for the open unarmed struggle. Every deviation from the straight path has meant a temporary arrest of the revolutionary revolution. I do not read 1942 events as does the brave lady. It was good that the people rose spontaneously. It was bad that some or many resorted to violence. It makes no difference that Shri Kishorelal Mashruwala, Kaka Saheb and other workers, in their impassioned zeal for the moment misinterpreted non-violence. That they did so, only shows how delicate an instrument non-violence is. My analogy is not meant to cast any refection on any parson. Everyone acted as he or she thought best. Spineness in the face of overwhelmingly organized violence would have meant cowardice. I would be weak and wrong if I failed to give my estimate of the doings of 1942.

"Aruna would rather unite Hindus and Muslims at the barricade than on the constitutional front. Even in terms of violence, this is a misleading proposition. If the union at the barricade is honest, there must be union also at the constitutional front. Fighters do not always live at the barricade. They are too wise to commit suicide. The barricade life has always to be followed by the constitutional. That front is not a taboo for ever. Emphatically it betrays want of foresight to disbelieve British declarations and precipitate a quarrel in anticipation. Is the official deputation coming to deceive a great nation? It is neither manly nor womanly to think so. What would be lost by waiting? Let the official deputation prove for the last time that British declarations are unreliable. The nation will gain by trusting. The deceiver loses when there is correct response from deceived.

"Let us face facts. The coming Mission is claimed to be a friendly mission, entertaining the hope that they will discover a constitutional method of delivery. But the problem is knotty, probably the knottiest that has ever confronted statesmen. It is possible that the mission will put forth an insoluble conundrum. So much the worse for them. "If they are intent upon finding an honest way out of the difficulties of their own creation. I have no doubt there is a way. But the nation too has to play the game. If it does, the barricade must be left aside at least for the time being. I appeal to Aruna and her friends to make, wise of the power their bravery and sacrifice has given them. "It is a matter of great relief that the ratings have listened to Sardar Patel's advice to surrender. They have not surrendered their honour. So far as I can see, in resorting to mutiny, they were badly advised.

If it was for grievance, fancied or real, they would have waited for the guidance and intervention of political leaders of their choice.

"If they mutinied for the freedom of India, they were doubly wrong. They could not do so without a call from a prepared revolutionary party. They were thoughtless and ignorant if they believed that by their might, they would deliver India from foreign domination.

"Aruna was right when she said that the fighters this time showed grit as never before. But grit becomes foolhardiness when it is untimely and suicidal as this was.

"She is entitled to say that the people 'are not interested in the ethics of violence or non-violence but the people are very much interested in knowing the way which will bring freedom to the masses—violence or non-violence.'

"The people have, however, imperfectly, hitherto gone the way of non-violence. Aruna and her comrades have to ask themselves everytime whether the non-violent way has or has not raised India from her slumber of ages and created in them a yearning, very vague perhaps, for Swaraj. There is, in my opinion, only one answer.

"There are other passages in Shrimati Aruna's statement which, as it appears to me, betray confusion of thought. But their treatment can wait.

"Needless to say that I have dealt with the message believing it to represent her opinion. If it does not, I apologise to her in advance. My argument, however, is not affected, even if it is found that the reporter has not correctly interpreted her's. For my argument is, after all, impersonal and directed only to the portions which are calculated to mislead the public, irrespective of their authorship."

The situation in Bombay having eased as a result of the unconditional surrender by the R.I.N. ratings. Aruna decided to leave for Calcutta as she had promised the people of Bengal that she would revisit their province as soon as she was free.

At the Howrah Railway Station Aruna was garlanded on behalf of the B.P.C.C., B.P.S.C. Socialist Association, E.I.

Railwaymen Mazdoor Union, Rubber Factory Workers Union and Chatkal Mazdoor Union. From the station she drove direct to Mr. Manbhai Bhimani's residence to condole with Mr. Bhimani's old parents who were in bereavement owing to the death of their son-in-law.

On the following day Aruna addressed a mammoth meeting of railway workers at the Mogul Bagan Maidan which was presided by Professor Humayun Kabir.

Aruna in the course of her speech told them that strike was indeed a very effective weapon in the hands of the railway workers who were discontented because their legitimate demands had not been fulfilled. But that in order to win their battle they needed unity, solidarity and organization.

Aruna warned them that the British Government would not hesitate to use force on the railway workers to break their morale. But no matter what came from them it was for the railwaymen to demonstrate through their solidarity, organization and iron-determination that they were not to surrender until their cause triumphed.

She appealed to the railway workers to place their grievances before the Congress Working Committee prior to resorting to hartal just as the Bombay ratings had done.

In the end Aruna called upon the workers to stand by the Congress and to strengthen the great patriotic organisation.

Aruna has originally planned to tour Bengal and Assam extensively, but on receiving a telegram from Maulana Azad asking her to proceed to Delhi she cancelled her Chittagong Students Conference programme and also curtailed her Assam tour.

She spoke to the people of Gauhati (Assam) about the policy the Congress ministers should follow during their tenure of office. She said that they should bear in mind that the Quit India issue over which the elections were fought will not have been carried out while British bureaucracy, military and the vested interests are entrenched everywhere.

Referring to Gandhiji's faith in office acceptance Aruna said, "this faith was a revolutionary factor. Gandhiji has the hope that his constructive programme can receive an impetus by the

Congress ministeries working it. This faith, if it was justified, must mean giving the programme a practical shape as the country was awaiting the unfolding of that plan."

She expressed her thought that the Congress Ministry in Assam would not be anything different from the Saadulla Cabinet or Section 93 Administration.

She asked the Congress ministers to win the Muslim hearts by action and for the removal of hatred by which the League leadership was functioning.

At Munsgung Railway Station a large crowd of Muslim Leaguers mobbed Aruna with lathis and brickbats. The angry mob demanded Pakistan from her and although the Leaguers were very provocative Aruna remained unruffled and quietly listened to all that they had to say. After they had finished Aruna told the leaguers that they should go to the British for wresting Pakistan. She said, "Who am I to give you Pakistan? I am but a humble servant of the nation. I have no power in my hands to make a gift to anybody. The power is in the hands of the British Government."

Then the crowed asked her to join the Muslim League. Aruna frankly refused. She added that she would not join the Muslim League because of Nizamudin Ministry's misdeeds, involving not only deaths of Hindus but millions of Muslims.

After her hurried tour of Assam Aruna returned to Calcutta and after a few days left for Delhi by air. Although Mr. Jinnah happened to be travelling by the same plane, he did not exchange a word with Aruna.

Immediately after her arrival in Delhi Aruna had a long talk with the former Congress President. After the talk she told the pressmen, "I told the Congress President that the ratings strike was spontaneous. In seeking redress of their grievances by resorting to strike and by wanting Congress intervention they have overstepped the convention and regulations governing the armed services. But in view of the war to peace time transition problems prevalent in the services and the disturbed political atmosphere the authorities would have been well advised to take the advantage of Sardar Patel's role as a mediator and not come out with provocative action.

I was summoned by the Congress President to Delhi in order to give him an eye witness account of the R.I.N. strike and subsequent happenings in Bombay; and elsewhere. I hope that only such a technical step will be taken against the R.I.N. ratings as may be necessary to satisfy the regulations and formalities". Concluding Aruna said "the navy in free India with its own government would not have occasion to resort to mutiny for removal of service grievances and racial discrimination."

Mahatma Gandhi gave the following reply to this trend of argument.

"The first principle of non-violent action propounded in the Congress resolution of 1920 at its special session in Calcutta under the presidentship of the late Lala Lajpat Rai is that non-co-operation with everything humiliating. It must be remembered that the R.I.N. was founded not for the benefit of the ruled. The men went with their eyes open. Discrimination stares one in the face. It cannot be avoided if one enters the service which is frankly organised to keep India under subjection. One may, one ought to try to mend under the conditions. That is possible only upto a point. That cannot be achieved through mutiny. Mutiny may conceivably succeed, but the success can only avail the mutineers and their kin, not the whole of India. And the lesson would be a bad inheritance.

"Discipline will be at least as necessary under Swaraj as it is now. India under successful mutineers would be cut up into warring factions exhausted by the internecine strife.

"India of the Congress has made little head way in the appreciation of the fight for Swaraj if it is true that hundreds would take their places if the present ratings resigned in pursuance of their campaign against humiliation. Can we have Swaraj for the masses if we are so degraded that hundreds of us are ready to swallow humiliation even to the extent of taking the places of humiliated fellowmen? The very thought is unworthy of Congressmen and that too at the moment when Swaraj is believed to be within sight.

"Those who hold that enlistment in the R.I.N. is their only means of livlihood must have a very poor opinion of themselves. A soldier's is hard life. He is a disciplined to work **in co-operation** and trained to work with the pickaxe and the spade. **Such a one** will disdain to think that apart from soldiering he has no means of livlihood. We have poor opinion of soldiers if we think that they cannot earn their bread by the sweat of the brow. A labourer is any day worthy of his hire. What is, however, true is that a soldier out of his calling will lack the glamour and the amenities provided for him. We have wasted precious twenty-five years if we have not stripped the possession of killing and destroying of the thick coat of varnish that has covered it for so long.

"Aruna Asaf Ali has been reported to have said that the ratings would have guined nothing by resigning. Will, they would have gained honour and dignity if they had manfully given up their jobs and taught the citizens of Bombay the way to save honour and dignity and they would have spared Bombay the senseless destruction of life, property and very precious foodstuffs. Surely this would have been an achievement not quite beneath notice.

"The last statement of Congressmen going to the legislatures for conserving the honour and liberty of the country is not the same as ratings serving for their livlihood with the possibility of being used against their own countrymen and their liberty. Congressmen who go to the legislatures are representatives elected by their voters and they go even if it is only to prevent those from going who will misrepresent their voters."

4

Underground Activities

The British Government offered a reward of Rs. 5,000 for the capture of the young absconder. But she, each time, proved too smart for the C.I.D. people who tried their best to hunt her down. How she drove the police almost mad is evident from the report of a police officer who after making frantic efforts to trace Aruna said to his boss "as against nine of us who are searching for her, there are nine lakhs in Delhi alone to offer her protection and quarter. It is an uneven game and you cannot blame us if we cannot succeed."

When after the Bhansali demonstration three lady Congress workers met the Executive Councillor he seemed desperate and shouted "Take me to Mrs. Asaf Ali and I'll explain everything to her." Nobody could say that they had met Aruna, like the elusive Pimpernel, she was here, she was there, she was everywhere and yet she was nowhere. There are a number of stories connected with her underground life. They tell of her sufferings, her sacrifices, her narrow escapes from the police and are enough to take one's breath away. Here are some of the stories.

Once she was warned that the place where she was putting up was no longer safe and that she should shift to some other place immediately. The notice was so short that she was at a loss to decide as to where she should go. Fortunately she got a brain wave. In the morning papers she had read an advertisement that an English family wanted an European paying guest. Aruna got into a taxi and dashed to the address advertised. The good old English lady was so captivated by Aruna's charming personality and manners that she decided to wave aside her stipulations in favour of an European boarder and accepted Aruna as her paying guest. When the police arrived in great triumph to arrest her they found to their bewilderment that the "mysterious bird had slipped out of their hands once again."

On another occasion Aruna fell ill. Dysentery from which she suffered was so serious that she was reduced to a bag of bones. Her underground comrades pressed her to take some rest and they arranged for her stay in a middle class family. On the second day a Government official a good friend of Aruna's paid a surprise visit to that family. Having known the family for a long time he walked into the house unannounced. To his amazement he found Aruna—the arch rebel, Aruna's host found himself in an awkward position but she came to the rescue of all. In her usual homely way she greeted him and talked him to as if he had come to her own house Delhi. The officer instead of reporting to the police said that he had been "privileged to have lived for a few moments, at any rate in the presence of living history." Despite police and C.I.D. vigilance Aruna once visited the residence of her sister, Purnima, where her mother was lying ill on her death bed. She could not, however, make it possible to be by the side of her mother during the last moments of her life.

After being released Asaf Ali went to Wellington Hospital for treatment. The police got the news that Aruna had gone to hospital to see her husband. They hurried to the hospital but felt foolish on learning that the lady who had called on Asaf Ali was Aruna's sister from Allahabad.

When Asaf Ali flew from Bombay to Simla, a nurse had accompanied him. Some police official got into his head that Aruna was attending to her husband under the disguise of a nurse. All sorts of enquiries were made so as to ascertain whether the nurse was real or false. Since the police could not come to any definite conclusion, a genius of the police official by a subterfuge got the measurements of the nurse. As the nurse was two inches shorter in height than Aruna, the police was finally convinced that the nurse in question was not Aruna unless she had chopped off two inches of her height.

Once Mrs. Bhimani came to stay with Asaf Ali. An officer of the Viceroy's household got the hint that Mrs. Bhimani was in reality Aruna. He carried the photograph of Aruna in his pocket and by a clever ruse confronted Mrs. Bhimani at a tea party. He was surprised that the guest of Asaf Ali resembled Aruna so much except for the fact that Mrs. Bhimani was two inches taller than Aruna.

It is believed that more than half of dozen persons including an architect, a pilot officer, (Mr. Patnaik) a garage owner and a Secretariat official were detained in prison for a considerable time because they were suspected of having given shelter to Aruna.

It may be recalled that after the release of political prisoners in 1945 a meeting of Congress Working Committee was held in Calcutta. The most important resolution passed was the resolution on non-violence. Even the Viceroy had accused the Congress of its violent activities and had stated that the wife of a working member had organized a strong movement of sabotage the Government's was efforts through violent means. The Working Committee after a five-day session passed a resolution re-affirming the Congress creed of non-violence and emphasising the Congressmen to stick to the non-violent creed in the struggle for freedom.

The following is the text of the resolution on non-violence :

"After the arrest of the principal Congressmen in the August of 1942 the unguided masses took the reins in their own hands and acted almost spontaneously. If many acts of heroism and sacrifice are to their credit there were acts done which could not be included in non-violence. It is, therefore, necessary for the Working Committee to affirm for the guidance of all concerned that the policy of non-violence adopted in 1920 by the Congress continues unabated and that such non-violence does not include burning of public property, cutting of telegraph wires, derailing trains and intimidation.

The Working Committee is of the opinion that the policy of non-violence as detailed in the Congress resolution 1920, since expanded and explained from time to time and action in accordance with it has raised India to a height never attained before.

"The Working Committee is further of the opinion that the constructive activities of the Congress beginning with the spinning wheel and Khadi as the centre are emblematic of the policy of non-violence and that every other Congress activity including what is known as the parliamentary programme is subservient to and designed to promote the constructives as explained by Mahatma Gandhi.

"The Working Committee is of the opinion that civil disobedience mass or any other, meant for the attainment of freedom, is inconceivable without the adoption of the constructive programme on the widest scale possible by the masses of India".

Immediately after the conclusion of the Congress Working Committee the Congress President Maulana Abul Kalam Azad explained at a press conference the various resolutions passed by the Working Committee during its present session.

The Congress President said that the resolution on non-violence was the most important of the resolutions passed in Calcutta during the last four or five days. "I emphasise," said Maulana Abul Kalam Azad, "the resolution is the most important one, because ever since the August 1942 struggle, people have begun to believe that the Congress creed of non-violence no longer binds the country in general and Congressmen in particular. There has been a growing feeling among people that it is not necessary to adhere strictly to the principle of non-violence in our struggle for political freedom.

This is absolutely wrong. It is for the purpose of removing this confusion and misconception in public mind that the Working Committee has thought it necessary to re-affirm the Congress creed of non-violence once again. We have reiterated our faith in non-violence as the only means to achieve our political objective with all the strength possible".

Aruna Speaks From—?

After reading this resolution of the Working Committee and the explanatory statement of the Congress President, Aruna Asaf Ali and Achyut Patwardhan sent from "somewhere in India" the following statement to Maulana Azad.

"The authors of the letter regard this resolution as a summary judgment upon the complete events of the past three years and request the Congress President to re-examine the issues more specifically and formulate specific charges and provide them with facilities on appearing before a duly constituted tribunal to vindicate their stand. The resolution they state is bound to he interpreted as a reflection upon their alleged lapse from the path of duty to the struggle for freedom and since they have no sense of wrong doing, they demand not merely a vindication of their self respect but also the respect that their point of view deserved in the ranks of the Congress."

The following is the text of the letter addressed to the Congress president by Mrs. Aruna Asaf Ali and Mr. Achyut Patwardhan from "somewhere in India."

The President,

Indian National Congress

Dear Maulana Sahib,

We have read carefully the resolution of the Congress Working Committee on the subject of non-violence passed on 11-12-1945. We have pondered the implication of the past three years and analyse its emphasis governing present policy and its significance in relation to any future struggle in which the Indian people may be involved. Your personal annotation of the same resolution issued in a press statement, has also clarified the perspective in which these policies are outlined. Since the resolution records the Congress Working Committee's considered views events and developments of the past three years, with some of which we have been vitally concerned along with other colleagues, it becomes necessary to define our position unequivocally and to bear our share of responsibility for our policies and activities during the period of your incarceration.

The resolution states in the first paragraph that after the arrest of the principal Congressmen the unguided masses . . . . acted almost spontaneously. This is not a complete accurate statement of facts. There were in Bombay about a dozen prominent workers from the various provinces who held responsible positions in the Congress organisation, after your arrest. Amongst us were several colleagues whose allegiance to Gandhiji's creed of truth and non-violence cannot be questioned. We were responsible along with these other colleagues for setting up an organisation to convey what we believed to be necessary directions to thousands of Congress workers and others who were still out of jail and who were anxious to implement the resolution of 8th August, 1942.

We all recognised the urgent necessity of providing some guidance to the vast forces that were being unleashed. Instructions, directives, appeals and proclamations and the day to day exhortations (broadcast by the Congress Radio) were issued from time to time after your arrest in the name of the All India Congress. If we speak of our doings it is only with the desire to assume personal responsibility for whatever policies were formulated and implemented in the name of All India Congress throughout this entire period. Our authority for assuming such responsibility was never questioned and we received the unsinted support of large sections of our people.

The spontaneous response of the people to the Congress call to act as free men is the greatest phenomenon of recent history yet once they had set their marching foot upon the path of revolt, they clamoured for effective and undaunted guidance. They asked to be organized to whatever degree the rerror regime would allow and their genius triumphed for a time over all the machinations and force of the white man's raj. With respect to dislocation, secrecy and intensive forms of social boycott and other attacks upon authority many specific instructions were issued. By large majority such advice was widely accepted. With regard to non-violence, Congress policy has been mainly pragmatic. From time to time it has defined its scope within limits of practicability. The Working Committee has refused to follow in the past the strict logic of Gandhian non-violence. There are its resolutions on record to prove this opinion. We have been ourselves profoundly influenced by the social valves of Gandhiji's philosophy.

But our acceptance of these valves is essentially pragmatic and electric. The recognition that we fight on unjust system than marely the personnel who admitted it, is the essence of our stress upon non-killing, respect for life and private property are also logical corollaries of the same.

These valves were stressed in all our directions issued under the Congress seal. Conditions of unprovoked military and police aggression, however, create situations which are by no means easy to cope with. The register has often only two alternatives. To resist with all his might in whatever manner seems practicable or to submit. Under the severest tests the Congress name was never tarnished by the counsel of submission.

We took our eve from the Working Committee's resolution of July 1942.

"That all aggression must be resisted, for any submission to it must mean the degradation of the Indian people and the continuation of their subjection. The Congress is anxious .... to build resistance to any aggression on India by the Japanese or any foreign power."

We also took note of Gandhiji's well known observations upon Polish resistance. The offer of armed support to Britain under certain conditions was fresh in our minds.

Again, the agreement in principle, after your release to join the Executive Council of the Viceroy when all that remained of the war was the re-conquest of Burma and Indonesia, did not suggest that our approach was contrary to Congress policy, otherwise it would lead us to the fantastic conclusions that certain specific acts are only permitted in alliance with the British, but those same acts become unpermisible when employed against it. It is, however, quite possible that under specific circumstances, even on pragmatic grounds, there would be room for honest differences. All that we have expressed heretofore relates only to the events during your forced detention. In so far as the resolution in question faces us with your considered judgement, we feel called upon to assume such responsibility as inexpiably devolves upon us. This is not intended to minimise the undoubted fact of vast elemental forces spontaneously released. All the same we deliberately provided a few grains of organisational direction to the thousands of tons of mass initiative for the lack of which this unrehearsed upsurge would have collapsed in a matter of weeks rather than months.

The Congress had proclaimed its resolve to launch a mass struggle on the widest possible scale non-violent lines. "Every Indian who desires freedom and strives for it" was to be "his own guide, urging him on along the hard road where there is no resting place." But it is obvious that initiative and organisation cannot be provided by each one for himself. A set of Congressmen and women sought to fulfil this obvious gap.

You have, however, deliberately ignored the fact that some of us have made a determined effort to provide direction and guidance in your absence. Further you are definite that the forms of resistance improvised were inconsistent with Congress policy of non-violence. This leaves us two loopholes. We can attribute all that happened to the spontaneous urge of a people's revolt of which we were on insignificant annoymous focus and treat your judgement as post factum advice for the guidance of future conduct. We may in the alternative disown our share and accept your judgement in silence. Honest conviction, however, prevents us from seeking this easier path. We were repeatedly warned that our activities might be disowned and our interpretation of the legitimate course of action repudiated. Nevertheless, we persisted in putting our faith upon one pragmatic test. "Whatever is calculated to sustain and effectively express the maximum potential resistance of the people and to vitalise their will to be free, is the legitimate path of resistance."

We feel an inner compulsion to reassert our conviction and stand by it and accept the consequences of such a step. We did not impose any dogmatic ritual of conduct upon our people. On the other hand, we studied their spontaneous improvisation with such powers of discrimination as we possess and strove to inform the widely separated strome centres of revolt with the experience and lessons gathered from far-flung sectors of resistances. Our directions have led thousands to risk their lives. It would be cowardice if we did not assume our share of guidance. We were not waging a private war upon the British System.

We submit the working committee have done less than justice to their own goods name for undaunted partisanship of freedom's cause by dismissing the momentous events of the past three years as a series of impulsive and heroic albeit undirected aberration. We remain unconvinced of our error although we may recognise the average element of mistake which persists in all organisational executive efforts.

As for the immediate implications of the working committee's resolution, it will lead to a totally fallacious postulate that a people's revolt hinges exclusively upon spontaneity. "Those who call upon the people to stake their lives upon one moment of total revolt bear the self-chosen obligation to provide an unbreakable core of guidance through organisation for the interchange of information and direction and for great co-ordination of all the available sources of resistance." This is not less necessary and becomes even decisive when the pattern of resistance is essentially decentralised. The question therefore cannot be evaded whatever honest differences there may be regarding the technique of revolt.

For lack of this recognition we witness the depressing fact of outstanding organisational talent being diverted in a lop-sided endeavour to generate enthusiasm without a corresponding effort to convert it for revitalising the instrument of resistance. Such a policy reflects an incapacity to comprehend the lessons that the last few years have learnt upon the understanding of the commonest unknown resister. The paradox of praising the dead men as heroes while obliquely disapproving the efforts which they fearlessly undertook along with others also defeats the linking up of enthusiasm with action.

This particular form of rigidity has in the past alienated from the Congress many sturdy fighters. We therefore plead for a re-examination of these weighty issued more specifically.

The Congress has more than once sought the freedom to interpret the general policy of non-violence in a form not acceptable to Gandhiji. On the 27th July, 1940, at the A.I.C.C. session at Poona, the Congress president threw a revealing light on these matters.

"The Indian National Congress is a political organization pledged to win the political independence of the country. It is not an institution for organising world peace. Honestly we cannot go as far as Mahatma Gandhi wants us to go. Most of us felt that we were not able to take up the grave responsibility of declaring that we would completely eschew violence when we have to deal with widespread internal disorders in this country of external aggression."

In view of a succession of deliberated deviations from the straight narrow path of non-violence some of which were initiated by Mahatma Gandhi himself (the Gelder statement dated July 2, 1940), it seems a little difficult for us to appreciate the relevance of this one-sided stress upon the implications of non-violence in the context of a total struggle.

We wish to make it plain that there is no influential section of political workers who advocate terrorism. The country in its upsurge of enthusiam today recognises the crying need for organising all available resources without which any heroic resistance would be nine days wonder.

It is this organization that is grievously neglected in the dust of election mock fights. We hope the threats uttered by the Secretary of State and repeated by the Viceroy and some Governors about closing the door of peaceful negotiations have not indirectly evoked this gesture of good behaviour.

We only hope our fears are without foundation.

On January 25, 1946, it was officially announced that the warrants of arrest against Aruna Asaf Ali were cancelled. The two cases pending against her; firstly alleged dissemination or prejudicial literature which was found in Aruna's writing in a house in Karol Bagh, and which, it is alleged, was intended for publication, secondly failure to surrender herself to the authorities as required by the order of the Chief Commissioner of Delhi, were also withdrawn.

It is amusing to note that although the higher authorities had cancelled the warrants against Aruna's arrest, the Court of Additional District Magistrate, Delhi, was quite ignorant of the fact. They still claimed Aruna as an absconder and would not give up her house in Delhi. Four days after the cancellation of warrants Aruna was spotted in Calcutta, by a reporter of the Amrita Bazar Patrika, driving home in a taxi. She appeared very much reduced. The excited reporter pressed her for a message and modest Aruna replied, "there is no question of feeling jubliant, leaving one's staunch comrades behind and I am not feeling happy at regaining the so-called civil liberty. While in India there are others in prison for doing what I and my other colleagues did who have yet to regain freedom, you cannot possibly expect to see me elated.

If anything, I am depressed." She added that nothing personnel should be mentioned about her as those were not the times for personnel things. Speaking of her comrades who were still underground she said that they did not except any magnanimity adding "we don't expect any quarter nor shall we give any." She said that she had done useful work while underground and intended carrying on that work, the only difference was that she would now work openly. Aruna was rather anxious to meet Gandhiji and have a talk with the father of the nation. It may be mentioned that the Mahatma while in detention in the Agha Khan Palace, in his letter to the Viceroy had condemned the violent action of those who were conducting the movement in the name of the Congress.

After his release he had requested the underground workers to surrender themselves to the police. Few had responded to Gandhiji. Since Aruna had not listened to him she felt it was her duty to meet the Mahatma and explain to him what had kept her and some of her comrades underground. She was disappointed to her that she could not have an urgent meeting as the Mahatma was on a tour to Madras. She sent him a telegram saying : "Desire to seek your blessings and pay my respects, please wire when and where it is possible."

Calcutta can boast of being the first city in India to hear Aruna's voice after an interval of three and a half years. A public meeting was held at Deshbandu Park where Aruna spoke to a large number of people from the land of her birth. The platform on which she stood had been most exquisitely designed by New Theatres Art Director, Souren Sen. The snow white platform represented the truth on which those who were fighting for freedom of India pinned their faith for final victory. The martyr's memorial ten feet high, consisted of a red winding pathway representing the youth climbing high and stopping at the foot of a white light, red representing the blood of the martyrs and the while light, the goal yet to be reached.

Aruna spoke to the eager crowd for more than one hour mostly in Hindustani, intimitantly in English and Bengalee. She called upon the people to boycott English goods. Criticising Lord Wavell's speech in the Central Legislative Assembly she said that there was no need for the British Government to fix a date for India's freedom, the Indians would settle it all themselves.

Being an enemy of the capitalists, she pointed out that she wanted the common man to be the real master of India. Bearing this idea in mind, she said, in the negotiations for India's political settlement which were afoot the people must remember that under any negotiated settlement, power only went to the powerful, but the power achieved through struggle remained with the people. The Indian masses therefore, she appealed, should carry on the struggle for freedom.

Aruna's admirers pressed her for a message and this is the message she gave them. "Messages from politicians are appreciated. For one who is essentially a field worker it strikes an odd note. However, if Bengal can give the lead in reviving Swadeshi movement of 1905 in 1946 spirit and bring about a total boycott of British goods, to some degree the Bengal famine deaths will have been avenged. Those haunting cries refuse to grow faint. Let us not stifie them." The terrible picture of the Bengal famine was still fresh in her mind so she asked her contrymen to avenge the wrong done to the people in famine days. In a pathetic tone she related that during the famine days, one night while walking alone the road she stumbled over something and to her horror found that it was a dead body. The cries of the hungry people were still ringing in her ears. She believed that the British Government would have to answer for this deed some day. "If not you and I," she said, "the future generation will see that these deaths are avenged."

Aruna had been asked over and over again by the Assam co-workers to visit their province. But as Aruna was leaving for Delhi, she expressed her inability to do so and wrote a letter to them saying "you can imagine my disappointment at not being able to be amidst you immediately. Although Assam and I have not known each other before 1942, it seems as if you were always known to me. As soon as I am in a position to make my programme for February, I shall let you know exactly when to expect me."

Aruna left Calcutta for Delhi on January 31, 1946. She was given a hearty send off at the Calcutta Railway Station. Originally she had planned to go straight to Delhi but no receiving a telegram from Pandit Nehru asking her to break her journey at Allahabad, she decided to do as he wished.

At every station crowds came to greet her. Even villagers, young and old, flocked to have a darshan of the heroine of 1942 revolution.

As the train, steamed in at Allahabad thundering shouts "Aruna Zindabad" were hearn. Many important Congressmen including Pandit Nehru were present at the station to receive and garland her.

A short time after her arrival, Aruna visited the room where her mother had expired. She stood for a moment outside the room then as she entered with slow determined steps, her old maid servant Basanti came and fell at her feet saying, "Ma Nahi" meaning mother is no more. Aruna whose heart was already heavy, at these words gave vent to her feelings and burst into tears. The scene touched Basanti and Purnima who were standing nearby and they also began weeping.

In the afternoon Aruna addressed the students at Parshotamdas Tandon Park. Speaking of some of the politicians who merely sit back and criticize the action of the leaders, Aruna said, "Let us all do our duty and not indulge in useless, mutual criticism. If Gandhiji the father of the nation gives a programme you dare not doubt his wisdom and dare not refuse to follow him. If Patel, the country's captain asks you to abide by certain decision, you dare not refuse him. If Nehru, the real leader of the people commands you to do certain things you dare not doubt his wisdom and sincerity."

Referring to the 1942 movement she said that it had shown the way to get freedom from unwilling hands. Although they had not achieved they goal the would not lose courage. She told the students that she could not tell them in detail what work she had been doing except that she had made a humble contribution on her part. She urged the students to sustain moral and revolutionary potentialities of the people which had come to the fore since the 1942 movement. She reminded the students that merely shouting slogans would not help in getting independence. What was more important, she said, was immediate, strong and revolutionary action, "Freedom's way is through battle," she said.

She warned the students to be prepared for the coming battle. "Freedom's battle", she said, "has to be fought and won by the strength of the people. Britishers will not free India voluntarily, you have to work for it and the strings of your bondage will be relaxed only when you are able to demonstrate your might and main beyond all-doubts." Concluding, she said "Do or die" was the mantram given by Gandhiji and she proposed to live up to it." On her way to Delhi from Allahabad, at a small station some soldiers of the Punjab Regiment headed by some officers approached Aruna and said, "What is your message for us?" Aruna replied at once "you must not charge on your unarmed brothers. This is my first advice. The second advice is organise boycott of foreign goods".

Mr. Asaf Ali went to Ghaziabad to meet his devoted wife. This meeting of the couple after three and half years was very touching indeed.

At Delhi Railway Station, outside as well as inside, crowds and crowds of people gathered to greet this heroine. As the train stopped at the platform the enthusiastic crowd cheered her heartily. With much difficulty she managed to descend from the train and allowed herself to be garlanded responding with folded hands and her sweet smile.

Once outside the station she addressed the crowd with the words :

> "Do not glorify me. You must glorify the martyrs of 1942. You must shout Jai Parkash Narayan Zindabad". The crowd repeated this slogan. Proceeding she said, "there is no occasion for rejoicing over the removal of restrictions on me. Until all the political prisoners and detenues are released, I shall not consider myself free. The truth is that I feel myself less free than I felt before January 25, 1946 when I was underground and refused to recognise the laws of the British Government that stand in the way of our struggle for freedom. By all means raise slogans of freedom but under no circumstances there should be any glorification of my personality.
>
> I am but a humble and disciplined soldier of India's great and unfinished fight for freedom." Continuing she said, "So far I have been working from behind the purdah and have come out in the open to serve you. The guiding star of my work is the same that inspired thousands of workers in 1942. And on the face of the shining star are written in gold the two words—'Quit India' the words that transformed cowards into heroes and the heroes into martyrs."

5

Socio-Political Ideology

Since the day of her emergence from the underground life Aruna had been pelted with requests from her co-workers of Punjab to visit their province. In spite of her best efforts she could not go to Lahore earlier than in the last weak of March. On her way to Lahore at the Ambala Railway Station she was given a rousing reception. At night she addressed a meeting held under the auspices of Students' Congress. Lady Congress volunteers presented a guard of honour with tri-coloured flags. A number of purses and gold bangles were presented to her.

The work which Bhagat Singh had started for India's freedom was yet incomplete. More than twenty years have passed but the goal for which he sacrificed his life has not yet been reached, though its vision inspires us all in our efforts. It is the duty of each one of us to strive every fibre of our nerves for the attainment of that cherished goal—the goal that promises the liberation of our down-trodden masses . . . the goal that will usher in an era of freedom from want and fear. Referring to the formation of the Coalition Ministry in the Punjab, Aruna said that it was a very diplomatic move on the part of the Congress.

She asked the people to forget the past policy and the atrocities committed by Sir Dhizar Hayat at the instance of the British Government. The Coalition Ministry had to face two enemies . . . the British Government and the Muslim League. The Ministry should put such a programme which would make the Punjab Muslims feel that it was the Congress which was really their well wisher and not the Muslim League.

In speech Aruna had vehemently condemned the Indian Communists for the statements they had made against Netaji Subhas Bose, adding, "our so-called patriots had the effrontory to call him a puppet in the hands of the Japanese. And they had the barefacedness to denounce him as the 'advance guard to Tojo.' There was not a derogatory objective that they did not use against the Indian National Army which had unleashed the sword from the frontiers of India to drive the British out. The brave men of the Azad Hind Fauj suffered and suffered so that from the womb of their sufferings the babe of Indian freedom may be born. Who does not know that there were suicide squads in the I.N.A., the members of which unit carried dynamites to blow up the enemy tanks. They carried death around their waists. They, for the honour of Mother India, challenged the will of God in fixing the hour of their death.

"It is a matter of positive shame that such fearless sons of India were damned by the Communists as traitors. It is not the soldiers of the I.N.A. who were traitors, but the Communists who maligned them and those mercenary and begging officers and soldiers who resisted them when they set their foot on the sacred soil of India.

"The soldiers of the Azad Hind Fauj are like the Jewels worthy to adorn the neck of Mother India and all those Indians who stood in their way, whether in the front line or in the rear, are like the stones to be thrown into the dust bin."

About the recent change in the policy of the Communists towards the British Government Aruna said, times have changed now. Russia, the god father of our Indian Communists has now become once again hostile to Britain. There is a clash of interests between Russia and Britain and how can our patriots side with Britain when Russia is working against that country.

These Communists today are thinking in terms of struggle and marshalling their forces against the Congress. I want my countrymen to be aware of their machinations. And now once again she warned the people of Lahore "the Communists are enemies at home. Beware of them. They betrayed the revolutionary forces in 1942."

When the British Cabinet Delegation arrived in India, Delhi became the centre of political activities. All the Congress leaders flocked to Delhi to see for themselves the important negotiations that were going to take place. Aruna also returned to Delhi as she wanted to watch the political drama closely. Besides, Maulana Azad had decided to stay at Asaf Ali's residence so she had to look after the comforts of the Maulana whose health since his release from the Ahmednagar jail had not been too good. Although Aruna had to entertain the members of the Working Committee who held their meetings at her house occasionally, she never neglected her own party work. She wrote articles for the Party paper called janata every week. During the Tripartite Conference she went to Simla for a few days.

The Congress Socialist Party, ever since the official announcement by the Lord Pathic Lawrence that a cabinet delegation was coming to India to negotiate with the leaders of Indian opinion for the transference of power to India, had been severely criticising this political mission. Aruna and her party felt that the Cabinet Delegation was coming to India just to gain time and to create further and greater differences among the political parties in India. Aruna had stated that the British Cabinet Delegation had not come to deliver freedom to India but to play the mediator between the Congress and the League. The British had created the so-called differences and that they were still trying to exploit them.

When the Congress Working Committee in its resolution dated May 24, 1946 issued from Delhi rejected the short-term proposals for an interim Government Aruna expressed her satisfaction at the rejection and dissatisfaction at the acceptance of long-term proposals. She said that the acceptance of the Constituent Assembly scheme foreshadowed many dangers. As the Constituent Assembly was far from the original idea of such an Assembly, it fell short of their aspirations. She maintained that the Constituent Assembly being a creation of the British it could never bring them freedom for which they had been fighting. Although the British Government had promised to accept the Constitution drawn up by the Constituent Assembly it would, nevertheless, be pulling wires in such a manner as not to allow the Indians to frame a Constitution which will be in consonance with wishes of the Indian people. She added that there were bound to be differences of opinion between the Congress and the League during the process of Constitution making.

At the A.I.C.C. Session held at Bombay on July 7, 1946 to ratify the Congress Working Committee's Delhi decision, Aruna, who is a member of the All-India Congress Committee, opposed the resolution and said that the policy of the Working Committee, since the release of its members had been out of tune with the spirit of Quit India resolution. The British power could only be overcome by a physical struggle and not by parleys and negotiations. Power by the people must come through their own struggle and stength.

If a Referendum were taken today, she said, the people would resent the present, policy of the Congress High Command as it was one of co-operation with the British. The Congress acceptance of a Constituent Assembly was a triumph for British post-war political plans. Realising their old method of repression it could no longer succeed in the changed circumstances. The British had changed their strategy, but they had not changed their hearts. The Working Committee had by its decision reduced itself to the status of the Muslim League which was the most reactionary political body in India.

The Congress demand of a Provisional Government had still to be met. The Constituent Assembly's suggestion was not acceptable to people, because it was being summoned by the British power, before the people had captured the citadel of power. She said she wondered how the British Government, which allowed Mahatma Gandhi to fast and die in the Agha Khan Palace in spite of the country wide demand for his release, could ever come before Mahatma Gandhi and offer whatever he wanted. It was an inconceivable thing.

Concluding her speech Aruna addressed Mahatma Gandhi and said, "we have listened to you all these years and it is now your duty to obey us."

Pandit Jawaharlal Nehru while answering some of the criticism of the opposition party said he was pleased to hear the fiery speech one of the women members had made. It was indicative, he said, of the temper of Indian womanhood. He said more and more opportunities should be given to the Indian women to participate in our public life.

On July 8, about 15,000 workers of the Delhi Cloth Mills went on strike as a protest against the refusal of the mill authorities to recognise the Textile Mazdoor Sangh and their refusal to accept the arbitration of the dispute by an independent

Panchayat. Yet the mill owner, Sri Sri Ram, declared that the strikers had no legitimate grievance. In a statement to the Press had asserted that the strike was not the result of economic reasons but was prompted by political groups who were trying to gain control over the political workers.

Aruna, who is the President of the Textile Mazdoor Sangh, contradicting his statement said that the Sangh enjoyed the overwhelming support of the general body of workers employed in the Delhi Cloth Mills and therefore, the question of political rivalry did not arise. Moreover, if the strikers had no legitimate grievances the mill authorities should have had no objection in placing the demands before an arbitrator. The fact that they did not do so clearly proved that they were conscious of the strength of the labour's case were fifteen days of strike. Mr. Asaf Ali, President of the Delhi Provincial Committee, intervened in the matter. The result was that the mill owner, Sri Sri Ram, recognised the Sangh and agreed to refer the dispute to arbitration. Aruna, the President of the Sangh, called off the strike on July 22.

Aruna Asaf Ali with her moving speeches had arrested the ardent favour of independence in the minds of many a youth. She with her message of courage, defiance and action had gained popularity in the student world.

During her tour to Sind, Mrs. Aruna Asaf Ali visited Shikarpur. A 16-year old lad named Ali Gohar Brohi was eager to see Aruna but his elder brothers dispute his requests, would not take him to the public meeting which she was to address. Ali Gohar, however, managed to reach the place of the meeting. Being unable to get near enough to the dais, Ali Gohar climbed up a high tree and saw Aruna. The branch of the tree on which he was setting suddenly gave way and Brohi fell down and was seriously injured. When Aruna heard the story she visited the hospital and was visibly moved by the youth's enthusiasm. The boy died the same evening.

ARUNAJI, AS I KNOW HER*

R.K. Garg

Arunaji was an inspiration in 1942, associated with the Quit India Movement. Gandhiji had decided to launch the Quit India

---

* R.K. Garg advocate, Supreme Court, Secretary General of Krishna Menon Society. I feel much beholden to the author.

Movement, on August 9, 1942. Jawaharlal Nehru was distressed with Gandhiji's obsession to do so. Having failed to dissaude Gandhiji, Panditji moved the Quit India Resolution at the A.I.I.C. Session in Bombay. This Movement, for compelling the British to leave India when Buckingham Palace was being bombed by the Germans, had spelt out no programme of action. All Congress Leaders were picked up and lodged in different jails all over India.

Congress Socialist Party, led by Jayaprakash Narayan, decided to go underground to carry on the Quit India Movement and to organise a Revolt against the British Rule. Aruna Asaf Ali also went underground and emerged as the most beautiful, romantic Revoluntionary inspiration in 1942. I was hardly a lad of 15 but had identified myself with the Congress fighting for Freedom under Gandhiji's spell in 1939 as a schoolboy. We boys too played truant from the school for months and delivered small unsigned slips carrying instructions 'sabotage and insurrection'. Arunaji was guiding this "Insurrection", which was fated to faint to but left deep impression in the sensitive minds of every Indian fired by the patriotic passion roused by Gandhiji's call to compel the British to Quit India.

In 1945, the War ended. Jawaharlal Nehru and Gandhiji were released from Jail. RIN (Royal Indian Navy) revolt came close on the heels of I.N.A.'s revolt led by Subhash. British rulers had gone bankrupt fighting the Second World War. Jawaharlal Nehru took the country by the storm, campaigning for the release of I.N.A. prisoners, General Shah Nawaz Khan, Captains Dhillon and Sehgal. Then came Freedom at midnight on August 15, 1947. Free India opened her eyes in the wake of darkness and gloom which had compelled Mahatma Gandhi to leave for Noakhali, when Pt. Nehru pulled down the Union Jack and unfurled the tri-colour from the ramparts of Red Fort on August 15, 1947. We, as a Nation, learnt to rejoice in our unbearable sorrow.

The wounds of partition were too deep for tears and yet the joy of freedom had created new hopes in the hearts of millions. These were for me intensely emotional moments in my teens. Arunaji was a Heroine in our hearts in her own right, even though, Gandhiji and Jawaharlal Nehru had been dominating the agony and ecstasy of this struggle for Freedom. But Arunaji had fired the hearts of us all for whom Indian Revolution was the greatest moment of our lives. We had not even seen her, but only heard of has as a woman of inflexible determination and unsurpassed beauty.

I saw Arunji for the first time castigating the National High Command at the AICC Session at Meerut for forgetting the heroic sacrifices the Socialists had made in the Quit India Movement. Gandhiji was present on the dais. Jawaharlal Nehru, Maulana Azad, Sardar Patel were in command of this historic AICC Session. Acharya Kriplani was the Congress President. Garmukteshwar Communal riots provided the background of this session. Kriplani's biting sarcasm and unimmutable sense of humour and Maulana Azad's chaste Urdu had left deep impressions of sorrow and shame of beastly communal passions, which had gripped the minds of Hindus and Muslims at a time when Freedom was won under the banner of Ahimsa and Truth. Gandhiji was a shattered man—shattered by the Partition and by the human sufferings caused by the communal violence.

Aruna Asaf Ali rose like the Sphinx with her magnificent presence and undaunted courage. With disdain, she reminded the leadership that there were heroes on the dais who had courageously carried on the fight for Freedom with their tremendous sacrifices and sufferings when the leadership was safely lodged in British jails. But for their sacrifices, how could the British be compelled to "Quit" India. "Where is the recognition of their share in rthe heroic sacrifices made?" She asked, with natural indignation. There was complete silence on the dais and in the pandal. Someone had to answer.

Sardar Patel was chosen to answer her back. That the Steel man that Patel was, had to answer her how intense must have been the impression her indicment had made. Sardar was in weak health but only physically. He was still a General in full command with a clear vision of Free India without Socialists or Communists having a say in shaping the destiny of Free India. He spoke sitting in a chair. Sarcastically he referred to Arunaji's incisive references to the patriotic contribution made by the Socialists. He spoke in Hindi like a Gujarati, as Gandhiji used to. That made his speech deadly. His words are still ringing in my mind.

He had said, "Some people say they brought freedom. It is pleasing to hear this. When beautiful and charming girls say so it is even more pleasing to hear it. But, I say that a cart was proceeding. Under it was walking a dog. That dog believed that he was pulling the cart." The message was clear that Socialists' contribution in the Freedom Movement was next to nothing.

Sardar's remarks were obviously intended to infuriate the Socialists and forced the Socialists to leave the Congress. That is precisely what was accomplished. Jawaharlal Nehru was the lone Socialist left to lead the Congress as the first Prime Minister of free India. Neither Socialists nor the Communists had joined the Constituent Assembly.

In 1952, Ajay Ghosh had somehow persuaded Arunaji to join the Communist Party of India. It must have been because of her undying faith in the Great October Revolution and its message of human emancipation and liberation of the people of every Nation. Even Jawaharlal Nehru had taught us all that Scientific Socialism was the only answer to the appalling problems of poverty of India. I have never understood to this day why Arunaji had to be a part of the Communist Movement of India at all? Our Movement was too regimented and her overgrown political personality could not be contained within the narrow confines of a rigid Communist Party of India. Inflexibility was the hallmark of its claims to Ideological purity, which was our strength and also our unsurmountable difficulty—responsible for all the good deeds we have done and also the impermissible mistakes we have committed ever since the Communist Movement was born in India.

We Communists never understood the difficulties of Pt. Jawaharlal Nehru as a leader of a great National Movement. Arunaji essentially belongs to this great National Movement, as did Jawaharlal Nehru. With Communists and the Socialists out of the Congress, it was easy to contain the irrepressible Jawaharlal Nehru, who knew well the importance of the Unity of the National Movement before and after Independence—both to win Freedom and build a modern just India, to wipe every tear from every eye. The Land Reforms were regulated and controller Non-Capitalist path was destined to fall. Capitalism had forced on us the logic of its own Laws of Development.

Socialism continues to torment us but even Socialist Nations are learning at tremendous cost that without ever-expanding production with latest technology, with inflexible respect for Human Rights, Socialism could not retain its claim as a superior system. Jawaharlal Nehru was the first World leader who did not accept Socialism without democracy, but even he could not forge instruments to create conditions of Socialism. Democratic Power was used for Monopolies to emerge in Jawaharlal's lifetime. Arunaji's dilemma has been she had accepted Socialism as an article of faith and did not abandon faith in Jawaharlal that he would fight the Growth of Monopolies and also World Imperialism. She was more right than all of us in knowing the durable aspects of Jawaharlal's leadership and also his limitations.

Jawaharlal Nehru, Sardar Patel, Rajendra Prasad, Maulana Azad and Rafi Ahmed Kidwai jointly built this India after Gandhiji had been assassinated on January 30, 1948. Their greatest achievement was that India was kept free and united and growth was linked with Social Justice but with the natural constraint of undying social, economic and political injustice often aggravated by the very process of Growth. Arunaji remained a member of Jawaharlal's family, and Jawaharlal encouraged her to be his critic as a Socialist. Jawaharlal Nehru never questioned her right to assail him and his Government both. His love and affection and support for her was always available to her to follow her own independent path. Jawaharlal was cynical if she could ever succeed in changing this cruel world of domination and exploitation.

Arunaji, Krishna Menon, Keshav Dev Malviya and Narayanan with Dr. Baliga got together to found "Link House" and bring out not only a Weekly "Link" but also a National Daily "Patriot". Narayanan was an obstinate Socialist committed to his views as tanaciously as was Krishna Menon. Arunaji and Keshav Dev were a benign influence on both. They formed one family of committed Socialists, who dared launch Patriot in the teeth of competition with powerful Dailies run from Delhi and now almost every important State capital.

I remember the day when Jawaharlal Nehru came to Link House to inaugurate the first Issue of Patriot. In that limited gathering, Jawaharlal Nehru shared his bewilderment at the very thought that Aruna should embark on such a "mad venture" as to bring out an English Daily from Delhi. If I remember, right, his words were, "Aruna came to me. She said she was going to start an English Daily.

I asked her, how could she do it? Who will give her the money? Who will give her the advertisements? How would she run it? But she has done it. I don't know how long it will go on. But, I am involved in it. I wish it to go on." And next morning, on the front page of Patriot was the picture of Jawaharlal Nehru engrossed in reading the first Issue of Patriot.

Krishna Menon and Keshav Dev Malviya were frequent visitors to Link House. Narayanan was always there. There were animated and heated debates between them. "How wrong was the Government and how much more was needed to be done?" Patriot was a passion with its Founders. Narayanan worked till 3 A.M. He was all over in the Press, even at the machines correcting the proofs and encouraging the workers. But, this "mad venture" could not see the light of day without the benign, saintly quiet dedication of Dr. A.V. Baliga.

He was the most outstanding Surgeon of Bombay. He must have "fleeced" his rich clients by his persuasive dignity and, I am sure, they were willing to be fleeced by him for a good cause. No less irrepressible was Aruna. Who could say "No" to her whenever Patriot or Link was in difficulty and all that was needed was money to run the Patriot. Even so, it has not been easy as sources of support are drying up. Socialism is being rejected as a dirty word even in the land of the Great October Revolution.

But, Narayanan never compromised his commitment to Patriotism or Socialism even at the worst of times. Patriot went through financial agonies, ideological insoluble dilemmas, which were enough to kill any venture. And yet, Arunaji's frail figure, with fire within, has kept it alive as a national force of ideas to spur the patriots to action.

O.P. Sangal and a whole team of dedicated Leftists assisted Arunaji and Narayanan to make Link and Patriot unique in their exposition of ideas with a national idiom free from classical Socialist jargon. Sangal was brilliant as a Journalist and a clear in his perception, which he had perfected under the great P.C. Joshi, when he was building the Communist Party of India. He was quite modest about the achievements of Patriot. He said, "Patriot may not have achieved much for itself but no English Daily could ignore what was published in the Patriot. Therefore, it had succeeded in changing the idiom of National Dailies in the debate on all national and international issues."

I have often wondered if Arunaji can ever withdrawn from active political life. Her response is ever intense and sincere beyond words. She reacts against injustice with indignation and feels exasperated at our feeble responses to great challenges threatening even the survival of free India or its unity. She is never tired of putting us to shame. "How can a Movement be built in small meetings held in closed doors? What has happened to you all?" She often asked with agony in her voice. "Why can't you go to the masses. If you have something to say but the masses are not moved, nothing is ever going to happen in this country."

How true it is when leaders are being made and unmade by newspapers, speeches on the radio and the television and not by the capacity to move the masses into action with a clear direction. The National Movement had in Aruna Asaf Ali a colossus. Something of the greatness of great causes sticks even to small men. But, great movements for emancipation of every men, and women needs renewal, freshness and creativity, which is somehow not within the reach of us mortals today.

We are fortunate Arunaji is there with us to share our griefs and to inspire us to a great future for this great Nation. I was deeply touched when I saw her sitting quietly in Nehru Museum at a meeting to pay tribute to Rajiv Gandhi after his gruesome assassination. Arunaji is a living monument of the heroic sacrifices made by millions to win and sustain this Freedom.

She has borne the assassinations of Gandhiji, Indira Gandhi and Rajiv Gandhi. She has known, how shattered Jawaharlal Nehru was after November, 1962, but she has so identified herself with the cause of Freedom, National Liberation and Human emancipation, that she always remains a flaming inspiration as she was in 1942. We need her just as desperately now as then, and perhaps even more.

A LOVABLE PERSONALITY*

My association with Mrs. Aruna Asaf Ali whom we affectionately call Arunaji, is nearly four decades old.

Vimla Farooqi

---

* Vimla Farooqi, social worker and fighter for women's rights. I am much grateful to the author for her new information.

I have found her to be a very warm and affectionate person who has a feeling and concern for her friends and colleagues.

Arunaji is a deeply political person who reacts to events spontaneously.

Her major commitments are to the defence of secularism, world peace and to procuring a better life for women, socially and economically and social justice for all. These issues are closely interlinked as women's position cannot improve in a society ridden with communal tensions or international conflicts.

Arunaji is a convinced anti-imperialist. She fought bravely against British imperialism for the freedom of India and has been fighting against imperialist aggression wherever it occurred and against their manoeuvres to plunge the world in another war.

Arunaji, has been associated with the National Federation of Indian Women since its inception in 1953, first as its Patron, then President for nineteen years and now as its Patron-in-chief. As its President she directed and guided the activities of the N.F.I.W. very effectively. Her stress was no intensifying grass-root work.

Arunaji acquired a rich experience of work among the people as a leading member of the Indian National Congress when it was fighting for the country's independence.

She has a broad vision and is acquainted with the needs the aspirations of the people. She does not put men's and women's problems in different compartments. Food and shelter is the first need of every women and man and women have to fight along with men for procuring them. It is a pleasure to hear Arunaji speak to women in 'bastis' and slums. I wish to underline the fact that Arunaji loves to go to these areas and never refused, unless there is a pressing reason to participate in the meetings or any other functions in these localities.

She reacts to their demands sympathetically and helps to get them relief in whatever why possible. She used to visit Dayalpur, a village near Delhi, regularly along with us. The women of that village complained about the non-availability of any medical facilities in the village. Not even a trained mid-wife was available for deliveries of babies. Arunaji look up this issue personally. She approached the authorities and in two months time a Child and Maternity Centre was set up in the village.

In another area, an outlying rehabilitation colony, she pressurised Delhi Municipal Corporation to improve the drainage by building proper drains and sewers. She participates in all types of actions not bothering whether they are big or small.

She led a demonstration of N.F.I.W. in Delhi against the non-availability of sugar and other rationed articles at the fair-price shops. It was not a big demonstration but Arunaji's presence enhanced its quality. Delhi administration has to take serious note of it and we could get some improvement in the distribution of rations.

Arunaji is deeply devoted to the cause of secularism. To work for communal harmony and national integrity is almost a passion with her. During the period when she was the President of the N.F.I.W. she led many all India campaigns aimed at promoting communal harmony among women. In recent years she visited Moradabad, Meerut, some places in Bihar when communal notes took place. She met people of different communities and helped to set up peace-committees. She appealed to the N.F.I.W. unit to collect relief material for the victims of notes.

Women's organisations were inspired to launch several joint actions in this direction throughout Punjab. She has visited Punjab a number of times at the invitation of the Punjab Unit of the N.F.I.W. in the recent years. I have seen her being very much emotionally perturbed when communal disturbance took place. For the progress of India it is a precondition that all communities live together in peace. This is a matter of faith with her and she will do everything possible to implement it. Arunaji is a confirmed anti-impedalist. She fought against the British to get freedom for India. She suffered many hardship lived in prisons and led underground life haunted by the police. But she did not lose faith, did not falter but stood firm for her convictions.

At the time when India won independence, Arunaji was among top all India leaders of the Congress Party but she did not accept any post in the Government. She continued to organise the poor, the deprived and the exploited people. She wanted to be with them and help them to strengthen their voice in moulding the affairs of Independent India.

Arunaji, took up the cause of world peace and came up as one of the prominent leaders of this movement in India. She was the recipient of Lenin Peace Prize in 1965.

As the President of the N.F.I.W., she was the Vice-President of the Women's International Democratic Federation for nearly two decades. There also she played an important role in formulating programmes for strengthening the world peace movement and for organising women to achieve a status of genuine equality, so that they can participate as equal partners in national and international affairs.

Arunaji, initiated and participated in many campaigns of solidarity with the people of Vietnam fighting against U.S imperialism.

As a leader of the N.F.I.W. and of several other organisations fighting for the defence of world peace and democracy she took active part in the actions launched in support of the people of South Africa. Chile, Palestine and many other issues as they came up.

Arunaji may look frail but is never idle; she has a tremendous store of energy for work. She does not believe in just speaking and passing resolutions but in action.

Arunaji thinks of problems and formulates the solutions beautifully. Her presidential addresses to the N.F.I.W. Congresses were always inspiring and formulated the current issues appropriately and set the tone for the discussions by the delegates from all over the country.

Inspite of her deep involvement in national and international responsibilities. Arunaji is a social and friendly person. She never neglects to attend marriages, birthdays or other functions hosted by friends and does not forget to lake a suitable present for the occasion.

She finds time to visit stick friends and help in whatever way required. Her warm affection is always there to cheer up the patient.

Whenever she finds time from her busy schedule. Arunaji loves to sit and chart with friends.

She is always happy to participate in the "pot luck" luncheons we sometimes arrange in the office of the N.F.I.W. It is an informal opportunity to sit and talk of light matters.

Arunaji is a person who inspires admiration and love in the people who know her.

Her simple and clean life is a rarity these days.

ARUNA ASAF ALI*

Manmohini Sahgal

I had my first glimpse of Aruna at the Students' Conference in Amritsar many years ago. She had evidently been recently married and was accompanying her husband Asaf Aliji who was presiding over this conference. In my mind's eye I can still visualise the attractive young lady dressed in all her finery. I attended this Conference in my capacity as the President of the Lahore Students Union (a student body founded by Shaheed Bhagat Singh).

We lost touch with both Mr. and Mrs. Asaf Ali until my family including my mother Lado Rani Zutshi, my two sisters Janak and Shyama and myself happened to be in the Lahore Female Jail serving our own respective prison terms when this batch of women satyagrahi prisoners were brought from Delhi. (Incidentally the Lahore Female Jail was the only Women's Prison covering the whole of the Punjab, the then North West Frontier Province and Delhi). There was instant rapport between Aruna and us; so much so that we shared the same accommodation and other 'facilities' provided by the jail authorities to 'A' class prisoners. So we got to know each other well. She was very found of my mother Lado Rani Zutshi.

Thereafter my family stayed with the Asaf Ali's in their house in Faiz Bazar in Delhi, whenever we happened to be visiting the capital city. Needless to say we were always most welcome and received a lot of affection from our hosts. If they were put to any inconvenience by our descending upon them so frequently, never by their attitude did we discern that.

During the Quit India Movement, all the leaders were arrested, and a vacuum was thus created. But Aruna and her friends had other ideas. They felt it was easy to court arrest and be imprisoned, but who would guide the public? Besides, this was time when Aruna and some of our notable Congress leaders had veered towards socialism. They advocated equal opportunities

* Freedom Fighter, Social Worker to whom I am much grateful.

in all spheres of life for all—as well as equal distribution of all the good things of life. To carry out this work needed a lot of courage and determination.

Irrespective of this ideology the authorities were out to arrest all such prominent Congressmen. So Aruna had to go underground. Life must have been hard but Aruna was and is courageous enough to face hardship cheerfully. Friends rallied round to provide the necessary protection for her but she never exploited her friends by staying on indefinitely. We had also the proud privilege of being considered in that category as she spent a couple of nights with us at our house on Raisina Road in the late thirties. My husband, although a Government servant, fully co-operated with me in this venture.

After Independence our field of work was different. As President of the National Federation of Indian Women she used to invite me to all their functions which I attended very regularly. So she persauded me to join this organisation and I became a full-fledged member. The warm reception I got from other members was very heartening. I am still actively involved with all their activities.

Aruna has inspired us all along with her great concern for the distressed and the needy. Incidentally this is not the only organisation through which she works; under the aegis of Dr. Baliga Foundation she has diversified her work and activities in other areas and fields. She is a good organiser and an excellent orator. She has great charm and a knack of carrying with her all her colleagues and friends in whatever field of work she is involved. Her international relations are second to none. She is a well respected figure in countries dedicated to the welfare of the deprived.

I am particularly indebted to her for including me in the delegations going abroad on Friendship Missions, thereby giving me an opportunity for a bird's-eye-view of their problems which are very similar to ours.

Aruna has become frail now but the indomitable spirit is still unquenched striving to alleviate the sufferings of her follow beings.

Truely she is a great person—a leader in her own right and a true daughter of Mother India.

I salute her.

ARUNA DI*

T.N. Kaul

Arunadi, as we affectionately call her, has been to my generation a heroine, ever since she joined the Quit India Movement in 1942 and went underground. Her grace and charm, her winning smile and sympathetic attitude won for her many followers and admirers, Jawaharlal Nehru and Mahatma Gandhi recognised her sincerity and spirit of sacrifice, even though they did not always agree with her rebellious moods and methods. She, in her turn, loved and respected them.

She would argue with them but often stick to her own view-point. Though she respected their advice she had a will of her own and held strong views on certain subjects—*e.g.* the role of women in society : the priority of the interests of the poorer sections of populations; the need to give equality of opportunity to all, irrespective of caste, creed, social status or birth.

Before Independence, Arunadi represented the younger leftist and revolutionary generation and often led movements sponsored by them. She became, in their eyes, a Joan of Arc—unafraid, bold and courageous in the pursuit of her convictions.

After Independence Arunadi continued her crusade for the oppressed and poor, women and youth. She was the first elected Mayor of Delhi and introduced some major reforms in the civic administration of the capital. It is a pity that she never agreed to stand for Parliament. This was perhaps partly because she could not accept the arbitrary diktats of any Party and partly because she wanted to concentrate on building up and mobilising public opinion in support of the causes she held dear. She was elected President of the All India Women's Conference and is an active worker in the women's movement in India and the world.

Arunadi also worked steadfastly for strengthening the World Peace Movement and was awarded the Lenin Prize for Peace. She donated the prize money to public and charitable causes.

She lives a very simple and somewhat austere life. She works from dawn till midnight and lives in small flat on Asaf Ali Road.

---

* T.N. Kaul Former Foreign Secretary. Ambassador to USA and USSR. Editor-in-Chief 'World Affairs'. I extend my respectful regards to him.

She does not believe in ostentatious living and feels completely at home with those living in *jhuggis* and *johmparies*.

Arunadi is a slim, frail-looking person but retains her strong personality, charm, grace and beauty. Clad in a pure handspun and hand-woven white Khadi sari and wearing ordinary chappals she roams round the villages in and around Delhi, floating like a cloud in the sky. She travels constantly by air to Calcutta, Bombay, Madras and other places wherever her work takes her. She shuns travelling abroad except on very important and unavoidable occasions.

Arunadi is a fighter for freedom—in all spheres of life-freedom from hypocrisy and cant, from superiority or inferiority complex, from dogma and fanaticism, from obscurantic social customs and conventions. She is a rebel at heart but looks like a gentle angel, outwardly at peace but inwardly seething with unrest and anger at the exploitation of women and the poorer sections of society.

A selfless worker, a dedicated believer in the equality of all human beings, Arunaji is an object of admiration and affection for millions of Indians and others. She is human in all her dealings with fellow human beings and never losses her temper or sense of fairness and equality. She always speaks straight from her heart and thereby wins the hearts of others. There are many such leaders in India or the world today.

We wish Arunaji on this day, many more 'happy returns' and offer our good wishes for her health, happiness and success in the causes she holds dear and works for.

6

Role in Freedom Struggle

What is causing real anxiety to many thoughtful people in the main, is the weakening of the national will to unity and desire for collective strength. This indifference to the welding of the nation is making our Republic increasingly vulnerable. Those who feel intensely perturbed by this unhappy development have reasons for doing so. The long and dark night of India's total subjugation rationally be expected to breed in us acute consciousness of the tragic historical consequences of disunity in her bitter years of servitude and humiliation.

These developments are reminiscent of the days when imperialism was triumphant. With the defeat of the forces of imperialism one should have expected a decline if got complete elimination of remnants of crude feudal thought and obsolete social habits. A generation that actively carried on the fight against these evils, making it a vital part of the national struggle, is being called upon to witness the evolution of a new irrational challenge to democratic and egalitarian principles and social decencies.

When assessing similar situations before independence, it often struck one that sowing dissensions and keeping the community divided was an important instrument of alien state policy and those who fought imperialism assumed that communalism as a reactionary force could be destroyed really only in freedom. When foreign domination ended twelve years ago, it was therefore taken for granted that as soon as state power was vested in the democratic national leadership that overthrew it, the roots of social dis-integration would wither.

That assumption has been proved wrong. These shameful vestiges have not been cauterised. This is painfully borne out by the communal ideologies that are permitted to permeate our political platforms and to use the instruments of our secular democracy like adult suffrage to subvert it! Obviously then, British power when it withdrew in 1947 had succeeded not only in dividing the country but in leaving intact the seeds of future discord also. The leniency shown to communal fanatics in the first year of freedom cost us the life of one who was the nation's most precious asset. After that experience it should have become impossible for the communalist to foul politics. But more than a decade later we find slogans devoid of any economic and social content being permitted to mislead the voter when he sets out to take political decisions in our parliamentary democracy.

There are two other factors that have contributed considerably to a weakening of our new nation state : The issue of language and linguistic states and a sharpening of local patriotism and consequential disputes about state borders. These dreadful debates have cost the nation a great deal in terms of human energy and emotion. But since the language controversy cuts across caste and communal barriers, it is less dangerous and its solution may be only a matter of time. Already the controversy has narrowed down and if a truly democratic decision is once taken with firmness it can heal the wounds the protagonists inflicted on one another.

The fact that we have as yet not achieved a unified understanding certain basic principles of nationhood and social justice cannot be ignored any longer. The prevalent national mood is so powerfully vitiated by currents of narrow sectarianism that if unchecked they are likely to do irreparable damage to the sense of national oneness that held us together during half a century of struggle. If this is not realised in time the political and material gains of the decade can be seriously jeopardised. Internecine resentments and tension, at almost every level, have reached such a point that forces opposed to socialism, secularism and parliamentary democracy find it the easiest thing to exploit the situation to their advantage. As a matter of fact, the reactionary Right has already realised this and feels that the opportune moment for it to strike has at last arrived. The recent emergence of a new political consolidation—the Swatantra Party—is the overt expression of this realisation. In a less spectacular and more piecemeal manner exclusively communal forces also are gaining ground. Wherever disillusionment born of discontent and disappointment with the performance of those in authority rise to the surface, we find reactionary elements rearing their heads and misleading the unwary.

In this situation can what is called the Left afford to allow minds in despair to gather round reaction or drift into passive defeatism?

The history of the rise of Fascism in the West is not so remote. What is wrote on the wall is not yet quite faint.

The Left India, to people of my way of thinking, is contained today within the two major political parties—in the Congress and the Communist Party of India. The rest are splinters consisting either of well-meaning individualists or confused good samaritans whose chief function is to sow confusion and help the very forces they want to defeat.

Neither of the two major parties, however, is likely to agree with this analysis. In fact both will emphatically disagree with it. And yet, judged by the political pronouncements of the Congress and Communist parties, a detached observer cannot but come to the conclusion that they are broadly in sympathy with policies and programmes that in current political terminology belong to parties of the 'Left'. One has only to study the Nagpur resolutions of the Congress and the documents of the Ooty Seminar and recent policy statements and resolutions of the Communist Party to discern a common approach in crucial matters related to economic development and international relations and, above all, in the role of parliamentary democracy in establishing a socialist society.

This similarity of outlook on basic national objectives does not rule out differences and dissimilarities in matters of detail, such as the order of priorities, the rate at which reforms should be implemented, the firmness required to check maladministration and corruption, etc. But, by and large both these parties are agreed on the fundamental role of an industrialised and planned economy as the only rational and scientific road to national progress. Indian Communists have gone further than they ever dared to go before and have removed the last barrier and accepted the validity of the Nehru formulation that given universal adult suffrage and compulsory education, parliamentary democracy can replace a capitalist society with a socialist order of production and distribution.

Similarly, in international affairs, these two parties have for many years now shared in an almost bi-partisan policy on major issues. With so much in common, it should not be difficult for the leaders of both the parties to see how interests both abhor are preparing to cut the ground from under democracy and socialism. Unless political power is seen as an end in itself it should not be difficult for them to realise that freedom as they understand it is in real peril.

Will such an understanding lead to the weakening of one or the other of these parties? When nations are confronted with major threats like world wars or civil wars, like-minded parties usually come together. With the restoration of normal conditions each component of the national coalition goes its way, content to place before the electorate at the proper time its own programme as opposed to the programme of the party in power. This has happened again and again in countries with political systems similar to ours and can and will happen here also. There is no question of liquidation of their identities or of mergers. It is merely a matter of defending the foundations of a commonly acceptable national edifice in periods of confusion or crisis.

I am of the view that we have entered a period of crisis with the emergence of the Swatantra Party. It has come earlier than anticipated and it is all the more significant that the challenge should come at a time when the Second Five Year Plan is far from fulfilment, the food situation has not improved and the army of the unemployed is claiming new recruits with every passing hour. If instead of recognising the dangers inherent in these developments, parties who ardently believe in the same things continue to weaken one another and thereby the progressive forces in India, they will merely hasten the beginning of the end of the dream of socialism.

The Congress as the senior party of the nation, a party that at one time contained within its fold nearly all the socialist parties and the Communist party as well, will naturally have to make up its mind without further loss of time and strength. It can once again unify the people around nationally accepted vision of the future. From the days when it nearly rejected socialism and ejected convinced socialists from its ranks, it has travelled far. From Avadi onwards it has again been approaching the goal of socialist understanding at an ever-increasing pace, Nagpur being the latest milestone.

Its allies should and can be from the Left, rather than the communal and feudal Right. Seeing in each other the main enemy of social freedom both the Congress and the Communists may find that reaction has made the best of this situation and put out the light that neither cared to protect.

Link, August 16, 1959.

MEMORIES OF '42

Much water has rushed down the Ganges and the Yangtze, the Volga, the Nile and the Mississipi in the eighteen years since 1942, when our people threw their final challenge to British authority in India, and memories of their exciting period in world history are already becoming vague.

As the years roll by, men and events that make history and shake the earth from end to end, become shadows. Even the millennial tragedies of war lose their grim appeal. Upheavals and gigantic conflicts that once seemed inescapably decisive take their orderly place in what is but a process, and particular occasions like ours in 1942 begin to appear almost unreal in 1960. There is nothing extraordinary or regrettable about this blurring of the distant scene. The past cannot and ought not to dominate the present. Great achievements, of intellect or physical heroism—or sordid deads and happenings of the past can be given precise and specific significance only at the risk of rank exaggeration, however, objective the writer of history be. Even so, for a correct understanding of present social situations a study of particular periods of history, and the separate events that made the period, is useful. Any event or occasion wholly forgotten, can make action in the present irrelevant and occasionally make it even look like reaction. Lack of perspective often vests human activity with purely superficial ends and exclusive satisfaction of current need brings on the scene the treacherous logic of opportunism. That is why it is good occasionally to look back.

The last pages of a book are usually the most interesting because they record climax. Often the whole book is judged by the manner in which the author ends his story, be it fiction or fact. This is true of the histories of revolutions also. The final result attracts posterity's maximum attention. Yet, without the countless preceding revolutions that ended in seeming failure and the sacrifices and sufferings of groups and individuals who resisted alien authority, the grand finale of the Quit India movement would never have been reached.

Therefore, although 1942 saw the beginning of the end of British rule in India, the credit for crowning the last phase of our struggle with success must go no less to those of our people who from 1905 onwards (if not earlier) surged forward again and again in defiant action, regardless of consequences. Later, had Gandhiji not ushered in the age of mass upheavals, the patriotic urge would never have seeped down to the people and the Second World War would probably have found the Indian masses in as subservient a state of mind as during the European war of 1918.

The courageous deeds of Individuals and small groups obviously are by themselves quite ineffective for wresting political authority from alien or domestic tyrants. But for Gandhiji's innumerable campaigns which drew together the masses as no other movement did, we could not have availed ourselves of the opportunities for revolutionary action which suddenly opened up when war came in 1939.

Wars, ancient and modern, are curious phenomena; while they bring death and desolation to many they also unshackle millions of serfs and liberate entire nations from the clutches of imperialists and despots. The paradox made what came in the wake of the World War of 1939 more significant than the war itself. Not only was the ghost of reactionary authoritarianism temporarily at least laid, but India and practically all Asia emerged into freedom. The brave who shed their blood and lost all that makes life worth living, had not perished and suffered meaninglessly.

They perished so that others may live not as slaves but as free men. The urge to intensify the struggle for India's liberation as soon as the West plunged into World War II, electrified and gave sharp edge to the thinking of politically conscious India. Jawaharlal Nehru's dramatic dash back from Chung-king, the Viceregal declaration that India was at war (without any reference to her true representatives), the withdrawal of Congressmen and Congress governments from Central and later Provincial legislatures came in quick succession. With every rejection of Indian advice and opinion by Britain, anger and resentment against Imperialism blazed as never before. Britain's contemptuous and arrogant ignoring of the Congress offer to cooperate for defence of democracy, was as intolerable national insult.. Many men and women of the then younger generation grew angry at the elder leaders' hesitation to embarrass the British Government.

The explanation that Britain was engaged in a deadly conflict with Hitlerism was regarded as weakness. In particular the urgent and repeated appeals to British Liberals and Britain's Allies irritated the hot-blooded. When the attempt to make the British Government (then led by Churchill) realise how absurd it was to expect Indians to offer themselves to defend their Imperial masters failed, there was great joy. Public opinion was eager to have done with endless talks with the Viceroy, the Cripps Mission, etc., etc. What was wanted was preparations for the "open Rebellion" about which Gandhiji had started writing and speaking. Nevertheless Congress leaders were eager to reconcile their desire to make India a party to the world struggle, with her passionate desire to attain freedom and the search for a compromise continued almost to the zero hour. Eventually a partial concession to the urge for action was made by Gandhiji when he permitted the launching of a "no war effort" campaign, i.e. the individual Satyagraha movement. It was a totally inadequate form of struggle and became wholly symbolic. It merely curbed the militant momentarily.

The final Quit India struggle of 1942 thus took a long time to materialise—for many of my generation much too long! This delay nevertheless proved a blessing. By July-August '42, the war was almost at India's doorstep. British armies had retreated from Burma and Malaya. Britain's great Empire was shaking. The Indian National Army led by Subhas Chandra Bose had declared confidently its determination to liberate India. The thought of imminent physical involvement in the great conflagration heightened the militant mood of the people.

When, therefore, on the 9th of August Integrated of gratefully acknowledging the Congress A.I.C.C. resolution as a sober and statesmanlike offer of partnership in the task of resisting Fascism—albeit on terms of equality—the British struck at the Congress, its cadres, its sympathisers, and even the nationalist press, the floodgates of pent-up Indian mass fury broke.

The sincere desire "to seek an honourable settlement" was spurned with Churchillian bombast. A reign of terror as had never been experienced in any part of the Empire began. Men, women and children were victimised for unarmed defiance of "Ordinance Raj". Arrests, imprisonments without trials, lathi-charges and firing on mobs, collective fines, confiscation of property and finally, physical torture—every weapon for crushing the spirit of rebellion was utilised by a handful of Englishmen and their hirelings.

This well prepared attack was totally unexpected by the revolutionaries. Gandhiji's exposure of the 'Puckle' circular which revealed what steps Government intended to take had been much too late. For the first few weeks every effort at organising resistance fell short of the desperate and menacing situation that confronted those who preferred revolution to non-cooperation.

One has today to refresh one's memory by reading accounts of what happened to the women of Chimur, the people of Ashti and Ramteh, to hundreds in Midnapore and Ballia, to recapture something of what one felt when they actually happened. But in '42, as the horrible events unrolled, every Indian grew cold with anger. Even moderates like K.C. Neogy and the late Shyama Prasad Mukherjee could not keep calm! And all that the victims had done was to resist the British will non-violently. Naturally the blast of British violence had some effect.

The brave new "republics" of Satara, Midnapore and Ballia had frightened the government even though they were short-lived. The increasingly "insolent" behaviour of the Indian army and navy terrified the White man. (Later after the 1946 naval uprising it was to demoralise them completely). But in the absence of a substantiating mass rising, the revolutionaries of

'42 began to experience an enervating spiritual exhaustion. But it is to their everlasting credit that they never surrendered. Young men and women who lacked leadership, experience and ideology plodded on unremittingly in the flickering light of the fire that was lit on August 9 in Bombay. They tasted misery in full measure and much suffering, but there was exhilaration and upliftment also.

Eventually came freedom but with it came also great sorrow and mourning. Imperialism's parting shot split our country. Was it necessary to allow this division? Top revent the division of India, it was argued would mean another struggle, possibly some form of civil strife and of course further suffering to all. This was not palatable to the leaders of the Congress because the fear of not being able to lead guide the struggle haunted them. Some of them had even repudiated many things that happened during the first instalment of open revolution.

Deviation from non-violent principles and the right path were put forward as the reason for decrying the role of the new leadership that had temporarily emerged. Marching with this distaste for new ways of defiance and new forms of struggle was another fear in the minds of a few in the Congress. In the next round, also with alien rule the influence of Indian privilege and property might also disappear.

The end, for those who had seen the vision of a completed revolution was dismal. Inexperienced, lacking dynamic leadership, their fine spirit of recklessness ridiculed by those who played for safety, the "Augusters" of 1942 grew dejected and gradually drifted away either to different groups or into complete inaction.

Will the lessons they learnt be of no use to the country? Or, as has happened elsewhere, will their disappointment help others who may read of their doings when history is written, to more intelligent ways? Only time will answer that question.

Link, August, 15, 1960

BEHIND LINK HOUSE

More often than not, ideals and ideals tend to remain in the clouds. Like aircraft awaiting landing signals they keep hovering in the air much to the annoyance of impatient passengers. That is how I can best describe the years and months during which the idea of organising United India Periodicals (the name came afterwards) was debated. That the venture would lead to building a mutli-storeyed structure was not the calculation of any of the sponsors in the first instance.

It was a dramatic enterprise to which we found ourselves committed in the course of our work. Mobilising resources from money to men and diverting them to a project that requires precision and efficiency is an adventure that requires above all business-like techniques which few of the originators of the scheme possessed in the professional sense of the term. Therefore for most of us the endeavour was adventurous and exciting with all the hazards attending such efforts. To amateurs like me the problems stemming from the decision to house Link and other journals that may follow it, and to set up an adequate printing press seemed infinitely complicated and at times tiresome.

But for the artist in our architect we could never have acquired an aesthetically satisfying place to spend our working lives in. How can we ever forget this voluntary gesture on the part of one whose time is very precious and whose organisation is in hourly demand by builders who range from people who want luxurious mansions to those interested in large educational and clinical institutions not to speak of scores of housing units.

Every age leaves the stamp of its peculiarities on the brick and mortar dwellings the people make for their use. The historic monuments of bygone years are mute witnesses of the sort of life lived by our forbears, reflecting their social and economic scheme of things. Wisdom lies in knowing that these old historic mounuments were modern when they were built and that the modern world's skyscraping towards when they in turn become ruins, may rouse nothing but posterity's causal curiosity after a few generations have used them.

While taking satisfaction in the completion of a programme one cannot but admit to oneself that in this phase of our national economic evolution mutli-storeyed structures are very incongruous. Invariably all around them lie huddled mud huts and rag and tin hovels reminding us of the tremendous distance between the many and the few in our country. That embarked as we were on a mission that required a base of concrete and steel and much modern equipment, a building of this kind was necessary was clear to us; but many a friend still wants to know why a band of convinced Socialists should have thought in terms of a multi-storeyed structure usually associated with multi-millionaries rather than ordinary folk.

The answer is that in social situaiton in transition towards industrialisation one either falls in line with all the requirements of efficiency or gets left behind. If we were to accomplish what we had set out to achieve, namely, a modern printing press in the heart of New Delhi's 'Fleet Street' area, we had to abide by regulations prescribed by Government for press buildings in the Capital. Hence the size of this establishment and therefore the cost. In an age of extreme competition between conflicting and contradictory interests the race to reach the chosen goal has to be run on terms set by the dominant group in society, those in control of the commanding heights—social, political, and above all financial.

Our aim of establishing an adequately large and efficient printing and publishing organisation owned and maintained by people who believe that the cause of spreading intellectual enlightenment suffers greatly if left to commercially oriented owners of concentrated property compelled us to follow apprently in their footsteps. The power and influence of the printed word can be mobilised either to debase or ennoble minds. They can either be used in the service of or against the fundamental interests of the people. In a society such as ours it is dangerous if not fatal to permit monopolisers of the people's wealth to became monopolists of their spiritual and intellectual assets also. Those who have sought to transform society have always felt the need to use means other than the spoken word for influencing thought and action. Gandhiji and his predecessors felt the need to propagate the message of liberation and to outline its tasks in journals and news sheets which in their times moulded public opinion far and near. Jawaharlal Nehru also had to turn journalist and author. Every leader of significance in our movement for freedom has been, in fact, a journalist, essayist and pamphleteer by turns because each one of them in their turn realised that as the craving for knowledge grows those who seek mere profit at its expense would exploit this necessity of man and divert minds into irrational and obscurantist directions.

There is no better example than Gandhiji for those who set out to organise the transport of information. Despite the stresses and strains of militant activities he never lost sight of his duties as a journalist, a writer of chaste prose in Young India and Harijan. He realised that all that is new and living has constantly to battle against the deadweight of past ages and that in this struggle is modern and efficiently organised press is a powerful weapon. Since both the forces of reaction and the forces that take life forward are able to utilise the same instruments there is no alternative to mobilising financial and technical resources in as big a way as one can. The challenge of big money compels us to adopt a course of action that calls for extremely hard and persistent work. And it does not good to notice the dawn of a new awareness about the job of the press in shaping social policies in our country.

This is perhaps inevitable because political freedom by itself can never be an end. Once free, a people, and particularly those who think for them and with them begin to feel the need for examining the social relationships that society imposes. The beliefs and modes of thought and life of earlier periods are examined and their validity in terms of existing situations questioned. To guide the traffic in ideas in such periods to transition, to direct them away from slogans empty of purposive content is the function of men and women who have assumed the responsibilities of intellectual leaders. Writers, be they journalists or novelists, poets or dramatists form the cultural vanguard of every society.

It should be their endeavour to explain continuously and cogently how ethics and morality are ultimately linked with economic and social realities, why the truths of yesterday can no longer satisfy the urges of today, how new values are the result of changes in social relations, and finally and most importantly, they must affirm and prove that truth, scientific or otherwise, is absolute only in the sense that it is a balance of continuity and change. To help men and women who are gifted to undertake this task of dispelling darkness, institutions such as the one to which Link belongs are necessary whatever the cost entailed. Jawaharlal Nehru's visit to Link House on Saturday marks the beginning of a new chapter. His presence among us will enthuse and inspire the workers who have laboured untiringly in the press, at editorial and administrative desks, Link's correspondents and representative everywhere, and last but not least those charged with the responsibilities of directing the affairs of this organisation. It is our sincere hope and earnest belief that we shall do our very best to deserve the privilege of his interest in our endeavour.

Link, July 1, 1962.

* * * * *

Link began publication on Independence Day eleven years after India had attained freedom and reaches its eighteenth year of existence as a weekly newsmagazine. Throughout these exciting years it has tried its best to live up to its first Editorial promise that "it will try to avoid prejudice and be true to fact. It will demand unprejudiced treatment from all in return, and always be ready to be judged by the purity of its purpose and the honesty of its methods". Naturally, it is for Link's readers to say whether or not it has been able to live up to its objectives.

If political life in India had been lacking in dynamism and had been following a straight line unresponsive to a rapidly changing national and international situation, it would have been easier for a news journal to keep to the straight and narrow path, rigidly following the beaten track. And Link could have yielded to the temptation to become "popular" only at the cost of giving in to unhealthy and retrograde trends in a social order that is on the whole trying to take the path of progress against heavy odds. Link's readers, however, owe it to this journal to point out its acts of omission and commission and thereby help in its improvement.

Eleven years after Independence was a fairly long span of time of come to the conclusion that the Indian intelligentsia was getting confused about the great objectives for which the people had struggled relentlessly decade after decade from the earliest years of 20th century. The promoters of this journal were well-known individual belonging not only to political parties, but almost all the major academic professions. Before it was actually published on August 15, 1958, V.K. Krishan Menon, Dr. A.V. Baliga, K.M. Panikkar, M. Chalapathi Rau, D.P. Mukherjee, Bishnu Dey, Pothan Joseph. S. Vaidyanathan Aiyer and a few of us decided that India needed a magazine that could every week carry out a summary of news, both Indian and world news, and that would provide basic information to those who were seriously interested in understanding India's role in shaping events.

This team of well-known advisers was assisted by young journalists who were dedicated to the idea that the Indian people's march towards the goal of peace and prosperity would not be easy. Despite the magnetic personality of Jawaharlal Nehru and his colleagues of the pre-freedom era, the quality of the rank and file of Congressmen had begun to deteriorate. During any struggle for emancipation the noblest in man comes to the surface; once political power, total and absolute, is achieved the finer characteristics slowly but surely recede and the elemental urges of personal ambition take the upper hand.

The result is the jettisoning of ideals and ideological moorings. Thus the men and women who flocked to the victorious Indian National Congress were by and large out to achieve selfish ends, forgetting the oft-repeated pleadings of Gandhiji and Jawaharlal Nehru that ends and means must always be such as to lead to the undoing of the wretched legacy of a long period of servitude—making the Indian masses aware of their rights and responsibilities, curbing the desire of the few to fatten on the toil of the millions who were the true masters of the motherland and, most important, restoring India's dignity in the comity of nations by working tirelessly to rid it of its backwardness.

Amongst the many messages Link's first issue received from distinguished compatriots, the one that was most thought provoking and meaningful was from Dr. S. Radhakrishnan, the then Vice President of India. I cannot resist the desire to quote it: "If civilisation consists of science and scholarship, of arts and letters, it is possible only in a democratic society. These are the results of what a man does with his solitariness, to use Whitehead's accounts of religion. The great achievements of science, literature and philosophy are the products of individual genius, its thought and meditation. They cannot flourish where injustice, discrimination, ignorance, superstition, and arbitrary power prevail. We must fight them within the nation if we are to quicken the minds of our people. Einstein observed : 'It is quite possible to assert that intellectual individualism and the thirst for scientific knowledge emerged simultaneously in history and have remained inseparable ever since.'"

By 1957 it was clear that Jawaharlal Nehru was aware that unless the Congress became once again the spearhead of national unanimity on all the major issues confronting the nation, its progress would be chequered and that obscurantist, acquisitive and anti-national forces would gain the upper hand, undermining the unity of purpose which is essential for a democratic socialist-oriented India, pulsating with the energy that a new sense of freedom should give the people and their leaders. He was equally aware that although imperialism had suffered a tremendous set-back with the emergence of free countries in Asia and even Africa, its tentacles were searching out for weak spots everywhere so that it may reassert its monopoly, whether be the new mantle it adopt. How correct he was in his assessment has been borne out by facts and events that are well known to every thinking and forward-looking individual in every country in the world.

Jawaharlal Nehru's thoughts and observations struck a sympathetic chord in the hearts and minds of the promoters of this newsmagazine and long hours were spent in working out the frame of reference for its contents, its name, size, manner of presentation etc. Krishna Menon, one of the chief architects of the plan, chose Link as the name because he felt (and all of us agreed) that this journal must link all those who shared the Nehru ideal of a new India. How to meet the cost of production of a journal that must not be drab in appearance, not indulge in sensationalism to attract a readership, not yield in its principle of working for a socialist order of society, remain unattached to any political party and yet appeal to the emerging intelligentsia were our major problems. But for the unstinted support of Jawaharlal Nehru and many of his distinguished colleagues, and above all the wholehearted generosity of Dr. A.V. Baliga whose fame and affluence were a legend in India, Link could not have dared step out and join the then existing fraternity of weekly journals.

The success of this endeavour is not to be measured in financial terms, or in terms of massive circulation. Many friends have complained that it is too serious a newsmagazine for the younger generation of today. They feel that we ought to be more jazzy in every sense of the word, not every critical of the Arts and specially the film word, have features which can excite the imagination of those to whom politics is a "bore" and cater to the modern youth's craze for "modernism" whatever the term may mean. However, it is difficult for men and women who believe that the educated elite must be identified with the working masses, at all levels, to respond to these well-meaning suggestions.

Certainly values do change but there are certain eternal verities of thought that cannot change and as far as possible sensitive minds must add to these verities and not degrade them.

As Link enters its 19th year, if faces many dangers but those who are not afraid of facing challenges do not deserve to survive.

It is my belief that Link will survive because a few can do much provided they are courageous and do not fear a life of austerity, long hours of un-rewarded work and a determination that the quality of life of our people must improve rapidly if this naiton of vast wealth is to make its long suffering masses the true masters of their future. I believe that such men and women will be found who will join the small band of workers in Link House and think that it is worth their while to serve the cause of intellectual integrity.

Link, August 15, 1976

* * * *

The poisonous seeds sown by the imperialists over the two centuries of their domination turned even decent men into insane beasts. Gandhiji and Jawaharlal Nehru and others laboured day and night to pacify the sufferers and resettle the mass of uprooted humanity. The healing words of Gandhiji had a soothing effect. However, despite the gradual calming down of passions, peace ultimately prevailed all over the country only after two fatal bullet shots had pierced the gentle heart of the greatest Indian of our century. Men who, somewhat hypocritically, pay lip service to their belief that freedom came to India in a uniquely non-violent manner, do not of course want to acknowledge these facts. In reality, freedom claimed the sacrifice of countless men who mounted the gallows, thousands who got killed, others who were ruined in the looting and burning of their possessions. And, finally, even the man who loved and cared for this country more than his own life had to be crucified.

Positively, the first decade of freedom was India's crucial and formative period. The evolution and completion of a democratic Constitution proved that politically conscious Indians were aware of the need to guarantee the people's social and economic freedom, their right to equal opportunity. The task of giving concrete shape to the many conflicting ideas and ideologies and reconciliation of contradictory aspirations and interests was undertaken in all seriousness by men and women chosen by the people to evolve a constitutional framework for the translation of their dream of a democratic, free and just social order into reality.

These first ten years after Independence were indeed full of meaningful events. Laying the foundation of a new Nation-State was the main occupation of a team of seasoned and dedicated political leaders under Jawaharlal Nehru's enlightened guidance. The basic features of modern India's superstructure owe their texture to his vision. He wanted India to be an equal among equals on the world scene. He wanted India to be a revitalised nation in Asia which should combine the pursuit of economic growth with the objective of the liquidation of exploitation in all its forms as its objective, a country that should be free of any involvement in imperialist and expansionist ambitions, dedicated to world peace.

This was also a crucial period in our relationship with the capitalist and socialist countries. Simultaneously, our attitude to peoples who were waging a struggle against imperialism in Africa, Asia and elsewhere was also taking concrete shape. Naturally, it was not smooth sailing for those who shared Nehru's beliefs because there were others who held the view that India could prosper only if it followed the trail laid down by the West European and American believers in a so-called "free world"—free for the gendarmes of aggressive imperialism and international capitalism.

In brief, this was the political backdrop when a group of men and women thought of producing a journal devoted to the task of explaining socialism to intelligent people. They believed it was not enough to be politically independent; that freedom was not an abstraction. Also it was important to convey through its columns the real nature of the subtle and aggressive forces at work all over the world to undermine the gains of victory over the Hitler menace.

The group that thought about the new journal was composed of men and women who had participated in many struggles from the thirties up to the "Quit India" movement launched on the 9th of August, 1942. Some of us "Augusters" had left the Congress after independence; we were free from any ideological aversion to Marxism—unlike some influential socialists who had gained considerable popularity during the "Quit India" movement but later turned anti-Marxist, anti-Soviet and joined the "cold war" brigade in India, equating Communism with what they called "totalitarianism". Our small "Left Socialist Group" had discovered that quite a few influential industrial workers who had joined the freedom struggle, some experienced and competent journalists, young lawyers, doctors, etc. in many parts of the country agreed that we should function independently of all known parties of the Left, Right and Centre in India.

By the end of the first decade of independence, i.e. from 1957 onwards, persons belonging to the Congress and others began to feel the need for an informative independent newsmagazine. The venture thus took shape in 1958. The motivating idea of such a journal, it was felt, should be to interpret the significance of scientific socialism in a situation wherein Parliamentary democracy was unable to provide expeditious solutions to the problems of poverty to any significant degree. Capitalist industrialisation by and large had failed in its 'mission' in India.

Our plans for Link would not have borne fruit were it not for the inspiration, guidance and concrete help of men like V.K. Krishna Menon, Dr. A.V. Baliga, K.D. Malaviya, Biju Patnaik and a band of enthusiastic young men such as P. Viswanath, K.V. Shambhu and many others who rallied round Editor E. Narayanan. Once this team had prepared the blueprint, the search for financial sustenance received Dr. Baliga's ever generous response and active co-operation.

It was left V.K. Krishna Menon to suggest a name and after checking and re-checking a long list, he asked us if Link would do. The name had to be short and suggest the main objectives of the weekly, which was to unite the Lift and progressive forces in the Indian National Congress and those outside the established Left parties. Link thus appeared, after months and months of planning, on August 15, 1958, twenty years ago.

Jawaharlal Nehru was consulted on many occasion while we were in the process of clearing the hurdles. His eloquent message to its Founder-Editor enthused the closely knit team of men and women. And when Link appeared on the news stands for the first time, it was hailed as something new in journalism, with reading material for serious students of politics, a journal produced by patriots. However, with each passing week Link became a subject of controversy. Its sharply critical approach offended the over-sensitive and its radical content annoyed the conservatives who believed that it was spreading "dangerous" ideas. Those hostile to any advocacy of a socialist solution to the problems facing the people accused it of allegiance to a "foreign" ideology, and V.K. Krishna Menon, who was then Defence Minister, became their favourite target. Politicians who could not tolerate his bluntness, his intellectual brilliance and caustic wit were particularly prejudiced against the magazine.

Link in its first decade of existence received more brickbats than bouquets. But it mattered little to us, for as long as we, who were responsible for its publication, were convinced that it would not be a plaything in the hands of power-politicians, nor a scandal sheet meant to denigrate individuals and that it would never compromise on the essentials of our national aspirations, we could look anyone in the face, meet any challenge. The difficulties of maintaining the standards set by its first Editorial team were enormous.

But it tried its best to live up to its own goals and when some talented young men, who had participated in various phases of mass struggles, came forward to work for the paper, our hopes soared. We began to feel that we were not quite alone. The sustenance we received from politically significant personalities, who were associated with the journal from its inception, enabled one and all to work hard, mindless of the meagre salaries and wages they received.

But for this courageous band of writers and workers, who did not use Link as a prop for successful careerism or personal benefit, it would never have survived the opposition of powerful financial interests and those who represented them in the power structure of our country. In the beginning of the second decade, from 1968 to 1978, our people's political maturity depended sharply. General elections indicated a gradual awakening amongst the millions people working in the fields and factories or wherever men and women toiled for their living. A determined will to fight for a better life and stepped-up organised action through trade unions became increasingly evident.

This had its own impact on the electoral front, wherever will defined political parties entered the contest. For the very first time, at least in an Asian country, the CPI (undivided) won a majority of seats in the Kerala Assembly which enabled it to form a Government led by E.M.S. Namboodiripad. While the masses all over India were jubilant, amongst the reactionaries even in the then ruling party (the Congress) there were adverse reactions. Nehru and his senior colleagues like Maulana Azad and Govind Ballabh Pant accepted the verdict of the people in a democratic spirit. But ironically the so-called "younger" generation of second-rank Congress leaders were violently agitated by this development. This and its consequences were an indication of the events were to follow.

Another significant event of the ten years from 1958 to 1968 was the liberation of Goa from the clutches of Portuguese Fascism. The downfall of this tiny enclave held on to by Salazar, an impudent director and oppressor of his own people, overjoyed the African freedom fighters in Angola, Mozambique and Guinea Bissau. Were Jawaharlal Nehru not the then Prime Minister and V.K. Krishna Menon his Defence Minister, Goa's freedom struggle may never have culminated in victory.

These events were land-marks in our post-independent years and Link can claim with a certain degree of satisfaction that it champion all the popular movements of those years. The success vindicated Link's understanding that if the Left forces unite in thought and deed reaction could ultimately be vanquished. The nation's and Link's greatest year of tragedy came in 1964 when India was plunged in deep sorrow as the news of Nehru's death hit the people—specially all those who looked upon Jawaharlal Nehru as the friend of the friendless. We felt like orphans; his death brought back memories of the day Gandhiji was assassinated in January, 1948. There was anger also.

It was common knowledge that he respected and loved the people of China and its leaders and always acknowledged their culture and civilisation, always espoused their cause in the UN and elsewhere. When China emerged victorious after its valiant struggles against Japanese imperialism and its allies, Nehru had been among the first who hailed it as the dawn of a new era. What saddened him greatly, besides China's teacherous and unprovoked aggression, was the reaction of his own countrymen, particularly members of his own party. Instead of rallying round him and the country, they derided Nehru's cherished beliefs, heaped ridicule on the basic features of his foreign policy and specially his assertion of friendship with Communist countries. Outwardly calm, he grieved inwardly, more so when his party men insisted on the dismissal of Krishna Menon, a life-long friend and colleague, a person on whom he had relied on many matters of international importance.

Link was, also, fatally afflicted by another tragedy the same years when news came from London that Dr. Baliga, its greatest benefactor, had passed away follwing a heart attack. Some years later, another tragic death took away Krishna Menon from our midst. With the passing away of these three magnanimous personalities, who were in their own way architects of Link, it lost its most sincere well-wishers.

Link and its contemporary Patriot have now entered a period which can be described as extremely hazardous. Death has taken its toll by robbing us of one, who though much younger in years than many of his older colleagues, literally slaved for Link from its earliest years : P. Viswanth, who died last year. However, Link must not enter its third decade in a spirit of defeatism. Many problems will confront it in a political climate that lacks rationality, many improvements will be necessary to make it a better instrument for clarifying the confusion prevalent at all levels. The concept of social revolution cannot be a static idea, it will have to evolve from decade. Link must never cease to strain every nerve to do so, however, uphill the climb.

Young men and women of vision with a progressive world outlook will surely join our depleted ranks, because very often adversity and danger attract the brave. History is full of instances where periods of stagnation are followed by periods of renewal. However remote the goal, Socialism has appeared on the agenda of almost every political party. The forces that yearn for the establishment of a socially free and equal society will reject "artificially manufactured" individuals who vulgarise it and claim to be national leaders—their "drill sergent" is "hunger", said Nehru. Therefore, eventually, they will be unified under their own leaders who identify themselves and share their hardships.

I would personally wish to think that when Link observes its 30th Aniversary, it will surely have justified the optimism of its promoters.

Link, August 15, 1978.

THOUGHTS ON AN INDEPENDENCE DAY

We are supposed to see ourselves as we are when reviewing national achievements and failures on national anniversaries. But do we dare to give expression to what we see in the privacy of our inner thoughts? Our attempts to speak the truth become in reality exercises in avoiding the unpalatable. Is this so because we are afraid of the effect of truth's acid on our audience, external and internal?

Glossing over facts, underestimating here and over-emphasizing there, reviewers normally like to give what may be called an optimistic account annually. Independence Day and Republic Day are probably observed not so much for a realistic stock-taking of the vast management of men's affairs but to impress upon them that however acute their individual misery, the nation has progressed according to plan. To make darkness look like light and crooked things look straight seems to be the primary function of utterances at such celebrations. It for a chance our planners and leaders could give a list of unattained targets, of what could not be achieved and why, the individual whom "the State" is supposed to serve, would benefit considerably.

If the vast body of individuals knew why they must earn what they do and not more, why prices should be as high as they are, why they must live in hovels, why wait for hours in a queue and so on and so forth such knowledge would help them bear their burdens more courageously. Broad generalisations are apt to confuse them because they contradict immediate and daily experience. If ordinary people could only know why disparities have to be tolerated, why some children can have four meals a day and their own little ones must content with one or less it might enable them to take the initiative necessary for altering their lot. If they knew why crime must follow punishment like night the day insofar as they and their millions of fellow citizens are concerned and yet some "at the Top" can evade the law by slipping in and out of legalities and regulations, could be effective allies of those who really mean what they say about rooting out corruption.

Why should equality of sacrifices mean less for them and more for the dwellers on the top storey?

Our "man in the street" audience would be grateful to all of us who assume the right to think for them if sometimes we could stop telling them what to do and what not to do, and instead satisfy their many curiosities about their own barren street life, their little world of small anxieties, their many desperate problems that never get solved. Nineteen sixty-three has been the most trying of all years since independence. Not only because it began when the whole nation was wondering why a friendly neighbour had suddenly turned into an enemy but also because it revealed the poverty of character of those who otherwise dash about giving the impression they were the inheritors of our independence. They panic knew no bounds and they were indignant with the Prime Minister for refusing to ask for American troops to halt the invading armies of China. If American soldiers could fight in Korea why not on the Himalayan heights, they argued.

They never bothered to think of the consequences of such intervention. What was uppermost in their minds was not that the nation freedom was in peril but that their petty wealth would vanish. And surely no price was too great for preventing such a catastrophy. Fortunately, this class and this type of individual is in a hopeless minority even among the wealthy privileged and they should not be taken too seriously. Even so the mentality of depending on others to defend our freedom by providing us with materials (if not men) has received much encouragement of late and reveals a serious flaw in our thinking. If the concept of independence does not imply fearlessness and absolute reliance on one's own resources how can we face our enemies and opponents as a free people?

It is our 480 million men and women who have to defend their country and not armies imported from across the seas. Why should others shed their blood for us in wars that may be forced on us by China or Pakistan? And during the nightmarish days of Chinese onslaughts weren't the millions ready to do and die for their country and demonstrate that they were not afraid? Should invasion be resorted to again by either of these inmical neighbours, the panicky and faint-hearted should rest assured that their own people are able to resist the enemy. The cup of our national humiliation will be full the day we think in terms of allowing others to defend our soil, to die for it, while we remain in the rear.

How do others see us as a people, as individuals? In the course of my recent tour abroad what was obvious was that India and Indians evoke a variety of reactions. The differ sharply from one country to another and the differences reflect the particular political and social ethos of the countries. In the Soviet Union an Indian is a much sought after person for several reasons.

They seem to like everything about us, the colour of our skin endears us to them and our eyes they say are beautiful, some very attractive. Soviet girls have married our boys because of these glamorous qualities. Soviet women these are fascinated by our feminine ways and of course our saries and salwars appeal to them very much. Those who study our languages, both men and women, adore our literature, our culture, our architecture and music. Our films have a special attraction for them and now after the Indian exhibition our consumer goods and tandoori cuisine have been added to the list of things that make India and Indians good.

The Soviet citizen's response to us is so natural, so free of all race and colour prejudice that it makes one wonder what makes the white-skinned people of the Western world so sure of their superiority. In the warm smile that greets one in Moscow's streets, hotels, lifts, taxis, etc., immediately makes one feel at home. But it would not do to think that they like us merely because of our romantic past and our old historical links with their country.

They like us because they yearn for peace and India's Nehru is a man of peace and therefore a friend. Fortunately, his image as a peace-make has not been blurred despite constant efforts by Chinese propagandists to paint him as a warmonger. This faith in Nehru's integrity is shared by statesman and commoner alike in the Soviet Union and their friendliness to us flows from this understanding. They see us as projections of India, ancient and modern, struggling to rise from centuries of stagnation, even as they had to struggle in the past against feudal oppression.

The spirit in which the English people react to us Indians is quite different. It is a queer mixture of contempt, affection, regard and romance. Having once belonged to their system, we are as yet not as apart from them as we would have been had that historic contact not been established. Of course, they will never forgive us entirely for having broken away but they are sharewd enough to see that there is no escape from co-existence with people one doesn't really approve of. Since our hybrid culture grew under their supervision and none can honestly admire imitation products, can we blame them.

And yet paradoxically enough England has the largest Indian population of any European country, with the number of Indian restaurants multiplying almost hourly. Nostalgic memories of days when Englishmen and women lived in India still haunt many of them but that does not necessarily make them warm up to us. We perhaps know one another too well to be impressed with our respective virtues of character and culture.

Illusions have also their uses. Very often they make life rich and interesting. Since neither the Indian nor the Englishman can have any illusions about each other we will perhaps go on glaring across the fence for some time yet.

Link, August 15, 1963.

ON THE DEATH OF JAWAHARLAL

Jawaharlal Nehru, our beloved, has taken leave of us. The unimaginable has happened. His tireless spirit has been stilled by the inexorable law that makes death the ultimate goal of all life. In innumerable homes in our country and the world over, there will be mourning for long.

For us the very thought of having to face life without Jawaharlal Nehru is alien and uncomfortable and full of desolation. How shall we reconcile ourselves to the fact of his absence from our midst? He meant so much to so many throughout these last forty years of Indian history that his sudden withdrawal has deprived us of our mainstay. A sense of insecurity unknown in his life-time has already begun to haunt us. A feeling of uncertainty about the shape of things to come robs our peace of mind as we think of the world without Nehru, of India without Nehru, and last but not least of the Indian National Congress without Nehru. Truly may we ask : "Whither India"? now that Jawaharlal Nehru has gone to rest, his voice silenced, his being a part of eternity.

As a great and good age of our history comes to an end and we wander through its corridors, many names of eminent Indians come to our mind. Men who thought and lived nobly, worked, suffered and died for freedom from bondage and stagnation. Will the era that now commences in India find an adequate leadership rising to heights of nobility and integrity, fearlessness and forthrightness, so that the proces of regeneration may flow on uninterrupted and unhampered, conquering all that is evil in humanity, rescuing it from violence, pettiness and greed? Or will we be compelled to acknowledge that henceforth only puny minds will be available to India because the best among us have vanished?

If this is the major challenge in our present situation, is it not our imperative duty to plunge afresh into the mind and thought of Nehru, discover what is imperishable therein and use it as a frame of reference for comprehending the forces with which we must reckon?

Collectively and individually, every Indian must be held accountable and responsible for the safety, well-being and progress of this magnificent land and its people to make up for Jawaharlal Nehru's loss. Thus, after Nehru, if we could justify his passionate and uncompromising belief in democracy, the problem as to who will now replace him will resolve itself.

If those whom the people have elected as their representatives rise above individual ambitions and carry on the gigantic struggle for uprooting inequality, war and poverty with the zeal and devotion of Jawaharlal Nehru, then only will he have not lived and died in vain.

We who have had the good fortune to live with him for the best part of our lives received our baptism at a common altar. He taught me and my generation to think clearly even as Gandhiji helped us to act instantly. We were fascinated by his scientific bent of mind, his impatience with conservatism, his utter unawareness of social categories of caste and religion and more than anything else his tremendous capacity to think in terms of the wide world and its problems.

Thus for the youth of the early thirties and forties of 20th century he was the symbol of everything new and modern. His ideas swept us off our feet because they were like a breath of fresh air blowing away the cobwebs of our feudal and colonial past, challenging us to revolutionize everything that stood in the way of absolute and undiluted freedom.

Every aspect of Jawaharlal Nehru's personality fascinated us and inspired us. He was our faultless and flawless idol, ideally perfect. In our own ways we tried to be like him, to live up to his expectations, and often to earn his approval was enough, the highest reward that the heart could desire.

Neither time nor age could blur the radiant image of Jawaharlal Nehru of our youth because we refused to allow ourselves to be overawed by the fact that he was India's Prime Minister. If ever there was a barrier between him and the likes of me it was because of this high office. To see him surrounded by hordes of careerists, both official and non-official, to see him yield to them where he should have resisted them firmly, dismayed and hurt us and at times we felt bitter and became cynical. Outwardly and even organisationally these moods often led to estrangement and aloofness. But these spells of withdrawal were merely passing phases because in every crucial test we found ourselves ranged with him and against those who questioned his fundamental social and political faith.

Will we be able to live courageously even after him, or will work and life become too much of a burden and drudgery? If the brave among the youth of today take over the torch that Jawaharlal Nehru lit our remaining years need not be dismal and dark. Should however a pall of ignorance and indifference keep them away from the field of action, our generation will truly be written off as a lost generation, aimless, empty and adrift.

Link, May 31, 1964.

THE NEHRU LEGACY

Base for Independence

This is the first Independence Day without Jawaharlal Nehru. He will never again address the nation from the Red Fort rampart. His voice, rallying and admonishing the people by turns, teaching them and pleading with them to think and act in unity, will not ring in their ears.

For sixteen years he held us under the spell of his personality and we either echoed his thoughts or reacted to them. There scarcely was ever a day when over the radio or in the Press his name was not mentioned in connection with some new event—or his opinion reported. He explained, annotated, criticized, encouraged a whole people as if they collectively were a single person. He told them their history, asked them to join with him in wondering over the marvels of their land and sea and rivers. This became news, interesting, refreshing and reassuring.

He discussed every problem in terms of its immediate applicability and relevance but always there was the postscript of its future significance. When reading his writings or hearing him speak, whether one agreed with him or differed, there was satisfying feeling that it was with a mind superior to one's own that one was in communication. His learning which he carried so lightly was great and his capacity for comprehension stupendous. He reminded us always of the past; but the assurance that in him we had a leader who reflected all the forward movements of the 20th century also, was complete. He wanted his country and his people to belong to this wonderful age of science and technology; but his objective was always a society based on equal rights and opportunities, and it was his utter devotion to this ideal that endeared him to millions of people not only in this country but all over the world.

Now that the post-Nehru era has commenced, inevitably the situation has changed. Gradually but surely the people will realize the need to assert their will and use the mechanism of the Indian Constitution with greater discrimination and sense of ultimate goals. Gone are the years when the people would vote as Nehru wanted them to and gone the times when their sense of security was confirmed by his physical presence, the cementing qualities of intellect and the boundless love he bore his people. As the years roll by new and as yet unpredictable forces will be released for good or evil. Much will depend on our collective ability and capacity for organizing ourselves. None of us can afford to think, feel and act as we did when Jawaharlal Nehru's genius and energy was at the disposal of the nation.

The seventeen years that Jawaharlal spent in leading and guiding were the years of preparation, the years during which the foundations of democracy and equality were laid. It is now time for every politically conscious individual and parties made up of such individuals to search their hearts and honestly assess their achievements and their short-comings and realistically resolve on patriotic programmes. A new pattern of political activity closely related to day-to-day issues which face our people will have to be created if there is not to be a general withdrawal of public interest from the activities and programmes of political parties.

In this great undertaking the Congress can set the example. As long as Jawaharlal Nehru lived and led there was no question whose opinions would count and whose advice taken. The millions who make up India looked over the heads of their political leaders and seeing him concluded that he himself would never stray from his course. This was particularly true of the Congress.

The bickerings between groups of leaders within it, the ever increasing talk of corruption, the pathetic deterioration of idealism and the constantly increasing influence of petty comfort on the lives of Congressmen brought in their wake feelings of revulsion and anger, but the people forgave those responsible because in their minds they were not truly important quantities. Beyond and above the stood one, incorruptible, stady of purpose and great enough to redeem all their sins of commission and omission. This great redeeming influence is gone and the Congress will be judged issue by issue and leader by leader, each aspect of policy and performance, each exhibition of pettiness or magnanimity being taken into consideration by a critical people.

It may be possible for a few months or years more, for Congressmen who have become influential or powerful through office or association with wealthy people to appear big and swagger about; but public opinion will judge them sooner or later, and the later it is, the more bitter will be the judgement.

The Congress is India's largest party. It is also one of the world's most important socialist parties. Its leaders cannot afford to behave hereafter as if they were representing different elements in a movement which requires from them only a minimum of agreement. Neither can they act as lucky individuals who have been placed in positions of power and influence by chance or a great leader who could be held responsible both for policy and performance.

The Congress will live or perish and those who lead it be able to claim that they partook in the progress of nation, or be compelled to confess that they utterly failed, according to the choice the organisation—that is the majority of active men and women in it—will make in the immediate future.

It is true that if the Congress organisation breaks down there will be for a time a "vacuum" in our politics; but such a situation will not continue for long. The people will find an alternative. The people, however, need not be forced to do this. If the Congress can find enough dedicated people within it who will accept responsibility without insisting on the formal privilege of power, who will lead the people without making a lucrative profession of leadership and who will honestly fight for ideals and an ideology the organisation will be able to consolidate all the forces of progress in the country and defeat every element of corrupt reaction and cowardly conservatims on our society. This requires in the first instance courage in the present leadership to insist on ideological and organisational discipline and to weed out whatever is unnecessary or unhealthy.

Ours is a rich heritage. No country can claim in one generation two leaders of the stature and qualities of Mahatma Gandhi and Jawaharlal Nehru. That they and not others were accepted and cherished by the people is proof that India's millions are politically mature and wonderfully sensitive. What these two beloved sons of India have left behind in terms of tradition, example and ideas constitute a peerless treasure house.

If me who knew them and were inspired and educated by them cannot put out inheritance to proper use, we will go down in history as a generation of futile men and women deserving nothing but obloquy and shame.

Jawaharlal Nehru's leadership has been described by Western sociologists as charismatic. The love and affection which the people of India heaped on him could have made a lesser man autocrat. In fact, long before independence in an anonymous article carried by a leading journal of those days, he had himself warned his admirers of the danger of his becoming a director. Conditions in India in the fifties were extraordinarily favourable for him if he wanted to assume dictatorship. In most of the neighbouring countries power was passing into the hands of extrovert individuals. Within the country, the influence of the Congress was declining but his personal popularity and influence were at their height. Inside the Congress there was no one to challenge his leadership.

As Chester Bowles has said, "Jawaharlal Nehru's political power was supreme to the point when he could easily have pursued the course of one-man rule which leaders in other developing countries have taken."

His true greatness lies in that he used his vast personal influence to strengthen and build safeguards against one-man rule; he changed the contours of existing political institutions, gave them a new content and provided a new meaning to their inter-relationship. He sought to demolish the social bases on which one-man rule could come about and the barriers that might retard the growth of democracy.

It fell to him to lead the nation in its transition from a backward looking, fragmented entity, held together only by the force of tradition, into a modern, integrated and self-moving community. He was aware of the "difficult and dangerous position" in which he was placed when he decided that he would lead the people's march to become a nation. He therefore laid down for himself a style of functioning which would enable him to play the role assigned to him by history.

Addressing a foreign audience he once said, "A prophet, as we all know, speaks the highest truth but is usually stoned for it. He is honoured afterwards, no doubt. But the leader has to adapt the truth as he sees it to circumstances in order to make it acceptable; because a leader is a leader, more specially in a democratic country, only insofar as he can carry his people with him . . . . therefore, a leader occupied a difficult and dangerous position. He wants to adhere to principle and truth as he sees it. But, inevitably, he tends to compromise."

But he went on to say, "Compromise with truth is a dangerous thing. Once you start compromising, you may go on compromising till you are at the bottom of the pit, because no standards are left. Nevertheless, there is no other way for a leader but to adapt himself (remembering always the principle) to circumstances to the extent that he must.

Therefore, while I lay down high principles, I recognize that countries cannot, as countries or as governments, function purely on the basis of high principles. I have to consider the facts as they are, the difficulties of a situation, the dangers in it, and adapt myself to them but remembering the principles all the time." Commentators, Indian and foreign, have often been baffled by his strong advocacy of radical policies and the compromises which he affected in actual practice. Some have ascribed his "lapses" to his awareness of the need for unity in the national movement. But that is only a partial explanation. The fact is that he was essentially a democrat and throughout his life he worked for building a democratic society in India, fighting against the separatist and divisive forces which weakened democracy, and in his definition of democracy, the role of the Opposition was always very important. To carry the largest number possible without making compromises on basic principles was his most important political objective.

During the struggle for independence, the demand for provincial autonomy and a federal structure at the top was a factor working for unity in the national movement but as a student of history he knew that federalism contained seeds of divisiveness and that in the past it was always disunity which led to domination by foreigners. Yet, a unitary government, he knew would not be acceptable.

As Chairman of three important committees set up to define the principles underlying the Constitution (the Committees for States, Union Powers and Union Constitution), he pleaded that a very broad interpretation should be put on the jurisdiction of Central subjects (Defence, Foreign Affairs and Communications). He wanted to leave minimum scope for divisive forces to operate and therefore sought for the Centre "powers implied or inherent in or resultant from the express powers of the Union."

Defending the provision for nomination for the Governors of the States by the Centre, he said, "We should always view things from the context of preserving the unity, stability and the security of India". He had also learnt from history that political instability had always opened the doors for outside intervention. While opposing the demand for the introduction of proportional representation, he said, "I can think of nothing more conducive to creating a feeble ministry and a feeble government."

Provisions in a Constitution alone, however, do not transform a tradition-bound society into a democracy. No one was more conscious of this than Jawaharlal Nehru. Through incessant campaigning from public platforms and in Parliament he sought to change our feudal outlook blinded by superstition, into a scientific, secular and modern approach to life. By his own example he sought to build conventions in Parliament to stabilise conditions in which discussion, exchange of views, persuasion and argument could be possible.

It is sometimes said that in the absence of a strong Opposition parliamentary democracy in transformed into one party rule which is no better than a one-man rule or at best the rule of a group. No one helped in building up the Opposition and in creating conditions in which it could function, as much as Jawaharlal Nehru did. Men like Jayaprakash Narayan expected him actually to organize the Opposition also for them. This of course he could not do.

However, he realised, as he himself said, that by itself political democracy was inadequate. On one occasion he posed the question "what is democracy?" and answered : "Democracy is something deeper than a form of government—voting elections, etc. In the ultimate analysis, it is a manner of thinking, a manner of action, a manner of behaviour. If the inner content is absent and if you are just given the outer shell, well, it may not be successful". He added, "Political freedom under economic pressure is very limited freedom".

For him democracy was not an in end itself. It was a means for building a self-generating society. When still engaged in our struggle for freedom he sought to place before the country the ideal of a socialist society. But characteristically before he made socialism acceptable to the leadership he brought it round (at the Karachi session in 1930) to accept the fundamental rights of the people which would give to a democratic society a socialist content. Step by step he got the leadership to accept the goal of a welfare State when the Constitution was being drafted. Later, it was recognized that such a State could operate only in "a socialistic pattern of society."

By the time he passed away even the opponents of socialism could not openly come out against the objective of socialism. It was in this manner that he sought to condition national thinking in terms of basic principles and ultimate objectives. Every compromise that he made in principle was a step forward in the direction of the ultimate objectives. The Constitution did not accept socialism. But, later, Parliament approved it as the national goal. In the Constitution, sanctity of private property was recognized. But he so changed our thinking in the course of years that the provisions of the Constitution are being amended one after another to enable socialist property relations to come into being. That was how he paved the way for further progress. But he created not only psychological conditions for our progress towards the goal; he also created an institution which could give the desired direction to our progress.

The Planning Commission did not have statutory powers; it may only be an advisory body. But during his life-time he made it an effective instrument for providing leadership to our economic effort. Progress is possible only if we are able to live in peace. The biggest danger to peace is the emergence of the armed forces as a decisive political factor. He sought to curb political ambitions in the armed forces by, on the one hand, creating in them an awareness of their responsibility and obligation to society—the speeches he delivered whenever he met men of the armed forces and the talks he gave in the army messes fully bear this out—and on the other by asserting the supremacy of the civil authorities. When an Army Chief of the Staff questioned the decision of the Minister concerned, Jawaharlal Nehru laid down the dictum that the decision of the Government was final.

From where he left us we have still to go a long way to reach the objectives defined for us by him. We can advance on the road he charted only if we have the integrity to strengthen the institutions he built and the courage to transform them whenever they become outdated.

Jawaharlal Nehru's vision of India was a harmonious blend of political and economic democracy. Striving to his last breath to make it real, he blazed a trail that no further leader of this country dare forget. When the great struggle to rediscover their national personality began in the last decades of the nineteenth century, the Indian people realised vaguely the need to look upon their task as not merely to end political subjugation but also to establish economic freedom. Yet it was only with the advent of Jawaharlal Nehru that the latter aspect of independence became meaningful to our teeming millions. Conscious of the class complexion of the National Congress, which he once desired as "petty bourgeois", he was alive to the socialist imperative—power for the working people.

He foresaw earlier than most others that the forces which three decades back were "weak but growing rapidly" would develop and demand their rightful shares of the fruit of the nation's independence. And it was to give the people a social philosophy that would explain and justify such a demand that he tirelessly worked throughout his life.

Jawaharlal has been variously called "Herald of a New Epoch" and the "Creator of our social and political clan". He himself never claimed such titles. All that he strove to do was to remind the people of their "tryst with destiny", and of the need to "redeem their pledge", for without doing that, they would again lose their personality. On his part he fought consistently to redeem this pledge, not as a leader seeking power, but as part of the national mainstream, that is the people.

The first occasion when he deliberately attempt to give the national platform a clear economic content was when he drafted the famous Karachi Resolution which said that "the State shall own or control key industries and services, mineral resources railways, waterways, shipping and other means of transport." Later, when Fascism "spectacularly" successful in providing employment to the German people, began to draw lurking admiration from certain sections of our people, he directed his own efforts to give a rational, socialistic orientation to the Congress programme. And as the Soviet model of planned development was the only scientific pattern that embodied this outlook, he felt no hesitation in advocating the need for integrated national planning on socialist lines.

"There can be no planning", he said in his note of December 21, 1983, "if planning does not include big industries; but not industrialisation alone. To make freedom real to the common people the organisation of economic life must (also) conform to the principle of justice to the end that it may secure a decent standard of living".

His keen sense of social justice as well as the need to free a predominantly rural economy from the fetters of feudalism to enable it to contribute its surplus for advancement led, Jawaharlal to lay stress on agrarian reforms. His live contact with, and leadership of, the oppressed peasantry of UP convinced him that the objective of all land reform should be to make the tiller the master of his land.

Rapid economic development through integrated national planning with industry as its core, and a radical transformation of the rural economy through land reforms were thus the key-points in Jawaharlal Nehru's programme for a Free India. He set out to emphasise their importance from the day he assumed the responsibility of office in the Interim Government in 1946. In the din of today's controversy about the direction of the Fourth Plan, it not often remembered that the question had been debate and conclusively answered by the Congress as for back as 1948. In that year the All India Congress Committee started in a resolution drafted by Jawaharlal Nehru, that "our aim should be to evolve .... an economic structure which will yield maximum production without the operation of private monopolies and the concentration of wealth, and which will create a proper balance between urban and rural economics. Such a social structure can provide an alternative to the acquisitive economy of private capitalism and the regimentation of a totalitarian state."

This declaration formed the basis of Nehru's famous "Middle Way" which, for all its "middleness" totally rejected India's development along a "capitalist" path. The "middleness" related only to the means to be adopted to reach the objective, and not to the objective as such.

These means, as he often stressed, had to be "democratic", that is, based on persuasion and consent, but always directed at propelling the economy and the polity in general towards the ultimate objective of a socialist society. This is evident from the different stages through which he made the Congress traverse before the heterogeneous organisation came to accept the establishment of a socialist as its specific objective.

Working assiduously on his colleagues, striking often unpalatable and embarrassing compromises with their conservative stand, and at the same time carrying on a ceaseless campaign of education among the people to make them conscious of the need for socialism, Jawaharlal attained his cherished objective of committing the Congress irrevocably to a socialist economy and a Socialist State.

At first all that it would agree to was the establishment of a "Welfare State" (1956). Thence to a "socialistic pattern of society" (Avadi 1955) and finally to an unmixed "Socialist State" (Bhubaneswar 1964)—the journey was no doubt, arduous, and not without detours that made the more impatient of his followers doubt the firmness of his convictions, but it was also a saga of a man's struggle to make his fellowmen drop ideological and other blinkers from their eyes and see the light of reason, as he saw it. The idealism of the National Planning Committee he soon discovered had to be tempered with the realisation that the Congress and the Parliament had to be accustomed to the idea of transformation, and planned, deliberate State action to that end. The first steps, therefore, had to be necessarily halting. The Industrial Policy Resolution of 1948, which today looks almost like a chapter from any of the FICCI brochures, embodied this approach. The First Five-Year Plan, with its accent on agriculture, and little or no provision for basic industries, reflected this early hesitant approach. Both aimed at familiarising the people and the Congress with the idea of planning without creating a scare amongst the conservative and the unconvinced. But later, when their hesitation had been somewhat overcome, and the people as a whole began to perceive in planning the only possible way to economic advance, Jawaharlal Nehru became more positive and the Second Plan reflected this.

The investment in the public sector in the Second plan was raised to a level twice that of the outlay on private sector projects in order to enable the State to have a "commanding position" in the economy as a whole. The "Nehru pattern" of planned economic development took another step forward, although, as the subsequent developments showed, it was still hedge in by vestiges of the earlier equivocal approach.

It also declared the Government's intention to undertake State trading, whenever found necessary. Besides reserving certain industries for the States Resolution also clearly indicated the "other industries, which are essential and require investment on a scale which only the State, in present circumstances, could provide, have also to be in public sector". The rest of the industries could, however, be developed in the private sector, with or without State participation.

The 1956 Industrial Policy Resolution, which formed the basis of the Second Plan, was in fact the expression of the Avadi Resolution of the Congress declaring the establishment of a "Socialistic Pattern of Society" as the objective of the organisation. It was no generalised expression either, but a concrete directive to the Government to propel the country towards socialism.

The Second Plan faced heavy weather when it was half through. The reasons for its crisis had little to do with its framing, or the economic policy guiding it. They were the reflection of a strange dichotomy between the objectives of policy and the apparatus of administration which was to plague him to the end. While sensing the dangers arising from this dichotomy, and always trying in his own way to correct it, he never allowed it to scare him. In fact, with every reverse his determination to pursue the course of planned development became firmer.

The result was the Third Five-Year Plan which, in spite of shortfalls in the preceding plan, was framed with the perspective of making the state a decisive factor in the economy. The hurdles it has come to face in its first years are again a reflection of the dichotomy which had marred the progress of the Second Plan.

In the sphere of agriculture, the famous Nagpur Resolution of 1960 was part of Jawaharlal's redemption of his pledge to the peasantry. Ceilings on land to get hold of a surplus to redistribute to the landless, and cooperative farming, the two cardinal principals underlying this resolution, could have certainly revolutionised our rural society, but for the fact that powerful elements in the Congress party scuttled its implementation at the State level.

Jawaharlal was not oblivious of this glaring gulf between what he—and the nation with him— proposed, and the administration disposed. In fact, in his last phase he was increasingly restive at the snail's pace of the country's progress. Bhubaneswar, with its categoric commitment not to a socialist pattern, but to a socialist state, was his response to this phenomenon. His agony was not without reason.

He could hear the rumblings of an approaching storm, of our people losing their faith in peaceful means unless the Congress showed the "necessary sense of urgency". Though the Bhubaneswar Resolution, and the Kamaraj plan, and a rigorous application of the principles embodied in them he wanted to sweep away the dirt and the cobwebs that had accumulated—both in the party and the administration–as the result of his liberal approach.

But he could not finish his task. Will those who claim the right to carry forward his policies have his courage and his vision? If they do, they should admit that the Industrial Policy Resolution is being flagrantly violated, even to the extent of allowing foreign participation in basic industries. Otherwise, too, foreign capital, against which Jawaharlal sounded the tocsin as early as 1956, is being openly courted and welcomed.

The most convincing testimony to nation sovereignty is capacity to exercise foreign policy. In the final analysis that nation is most independent which can choose most freely and practise without restraint its policies in regard to others. By this test India is one of the most independent nations in the world today and, no amount of sarcasm about our poverty or our dependence on economic support from foreign countries in the press or in pot-boiled books can hide that fundamental fact. Indeed much of the gloating references to our indigence in the newspapers of American and other Western countries can be traced to a sense of anger caused by the awareness that in spite of acknowledged economic and military superiority Western powers have not been able so far to make any dent in the independence of our foreign policy.

Jawaharlal Nehru was solely and completely responsible for this great national achievement. The magnitude of his success can be grasped only if the obstructions he had to face and the peculiarities of the decade in which he defined non-alignment and practised it with supreme virtuosity are borne in mind.

The Second World War ended the epoch of formal or explicit imperialism. But it created a situation in which many people were convinced that only such nations as allowed themselves to be herded around a commonly accepted master-nation could hope for true security.

Mr. Walter Lippman, for example, wrote towards the end of the war that the world would soon be divided into the Atlantic, the Russian and probably the Chinese spheres of influence, these three super-nations providing security for satellite neigbours and therefore, also laying down that would govern their relationship with the rest of the world and between themselves. Mr. Lippman, it is true, was not thinking of a Communist China then but of possible stabilization of the authority of Chiang Kai-shek. That detail, however, did not fundamentally invalidate his short-sighted analysis.

What was the reaction to such a polarization in this man who was writing in jail? He answers it with a question : "Where do the hundreds of millions of Asia and Africa come in this picture?" They would decide, he asserted, after getting answers to some more questions : "Does it (the polarization into blocs) help towards our liberation? Does it end the domination of one country over another? Will it enable us to live freely the life of our choice in cooperation with others? Does it bring equality and equal opportunity for nations as well as groups within each nation? Does it hold forth the promise of early liquidation of poverty and illiteracy?" He admitted that these questions were "nationalistic" but explained that "this nationalism seeks no domination over or interference with others". These questions he asked on behalf of as yet unfree Asia and Africa defined the scope and purpose of non-alignment which he later made the linch-pin of his own foreign policy and which he repeatedly said was no negative retreat from responsibility. Non-alignment on which he staked his own and his nation's fate immediately after he assumed office, was for him, from the very beginning, a positive and dynamic attitude vitally necessary for all developing countries both for economic growth and for escape from the suffocating grip of geo-political gangs of disillusioned Governments who had sold themselves blindly into the bondage of "blocs".

And study of Jawaharlal Nehru's foreign policy therefore becomes a study of how he practised non-alignment. The attitudes of satellite countries being entirely decided in the early post-war years by Washington and Moscow, his main concern when the began his career as Foreign Minister of India, was to define his relationships with these two powerful Governments. His assertion that he would remain uncommitted was viewed with anger and sometimes contempt in both the camps. Every move he made was viewed with intense suspicion. When India voted for the Veto in the U.N. in 1948 the American Press and its jackals in India howled. When anything he said or did appeared to be in the least differnt from the rigid "lines" that Stalin drew for every section of humanity, he was attacked by the Soviet Press and the Indian Communist Party. But between 1948 and 1950 he laid the foundations for independent action in the United Nations, made it clear to both the super-powers that neither wheedling nor bullying would divert him from the path he was marking for himself and established a relationship of freindship that was totally sincere—on his part—with China.

Unaware of the basic role that machiavellian opportunism plays in the political philosophy of Mao Tse-tung, Jawaharlal Nehru accepted China's Asianism as a sincerely cooperative approach to world problems. The fairly obvious indications of Chinese differences with the rigidities of Stalinism perhaps made him totally unsuspicious of China's true intentions in Asia. The acceptance of Panch Sheel by Peking, hypocritical as later events proved it, convinced him for a time that Indian non-alignment would be respected by the Chinese leaders.

He never regarded relationships with close neighbours like Pakistan, Burma and Ceylon as entirely in the sphere of foreign policy. He was always ready to make the maximum concessions to them and never lost the hope that the utter sincerity of his attitude of equality and cooperation would sooner or later be accepted and welcomed by the Governments of these countries. As soon as Burma and Ceylon began showing signs of enthusiasm for socialist reorganisation of their economies and stated their foreign policy intentions in terms of non-alignment his approach to them became uninhibitedly warm. As for Pakistan, the continuous efforts by her Government to interfere in the communal affairs of this country, to its insistence on continuing the aggression in Kashmir and its unprincipled alliance with the Western military bloc made him intensely suspicious. He regretted till his last days the need for spending so much on defence because of Pakistani aggressiveness and was always ready to come to terms provided Pakistan acted independently and honestly.

The changes in the foreign policies of the U.S.S.R. and the U.S.A. following the death of Stalin and John Foster Dulles were profound; but in regard to India they largely consisted of openly admitting the validity of Jawaharlal Nehru's propositions. This recognition that the Indian attitude stemmed from the love of independence was spontaneous, warm and patently sincere in the case of Prime Minister Khrushchev. It was forced, inhibited and opportunist in the case of American leaders. Naturally Jawaharlal Nehru's reactions were conditioned by the quality of the recognition. In post-Stalin Russia and its great leader, Khrushchev, Jawaharlal Nehru found a firm, understanding and courageous supporter of non-alignment. He responded to the sweeping changes that Khrushchev brought about in the Soviet Union's foreign policy with uninhibited and unreserved welcome. Indo-Soviet understanding indeed became, from 1954 onwards, the most important factor in India's own foreign policy and a compulsive influence on the foreign policies of many other countries. But for the undeviating attitude of friendship between the Soviet Union and India which was cemented by a mutual personal regard, rare among the leaders of big nations, between Jawaharlal Nehru and Khrushchev, the American and the British attitude to non-alignment would have continued to be one of contempt, and suspicion. That it had to be changed, at least officially and formally, to one of grudging tolerance was a great triumph for Jawaharlal Nehru, not because it brought in its wake any concrete advantage to India, but because withdrawal of open opposition to non-alignment by the American Government loosened the frozen attitudes of several satellites of Washington. America's interest in such mischievous contraptions as the Seato and the Cento became less intense, disillusioning in the process, a number of Asian yesmen who had till then been more loyal than the King.

Another consequence of Indo-Soviet friendship becoming a major factor in our epoch's international affairs, was the total exposure of Chinese chicanery and opportunism. In the course of the rabid attacks made by Chinese leaders in the last few years on this friendship, the political philosophy that Mao Tse-tung claims to be Marxism-Leninism has been proved to be nothing more than an Asian version of geopolitics, its objective being the gathering together of a number of client countries that will serve as a protective cover immediately, and eventually as a field for exploitation.

Jawaharlal Nehru advocated non-alignment in no isolationist spirit. His goal in trying to release small nations committed to the great powers was to create conditions for a world order of national entities whose equality of status is acknowledged irrespective of their military capacity or political ideology. He succeeded splendidly and many Western critics who had scoffed at him in the beginning had to admit before he died that but for him and his insistence on non-alignment for all developing countries the world on several recent occasions might have slipped into a war no one wants. He himself never made any such claims on behalf of the theory of non-alignment. He often said that whenever India was free the tendency had been towards non-involvement. He was always humble in regard to the role that this country has played or can play in world affairs. In 1950 he said, "I do not say that India as she is can make a vital difference to world affairs. So long as we have not solved most of our own problems our voice cannot carry the weight that it normally will and should". But he taught us that even when all our problems are solved and we are capable of exerting our real strength, it will be worthless unless it is exerted on the side of freedom for all peoples and fairness in the dealings between the richer and the poorer countries, between the so-called Great Powers and the small nations.

Nehru first came into touch with revolutionary Arab leaders during the World Conference against Imperialism and Colonial Oppression at Brussels in 1927. This was the time when the Arab national movement was just beginning to acquire organisational shape and several young Arab revolutionaries had come to Brussels after overcoming innumerable obstacles. Jawaharlal admired their revolutionary optimism and wrote in his report to the Indian National Congress : "The Arabs from Syria and North Africa were very different. Typical fighting men, who understood independence and fighting for it and cared for little else, and were wholly untainted with the slave mentality of more intellectual races". In the conference Nehru drafted and moved a resolution on Mesopotamia (Iraq).

After Nehru's return from Europe, the Congress policy towards the freedom movements in other countries underwent a radical reorientation. As Congress moved towards a redefinition of its national objective as Complete Independence, it also got rid of its inhibitions in extending full-throated support to the other countries fighting against imperialism. At its Calcutta session in 1928 the Congress, on Jawaharlal Nehru's advice, adopted a resolution on the Arabs' struggle for freedom and expressed its "full sympathy with them in their struggle for emancipation from the grip of Western imperialism which is, in the opinion of the Congress, a great menace to Indian struggle for freedom".

The Arabs reciprocated the sentiment. Chedly Ben Mustafa, the renowned leader of Tunisia's Destour Party, who had met Nehru at Brussels, in a message to the 43rd session of the Congress, wrote to Motilal Nehru : "We realise also that your fight is only as episode in the great world movement for the liberation of all oppressed people . . . . At the moment when you affirm your wish to have no compromise with imperialism, our party sends you its sympathy, its encouragement and assurances of its solidarity with you. . . . I should assure you, my dear comrade, that the people of Tunisia have the most ardent wish for the triumph of India's cause".

The Wafd Party of Egypt, first under the leadership of Saad Zaghlul Pasha and then Nahas Pasha, kept close touch with the Congress and its leaders, Mahatma Gandhi and Jawaharlal Nehru. Saad Zaghlul called Mahatma Gandhi the "spirit of resurgent Asia". The two leaders met when Gandhiji was coming back from London after attending the first Round Table Conference.

The great Egyptian poet Shouqi hailed their meeting as the coming together of two ancient cultures and the confluence of the Nile and the Ganges. A few years later, on his way to Europe on the eve of World War II, Jawaharlal Nehru paid a visit to Egypt and held long discussions with the Wafd leaders on the possibilities of coordinating the anti-imperialist struggle in the two countries.

He invited Nahas Pasha to attend the forthcoming Congress session. A year later, a five-member Wafd delegation was given a rousing reception at the Tripuri session of the Congress which felt "proud" in extending warm greetings to the Egyptian leaders whose presence "symbolised the solidarity of the movements for freedom in Egypt and India". Subhas Chandra Bose in his presidential address paid warm tributes to the Arabs for their "courage determination and the sacrifice made by them in their struggle for national freedom which naturally evoked the admiration of the Indian people who wished for the complete success of the Arabs in the attainment of their objectives".

As India's struggle for freedom gathered force, Jawaharlal became a symbol of courageous and uncompromising anti-imperialism for the Arab youth and intellectuals. Young students in such far off places as Khartoum memorised Nehru's speeches and writings which were smuggled from Cairo. Several faced corporal punishment because they refused to part with his books and insisted on displaying his photographs.

One of the main reasons for Jawaharlal Nehru's universal popularity in the Arab countries was his unequivocal opposition to the British policy in Palestine. As early as in 1937 the AICC. acting on the advice of Nehru and Azad, passed a resolution condemning the "reign of terror" established by the British in Palestine "with a view to coerce the Arabs into accepting the proposed partition of Palestine", while a few months later the Haripura session of the Congress denounced the British decision to impose "partition of Palestine in the teeth of Arab opposition." It asked the Jews in Palestine "not to seek the shelter of the British Mandatory power and not to allow themselves to be exploited in the interest of British imperialists".

The Tripuri session, after welcoming the Wafd delegation, strongly deplored the Zionists' role of aligning themselves "with the British armed forces to advance their special privileges". The partition of Palestine a few months after India's bifurcation shocked Nehru who on his way to London stopped at Cairo, visited the Arab League headquarters and personally conveyed to Azam Pasha, the Arab League Secretary-General, India's concern at the establishment of Israel and her sympathy with the Arab refugees.

Unlike many other world leaders Jawaharlal Nehru was quick to see the potentialities to the Egyptian revolution which India welcomed as enthusiastically as she had earlier welcomed the Kemalist revolution in Turkey. After Bandung where Nehru and Nasser developed an intimate friendship, India began increasingly to exercise a direct influence on the minds of the Egyptian leaders. Nehru seldom went to Europe without breaking his journey in Cairo where each time, in Nasser's words, "he talked and we listened to him for hours". Socialism, planning, land reforms, positive neutrality—all the chief components of Nasser's policy were to a large degree hammered into shape in these discussions.

The impact of India on the countries of Africa has been at two different levels. At one level the educated Africans watched with great interest the Indian struggle for political and economic independence. They assumed that the freedom struggle which India was waging would have immense consequences for their own countries; they looked upon Gandhi and Nehru not only as the leaders of the Indian national movement but also as the leaders of a world-wide movement against colonialism and fascism.

At another level the Indian settler population in East and South Africa was observed with suspicion. Wherever Africans came to know Indians as merchants, traders and civil servants, they appeared to be the tools of British imperialism, mercenaries, who were satisfied with the crumbs of exploitation.

Nehru saw the Indian struggle in its international setting more clearly than any of his contemporaries. He realised that any strengthening of European domination in Africa would affect India adversely. He also realised that in the final analysis British and other European imperialisms would be liquidated totally only when the struggle against them was truly Afro-Asian. He was one of the stoutest champions of the Ethiopians in their struggle against Fascist Italy's unwarranted aggression. At the same time the Indian National Congress under his leadership did everything in its power to see that the British settlers did not discriminate against the Indians in South and East Africa. As long as Africa was held in bondage in his opinion there could be no peace in the world. Repeatedly at the United Nations, the Indian delegation, under his instructions, attacked colonialism and gave every support to Africans. Till some of the African countries became independent, and could themselves press for the liberation of those territories which were under colonial rule, it was India that championed the cause of African independence.

Jawaharlal Nehru believed that efforts would be made whenever possible, but imperialism to return by the back door after ceremoniously walking out of the front. This happened in Congo and he did everything in his power to help the United Nations to establish a truly independent government in Congo and to minimize the dangers of great-power intervention.

There is one part of Africa where India has a special interest—East Africa, consisting of the territories of Uganda, Kenya, Tanganyika and Zanzibar. In all these countries there is a settled Indian community. It was expected that on the achievement of independence, India would pursue a more active policy in protecting the interests of Indian settlers.

But from the very beginning Nehru made it clear that the Indians who had settled in these countries should regard it as their home, and their loyalty was to the land they had adopted. The Indian High Commission instead of behaving as the custodian of settler interests cultivated African politicians. The Corfield Report on the origins of the Mau Mau in Kenya, in fact, blamed the Indian High Commission for having actively encouraged Africa nationalism.

7

Literary Pursuit

A YEAR WITHOUT NEHRU

A whole year has gone by without Jawaharlal Nehru amongst us. Even so the dull ache of final separation refuses to subside. Banal efforts to remind ourselves of what he meant to us and the world, to mourn and sentimentalize over our loss will continue, but they cannot really express adequately the degree of our impoverishment.

'Had we but world enough and time' to ponder and muse over the inner meaning of events which Jawaharlal Nehru shaped and to which he contributed so much, our grief and sorrow would have purified us. Instead, we are pushed from crisis to crisis unable to overcome our weaknesses and regain self-confidence as individuals or as a people.

In fact as the shadow-filled year since he passed away comes to its end, we are still missing him intensely–almost bitterly angry with him for having allowed death to have its way, to deprive us and to prevent him from keeping his unfulfilled promises. Why could he not have lived on, is the petulant irrational question one asks again and again because there seems to be no substitute for his personal guidance, as the threat to our freedom and security and to peace in the world increases hourly.

A thousand fleeting memories crowd in as I think of the long years of my apprenticeship in the era in which Jawaharlal Nehru led us. In the early years of our struggle we looked at him as we do at a distant star. He was ever so much more remote than Gandhiji because somehow we felt that to establish communion with Jawaharlal Nehru one had to attain a degree of intellectual comprehension and sophistication to which I felt I had no claim whatsoever. With Gandhiji it was quite different; there was no need to be inhibited, he took us as we were, raw but robust, questioning us and arguing with us, almost encouraging us not to think but act instinctively, setting at rest all intellectual doubts, urging us to have faith in the principle of ahimsa and resistance to evil.

When in later years I began to think (almost in spite of myself) I suddenly found that I was agreeing with Jawaharlal Nehru's approach. Gradually the compulsion to take sides on controversial issues like negotiating our way into freedom or resisting to the very end, of accepting compromises which smacked of surrender or of adhering to the path of continuous struggle against imperialism became inescapable. I still remember strolling with Gandhiji one evening in the early forties and telling him how torn some of us felt between him and Jawaharlalji—"the heart" led us to him but the head to the latter and Gandhiji's smiling advice; "If I were you I would allow the head to be where the heart is!"

In reality neither Gandhi nor Nehru did anything to consolidate either of the trends because it is my belief that they were essentially opposed to anything that smacked of sectarianism. Miles apart in many ways, the two were in absolute tune with one another and never encouraged any tendency that could lead to a clash in organizational terms. They agreed to differ when unable to arrive at a common understanding and were governed by a code of conduct unique among two leaders of such magnitude.

Their own writings provide ample proof of the mutual regard, affection and comprehension, and despite the attempts of radically-minded individuals who preferred to owe allegiance to him exclusively, Nehru discouraged any organized opposition to what was called the Gandhian approach. Nevertheless his impatience with those who vulgarized Gandhian values and boasted pretentiously of their moral superiority was equally vehement and devastating. Nehru's reluctance to lead and unite his progressive colleagues who were by and large influenced by him into accepting socialism as a belief, was resented by many of them. It was quite inexplicable why he could not see the advantage in organizing the vast working masses and disciplining them for the attainment of a goal so near his heart's desire.

And yet paradoxically when some of us took the initiative and went ahead and exerted our point of view demonstratively, we found him appreciative of our work. There are ever so many instances of his approval, but reminiscing over such a long stretch of time–nearly thirtyfive years—it is difficult and almost impossible to record every encounter with Jawaharlal Nehru.

For me personally glimpses of him became more frequent after the main battle was over, for the simple reason that I happen to be a citizen of Delhi, which became his second home in post-independent India. My meetings with him were invariably in connection with incidents and events relating to social and political developments. As I have said, even though he played no direct part in providing day-to-day guidance to my activities, I always got the impression that not only did he hear me, patiently and indulgently, but I sensed sometimes in his silences and sometimes by the way he looked that he approved of my action. We had many arguments and who can ever forget his indignant retorts, his frank exhibitions of annoyance when displeased and then that sudden faraway look, that calm gaze signifying partial acceptance of what was so hotly denied a few moments earlier. I shall never forget my amazement, and a sudden realization of myself as an entity of which he had become aware, when immediately on release from his last imprisonment in 1945 he sent me his greetings through the Press, not knowing where I was.

The apprehension that I might not have been acting correctly in deciding for myself what task I should perform for four whole years of bitter struggle vanished and, I knew that he (as also Gandhiji) had not really disapproved of our acts of revolt against imperialist Britain. Similarly, when during the RIN mutiny he responded to my urgent appeal to him and cut short his holiday in Kashmir and came over to Bombay and heard what the brave young ratings had to say, I knew we had his support in sealing the final doom of British power in India. Again, when in the early fifties I had made up my mind to go abroad for study and told him of my intention to visit the Soviet Union and other socialist countries with a view to observe for myself how socialism operates he readily endorsed the plan.

On my return when I reported to him (as was the wont of all who were near to him) my decision which amounted to a total break with the Congress, it never occurred to him to dissuade me from carrying out my plans. Nor did my subsequent efforts to make the working class and peasantry conscious of their role in working for a socialist society throw up any barriers between us. I could always be sure of a warm and affectionate welcome and sound advice. The final struggle for Goa's liberation was undertaken against heavy odds as we all know.

Our efforts went on despite them and there were moments when he was made to believe that a military solution would invite world criticism. But Nehru knew that his tryst with destiny would remain incomplete if this tiny pockets symbolizing Portuguese aggression and barbarism was not liquidated. His sense of the historic prevailed and Salazar's forces were humbled and forced to withdraw. Again characteristically, although he had never given his formal approval to the campaign for Goa's liberation, yet when he realized that the demand for action was supported by every section of our people, he accepted the challenge.

How shall we cherish the memory of our trusted leader? Several ways and means will suggest themselves to each of us according to our understanding of the times we live in. What would he have his country and his people do in his absence? He has left us enough words of wisdom to guide us individually till life's journey ends. Let us be true to them in remembrance and constantly measure ourselves with his message that "only those can sense life who stand on the verge of it, only those whose lives are not governed by the fear of death . . . . thus have we saved ourselves from triviality and an inner shame and cowardice".

The heart-breaking and unbelievable news that Gandhiji had been shot dead in New Delhi reached me in New York. I was to leave for India on the 29th of January but was delayed as all air journeys had to be cancelled due to bad weather. It was an uncommonly severe winter in North America and yet what froze every pore of one's being was not the icy winds or the chill from the snowstorm as it raged through the day, but the guilt of patricide.

"What would the world think of us?" "How could we ever explain away this criminal act?"—were the questions uppermost in my mind as I sat huddled in my seat, not daring to look at anyone around. As a matter of fact I was told when I arrived at the London airport that Sir Stafford Cripps had already referred in sneering terms of the incapacity of free Indians to protect the man whom they professed to worship. Indeed, those were moments when it was difficult to look anyone in the face, so deep was the feeling that we had disgraced ourselves.

Those who shared the agonising experience of Gandhiji's assassination were unable thereafter to recapture the elation that freedom had brought; our hour of triumph had been cut short and we shrank in our own estimation as a people. The martyrdom of Gandhiji, had it come about in the course of the struggle against imperialism, would have enabled us to share in it—but coming when it did; it only revealed the ugliness beneath the surface of our boastful claims to a "spiritual" heritage.

I am asked very often why such men and women who were many years younger to Gandhiji and were very often critical of his religious and ethical approach to life should have clung to him in all essentials. I wish it were easy to give a satisfactory answer to this question because illogical as it might appear, those who most sharply disagreed with him were often his most disciplined disciples.

It was one of the peculiarities of the national response to Mahatma Gandhi that people of every class and almost all shades of radicalism were influenced by him and even if they differed from him on important issues they finally could not but fall in line with him when he launched his movements for the larger cause of freedom. No alternative paths were available to our generation which was politically most active from the early thirties to the late forties. There was nothing more acceptable to the masses of our people. The people were not prepared to support any movement that did not have his blessings. And, therefore, Jawaharlal Nehru was quite right when he wrote in reply to an armchair Marxist's attack on Gandhiji : "He functioned inevitably within the orbit of nationalist ideology, but the dominating passion that consumed him was a desire to raise the masses.

In this respect he was always ahead of the nationalist movement. . . . Through nation-wide action he sought to mould the millions, and largely succeeded in doing so, and changing them from a demoralized, timid, and hopeless mass, bullied and crushed by every dominant interest, and incapable of resistance, into a people with self-respect and self-reliance, resisting tyranny, and capable of united action and sacrifice for a larger cause. He made them think of political and economic issues, and every village and every bazaar hummed with argument and debate on the new ideas and hopes that filled the people. That was an amazing psychological change".

Obviously, the most revolutionary ideology becomes meaningless if those who believe in it are unable to carry the masses with them, hence commonsense made us accept Gandhiji's advice leadership. Inevitably, therefore, during this period all reads led to Wardha or the Bhangi Colony or the III class compartment in which he travelled or even to Birla House, because he was available to all from the highest to the lowest. His opponents, foreign and domestic, used to indulge in all manner of insinuation and aspersions for the very catholicity that drew people of all shades of opinion to him. For one who had set his heart on the liberating not the country alone but the minds of men, such individuals who had doubt about the efficacy of his methods and were not in complete agreement with him, were specially welcome.

He was anxious to share his faith with them, to communicate his passionate beliefs because he realized that these people were sincerely and honestly (if somewhat impatiently) trying to test out ways and means which differed from his. Essentially a man of crystal like integrity he was always prepared to grant others the right to defend their beliefs. Gandhiji had another very rare capacity, namely, never to loss his poise or grow bitter and sour while arguing against points of view with which he was in total disagreement. Was this an attitude of mere tolerance? He denied it by saying, "Tolerance may imply a gratuitous assumption of the inferiority of other faiths to one's own . . . . . "What is more, he believed that "intolerance of criticism even of what one may prize as life itself, is not conducive to the growth of public corporate life". The criticism and views of friend or foe was not only acknowledged by Gandhiji but discussed in the columns of his weekly, Harijan.

When the Quit India movement went beyond the discipline enjoined by his non-violent non-cooperation, we were warned that he would disown and denounce us. Later when we explained at length how circumstances forced us to cross the limits, while he never agreed with us, instead of castigating us, he praised so warmly that our critics were completely confounded. At several prayer meetings after his release in 1944 he referred to "the Underground" and talked of their misguided methods but always qualified such statements by commending their fearlessness and courage. We all knew that he disapproved of secrecy and yet when I was eager and anxious to meet him secretly he never denied me that privilege. Sometimes when he wanted to communicate to some of us he would not hesitate to write and took good care to see that his letters reached their destination, wherever it was.

Gandhiji could have very easily ignored the 'rebel' group, but a study of his writings and speeches during the closing years of the most exciting period of our history proves that we were very much in his thoughts, individually and collectively—always "the intimate friend and colleague". His affectionate interest in our personal well-being and concern for our political future, even though we were not able to live up to his expectations proved how free he was from every form of bigotry, narrowness and sectarian prejudice.

It must be borne in mind that Gandhiji had necessarily to function on the nationalist plane and did not think in terms of class conflicts as such, but whatever he said or did stirred the masses to the depth of their being and made them aware of their class and caste subservience—the deep-rooted cause of their social backwardness as against the social prosperity of the privileged minority—and changed their attitude towards those who lived at their expense. In Jawaharlal Nehru's words. "Throughout his life he thought of India in terms of the poor and the oppressed and the downtrodden. To raise them and free them was the mission of his life. He adopted their ways of life and dress so that no one in the country might feel lowly."

There were many who thought he made a fetish of simplicity and austerity. But the austerities he practised had nothing to do with religious asceticism. He wanted all of us in the movement, whatever our social status, to give up ostentious habits so that we could evoke feelings of comradeliness among all our fellow workers, who obviously could not afford the good things of life. I can recall ever so many occasions on which he argued (as with Sarojini Naidu) against the use of silk even if it was hand spun and woven, because he felt that simpler our apparel, the more easily would people be drawn into the struggle.

Thus, during the life-time of this epoch-making person—the noblest Indian of our age—even we who were no more than mere speaks were given opportunities to work under his direction. This gave us a tremendous measure of self-confidence, a belief that our inadequacies notwithstanding we could be instrumental in bringing about historic changes.

With his passing away went much of the reflected glory in which we revealed. But the memory of having lived and worked for the liberation of India under "this mighty person" can never fade.

Link, January 30, 1996.

THE NEW CHALLENGE

"We end today a period of ill-fortune and India discovers himself again . . . The achievement we celebrate today is but a step—an opening of opportunity to the greater triumphs and achievements that await us. Are we brave enough and wise enough to grasp this opportunity and accept the challenge of the future?"

—From Jawaharlal Nehru's speech to the
Constituent Assembly on August 14, 1947

Old memories can achieve new meanings on anniversaries, which are formalised and institutionalised efforts to recall significant evens in a nation's history. It has become a custom with us to observe every year the birth of freedom from colonial rule in the month of August. But this month is important not only because it saw, nineteen years ago, the end of British rule over India, but also because five years prior to it in 1942, it was on the 9th of August that the people of this country rose, in vast numbers, resisting with all their strength, organised and unorganized, the will and authority of the then invincible empire of Great Britain. In the twenty old years that have intervened since that mighty upsurge shook us out of our slavishness and torpor, a new generation has come into existence. This generation's knowledge and experience of life has been conditioned by a chain of circumstances entirely different from those of my own generation. They have learnt to look upon the 15th August as the day of Indian Independence, as the day of our deliverance from foreign bondage; but awareness of the long and grim struggle that preceded it and contributed to make freedom a living reality has never really been a part of the young Indian's consciousness. They may have heard and read of vague happenings in those stirring times from their elders but the story of the courage and sacrifice of the millions who suffered and perished has scarcely affected their thinking.

Mechanically imparted anecdotes and incidents, cursory references to our great patriots and savants and the efforts of Jawaharlal Nehru constantly to educate the people notwithstanding, the post-freedom generation has not been given a thorough and systematic understanding of the politics and ethics of the Indian revolution in its entirety.

Therefore, if the new generation takes it for granted that the free air they breathe and the opportunities they enjoy today, did not involve a revolutionary effort, they are not really to blame. The tradition to which they are heir has been different because the intellectual norms that have shaped their thinking have ignored by and large the historical setting in which India's Independence was achieved.

The stimulating idealism that invigorated several generations of Indians in the earlier and later British periods of our history, has been replaced by a peculiar amalgam of opportunism, revolutionary catchwords, phrase-mongering and a cynical disregard of basic values. Gandhiji's assassination typified the emergence of this amoral, socially callous and unethical trend in our social organism. After that tragedy Jawaharlal Nehru's single handed efforts to keep the old fires burning in our hearts and minds were inadequate because the organisational form available to him failed to deliver the goods.

These harsh words are widely applicable but more so to such of us who in one form or another were participants in the movement for national independence. Most of us seem to have succumbled to the temptation to take to easy work and live in soft surroundings mainly because—be it the Gandhians or

Harijan Sevaks, the Kasturbaites or Bharat Sevaks, progressive authors, artists or journalists—we have all arrived at the escapist conclusion that patchy social reform is all that is possible and not social revolution. When people at the helm of social, cultural and political affairs reach the end of their mental tether, moral exhaustion is inevitable and becomes a noticeable feature of the times. Therefore, when appeals for sacrifice and hard work are sent forth from ministerial or from other elevated levels in the present Establishment, the response is one of indifference and irraverent rejection. Young men and women do come forward but only to ask for jobs and jeeps and all the bureaucratic paraphernalia that has sprung around "social work".

They refuse to go to the people living in villages and city and slums unless they are provided with everything that our MPs, MLAs, our Ministers and our business executives, are equipped with, may be with some modification. A slightly older age groups expects to be equated with candidates for either Municipal, State or Parliamentary bodies!

Why did the Do or Die call of Quit India days evoke quite a different set of reactions? These who enlisted wanted to plunge into the struggles, wanted to know about their form and content and they were completely unafraid of the consequences. Facing lathis and bullets or being led to prisons and even the gallows, nothing mattered to them in those years of feverish fervour. The moral timbre of the leadership at that period as also the objective situation in which it functioned was vastly different from what it is 24 years later. The manner in which post-independence social and political developments have taken place has divided our peoples sharply because the gains and losses of this period are not shared equally.

These divisions into classes and categories, some with too much and others too little (and some with just enough in between) explain the divisive processes at work, resulting in a bewildering variety of groups in almost every articulate section of the people. Those who have gained name and fame and wealth in the present order are unable to see why they who live by the sweat of their labour alone, should agitate and not submit and accept the current load of hardships in a spirit of resignation.

Aspirants to political leadership in the near future are being warned well ahead of the general elections next year that when making promises they must take care that they are fulfilled. August 1942 saw the beginning of the end of British rule in India. Is August 1966 witnessing the emergence of forces which will insist on placing social liberation on the agenda? The disinherited millions were willing to wait patiently all these 19 years because they loved and trusted Jawaharlal Nehru, their friend and guide of many many years.

I do not know how or when this new order will come to India. I imagine that every country will fashion it after its own way and fit it in with its national genius. But the essential basis of that order must remain and be a link in the world order that will emerge out of the present chaos. He did not live to see all this and there is no knowing yet when this dream will materialise but it is good to know that the outlines of the goal are clear and categoric.

The progressive forces in our country will have to reckon with the fact that an ex-colonial economy cannot be released from its feudal and semi-feudal heritage in a matter of days. Tall talk of militant programmes and action will not change the hard facts of life. The formidable task of solving the individual problems of nearly 500 million men and women has to be approached seriously and patiently. If a "national consensus" is essential in any socio-political sphere, it is imperative for the winning of economic independence. Every ounce of our national energy should have been devoted to overcoming the humiliating spectacle of poverty and the evils it has bred. Then only could the successive five year plans and their achievements have provided a more solid base for our independent development. Their failure lies in the fact that despite the development that has undeniably taken place in the 19 years of political independence, India finds it necessary to knock at the door of every developed country for aid and assistance.

The present-day talk of reviving the 'Swadeshi spirit' is a pathetic admission of independent India's dependence on foreign props and crutches. Can such a national consensus for rebuilding the economy be brought about in our system of multiparty parliamentary democracy? During the aggressive assaults and attacks of 1962 and 1965 there was a near-unanimity for the defence of the motherland. Then surely the realisation that unless we win the battle against economic backwardness our existing freedom might venish should bring about the unity of all our patriotic and progressive elements. The crisis of poverty can be overcome by resolving the crisis of leadership.

We in India have need to hasten the pace of our development before a new and disasterous war once again destroys world peace. The death-defying bravery of our fellow Asians in Vietnam against American imperialists can at any moment provoke the latter into waging a nuclear war.

It is our international and continental duty to prevent this world catastrophe. These are tasks that can unite us as a people once again, even as we were united long ago before Independence and restore in a large measure our confidence to think and act as free people.

As the ninteenth year of independence draws to its end, there is a new tenseness in the atmosphere. While the clash of ideas, factions and personalities is reaching new heights, the people's opposition to unpopular decisions and their ever-increasing burdens is bringing them into conflict with authority in almost every part of the country.

But this shyness must go and they must step out of their seclusion and participate in the task of leading and running the nation. Socialism in its most fundamental sense will elude us if the producers of wealth continue to "rule" by proxy. Whatever the obstacles, be it the British patterned ways and methods of law making, or the highly complicated Whitehall-oriented administrative machine, they must brush them aside and take their full share in administering the country, because they constitute the overwhelming majority. The present order is reaching the evening of its day, let new classes and their new leaders begin India's tomorrow.

Link, August 15, 1966.

DELHI AS A SYMBOL

Modern Delhi has risen on the ruins of many an empire. Its ancient monuments bear testimony to the important role this city has played over the centuries. They lie scattered all over and if only stones could speak we could hear them tell the story of our forefathers, depicting life as it was lived in their time.

They would be stories of storm and struggle, of war and peace, conquest and submission, fascinating and rich.

These silent monuments appear to watch the new city and its people with scorn because they feel outraged at the vulgarity of Delhi's present day architecture and the crudeness of our hybridised culture.

Nevertheless, time cannot stand still, and the cultural monstrosity that is Delhi today will sooner or later reflect the refinements that the new age of industrial growth, science and abundance will bring. The emergence of a new administrative structure for Delhi has roused a great deal of interest. Will it give birth to a modern and egalitarian Capital? Since every national metropolis mirrors the level of a country's social, political and economic development, as thing are, Delhi's street scenes are typical of an India in transition.

The bullock cart and the limousine, asphalted thoroughfares with bright lights and narrow unlit streets. Cows and buffalows roaming alongside horse-driven tongas and the latest in scooters. It is indeed a baffling spectacle.

Sophisticated tourists from countries which have swept away these relics of pre-industrial order, are naturally thrilled at the exoticness of it all. As a matter of fact, they get their money's worth only when they can photograph on Indian street scene, its temples and mosques, with urchins, lepers and women begging and imploring them for no more than a small coin. But do we wish to preserve these conditions as attractions for exciting the jaded nerves and satited appetites of foreign tourists? Or is it time we put a step to these obscenities by enacting measures that will help us to clean up the city and its environments?

Members of the Metropolitan Council and those who occupy its executive offices can, if they so desire, bring about a sea-change in the affairs of Delhi because they know why it is so unkempt and how the people who live here are suffering. They have neglected Delhi for a variety of reasons, but there is a fresh opportunity for Delhi's politicians to bury past differences (personal and factional) and work for the welfare of Delhi's teeming thousands. To be effective, Delhi's leaders must draw up a list of priorities and implement decisions by exercising tact and patience. The administrative personnel and the people can be brought into a more harmonious relationship if those who are at the helm of affairs want to the former and not merely score debating points.

Delhi should be the pride of the Indian people. With the introduction of these reforms it should be easier henceforth to work towards this goal.

Link, October 9, 1966.

WILL THE CONGRESS SURVIVE?

The shadow of a momentous event has enveloped the Indian landscape. Once again the hour approaches when a sixth of the human race will be expected to exercise its constitutional right to delegate its political authority to known and unknown individuals. With every passing day excitement is increasing because those engaged in the electoral battle are doing their best to stimulate the peoples' interest in the coming contest.

Sitting in hamlets or huts, in mansions or living in their world of slums and tenements, countless men and women are engaged in the fascinating process of making up their minds. Although they live in different and mutually exclusive compartments their is a commonly-felt awareness that the general election next month will be more significant than the preceding ones.

The mere absence of Nehru, who piloted India's ship of State for 17 long years has invested the situation with a peculiar gravity. In spite of their disappointments and doubts in the closing years of the Nehru era, they had that indefinable thing called "faith" in his dedicated leadership, which gave them a feeling of security and confidence. Without him not only has the present centre of authority ceased to inspire respect but it is widely believed that those who rule today do not have the ability to meet the dangers and difficulties facing the country.

In this atmosphere of doubt, despair and cynicism a drift to wards a directionless order of things has begun. The baffling confusion of the pre-election scene are no more than a reflection of our rudderless existence.

Future analysis of the history of our time will be in a better position to reveal as to why the Congress after the British had quit, failed to achieve nothing very much more than a superficial transformation of our social and economic conditions. However, an immediate explanation of its inability to create conditions that could eliminate the accumulated obstacles and the country's inability to take rapid strides on the road to progress is essential. Therefore, some rough and ready conclusions should be attempted even though they are not the result of a profound study of the periods immediately preceding independence.

In its essentials we must admit that the Indian anti-imperialist struggle was from its inception more protestant than revolutionary. Even after the Indian National Congress had ceased to be the mildly liberal organisation it was in its earliest days, the Gandhi Nehru Congress at the most militant periods refused to permit the anti-British movement to go beyond the framework of civil disobedience. What is more, it refused to encourage or support any anti-feudal or working class uprisings lest they lead to violent armed struggles.

We can recall ever so many instances when the anti-imperialist mood and temper of the masses was diverted into channels of passive resistance of a demonstrative character and their urge for militant action contained within the limits of non-violence and satyagraha. Whenever there arose a possibility (as in the 20s, 30s and 40s) of insurrectionary and revolutionary struggles that might have at one sweep weakened if not destroyed both foreign and Indian vested interests, Gandhiji's anguished appeals not to go beyond the limits of non-violence acted as a devastating veto. There are numerous instances of national leaders disowning and denouncing those who resorted to armed resistance or advocated guerilla methods against the British ruling force.

It was bcause of the destruction and demoralisaiton after World War II in England that the Congress gained an advantage over its adversary. The fact that independence was wrested not on India's terms (of a united India) and that we had to compromise on the issue of partition, supports the contention that we were forced to bargain from a position of comparative weakness and not from a position of strength.

On the other hand, it my personal belief that had a truly revolutionary process with organisational roots among the peasantry, proletariat and the middle class continued to challenge British rule over a longer period, it would inevitably have united the people irrespective of their religion, caste and community and dealt a crushing blow not only to imperialism but its allies and friends here.

But this was not to be for the simple reason that while the Congress was primarily committed to free India from foreign bondage, it was not prepared to be a party to bringing about conditions in which a radical change in property and social relations would be inevitable. Therefore, had the mass revolt against British rule not been inhibited by the appeals to limit its scope it would have not only put an end to imperialism but brought about the demolition of the entire social structure on which it rested.

The refusal of the Congress to be a party to any such movement, in fact its active opposition to such national trends, should have warned us as to its future role in Indian politics. Such speculations are, as rule, brushed aside as futile—the usual "ifs of history—but they do help us to understand even if to a limited extent, the currents and cross currents in which we seem to be caught up. Thus the political student of these times should consider whether there was any justification for the widespread belief that Congress was destined to lead both the forces of national and social liberation, whether its successes and failures should be measured by yardsticks one applies to political parties composed of men and women with firm socialist convictions and bound together by a code of strict party discipline.

Besides, for one who has lived and worked under the banner of the Congress in pre-Independent India there need be no illusions as to its ideological content and social composition. We know of course that there were the pulls and pressures to the right and left of its main driving force, Gandhiji. But the power politicians among Congressmen even in the pre-independence days never felt the need to be guided by well-defined principles, and their thinking was either rightist or reactionary. However, there were always a few Congressmen eagerly in search of new concepts and patterns of behaviour and they used to be drawn either to Gandhiji or to Jawaharlal Nehru.

Gandhiji's dream of a people who would be simple in their needs self-reliant and self-sufficient was in sharp contrast to

Nehru's vision of a socialist and industrialised order, wherein, material incentives for a higher living standard would not be discouraged. The former abhorred the thought of violent class struggles and the latter accepted the theory at any rate, of its inevitability, if parliamentary methods failed.

The impact of their public debate and loud thinking acted as a phenomenal stimulant for the masses and the intelligentsia. Through the speeches and writings of Nehru and the prayer meeting utterances of Gandhiji the Congress acquired its aura of high idealism. And yet it would be incorrect to conclude that the moral precepts of Gandhian utopia or Nehru's socialism were sincerely accepted by the Congress leaders.

With the passing away of Gandhiji and now of Nehru a process of disillusionment has set in because governments led by the Congress have failed to implement even the elementary social and economic reforms they had promised over and over again. The unrivalled moral prestige enjoyed by the Congress has withered away entirely due to its cynical disregard for putting into practice what it preaches.

Thus the Congress brand of socialism is looked upon as a sickening amalgam of political opportunism and ideological hypocrisy meant only to retain mass loyalty for the purpose of securing its political suffrage. Seldom has the socialist concept and principle been debased by misuse as in India since 1947. In its eagerness to hold on to political power and privilege and Congress has abdicated its earlier role and can no longer carry on the fight against oppression and human misery.

Between the vast multitude of men and women who long for relief from poverty, drudgery and drabness and the handful Indians who have exploited every opportunity to enrich themselves, there are as yet insurmountable barriers. Having consciously served the affluent and prosperous classes of this country so faithfully, it should cease talking of guarding Jawaharlal Nehru's legacy of socialism or of completing his unfinished tasks. It should stop repeating the formula *ad nauseum* that the Congress alone can be the nation's vehicle for strengthening freedom and democracy, for abolishing social inequalities and injustice because it convinces none. If belief in its political integrity is not to be shattered completely the least it can do is not to confuse and confound public opinion.

The Indian National Congress, Gandhiji said in the closing years of his life, derived its strength from the people. If it betrayed them, they would fall a prey to the white-robed 'goondas' of society. He was disturbed and perturbed by events not it tune with his understanding of political uprightness. "A living organism", he said, "ever grows or it dies". The Congress has won political freedom, but it has yet to win economic freedom, social and moral freedom. These freedoms are harder than the political, if only because they are constructive, less exciting and not spectacular. All embracing constructive work evokes the energy of all the units of the millions.

"The Congress has got the preliminary and necessary part of her freedom. The hardest has yet to come. In its difficult ascent to democracy, it has inevitably created rotten boroughs, leading to corruption and creation of institutions, popular and democratic only in name. How to get out of the weedy and unwieldy growth?"

His advice that the Congress should disband itself because "as a propaganda vehicle and parliamentary machine it has outlived its use" was ignored and caused much eyebrow raising. But unmindful of the opposition in high places he drafted a resolution which he could have a placed before the AICC had he lived. It give a complete blue-print of a new organisation—Lok Sevak Sangh—which would replace the Congress and become the spearhead of a movement to attain social moral and economic independence in terms of India's 70,000 villages. None among his erstwhile devotees cared to give his suggestion a second thought.

It can of course wield power on behalf of the latter for some time but by doing so it will have betrayed the legacy it inherited irrevocably. To save it from this sad fate the task of ousting antisocialists from the Congress organization has to be given high priority. It has failed so far because the effort lacked a dynamic leadership. Nor was the search for this leadership within the Congress undertaken seriously.

So what of the future? Let me repeat that if the Congress is to survive, it can do so only as a force that is willing to lead the march towards the goal of a socialist state. If there are Congressmen who believe that it is possible then they have to undertake the herculean task of bringing about elemental changes within the organisation. With faith in themselves and their cause they can and should make a final effort. Otherwise the angry waves of India's desperate millions will engulf it.

Link, January 26, 1967.

LOOKING BACK

"I do believe that, where there is only a choice between cowardice and violence, I would advise violence. I would rather have India resort to arms in order to defend her honour than that she should, in a cowardly manner, become or remain a helpless witness to her own dishonour".

—Mahatma Gandhi

"It was better to jump into the uncharted seas of action and do something rather than be the tame objects of a malign fate".

—Jawaharlal Nehru

A Quarter of a century has rolled by and the period of storms and upheavals known as "the Fortytwo" the "9th August" or the "Quit India" Movement, belongs to a past that is becoming shadowy and remote with every passing year. Those years from 1942 to 1946 being to a heroic phase of our history. Though to those who lived through it or took part in its activities it was chiefly a period of romantic adventures and legendary acts of courage and daring, it nevertheless represented a period of revolutionary mass awakening unprecedented in recent history. Thwarted and humiliated, unarmed and unprepared, the working and middle classes both in the towns and the villages countered with all their pent-up fury the savage and planned attacks unleashed by Englishmen who had been instructed by Churchill to crush such Indians as dared talk of freedom.

But it was not merely this brutal violence that made the mass revolt of '42 incomparable and so different from earlier uprisings. The reason why, for several weeks, large numbers of men and women desired to brave all hazards with reckless indifference to the consequence of their action lay in the fact that they felt they were part of the prevailing world turmoil. Dramatic developments associated with the rise of the Hitler menace in Europe in the thirties of 20th century had created tensions in every part of the world. When they culminated in war on a global scale involving Britain and its allies, it affected every section of the politically conscious India.

The Congress had declared again and again that India would not be a party to Britain's war for "colonies, raw materials and markets" and that in no case would we allow our manpower and resources to be used against our will. Therefore a clash with the British, who were determined not to yield, seemed imminent and inevitable in the eyes of most people as the war progressed. But would the Congress fight? Was Gandhiji prepared to risk a struggle that might not remain peaceful? Doubts had arisen not only about Gandhiji's willingness to challenge the British in their hour of distress but about his technique and their effectiveness for dislodging the British army of occupation.

Before the outbreak of World War II, Britain's invincibility was taken for granted in India and people had come to believe that freedom was a distant, almost unattainable goal. Gandhiji's noble efforts and Jawaharlal Nehru's inspiring guidance notwithstanding, they had come to the conclusion that we were the victims of an enormously superior equally enormous resources.

The fact that an alien people from a distant and a tiny island had the capacity to subjugate the million in a country as vast as ours (and continued to do so for nearly a century and a half), had engendered feelings of intense hatred for it. It was also becoming obviously that we Indians, however glorious our past, were unable to throw out this foreign usurper. Therefore, it was but natural that when the European crisis exploded and war on a world scale began, the reaction of the Indian people to this catastrophe was one of unconcealed relief! A weakened empire would have to loosen its grip and this realisation was enough to lift us out of the mire of defeatism and apathy. This did not, of course, apply to the intellectual elite in the Congress and the Communist parties. For Jawaharlal Nehru, specially. It was a cruel dilemma. While he could not reconcile himself to the role of a helpless spectator by refusing to respond to the peoples' demand for swift action he found it difficult to say or do anything that might help the fascists in their plans of global conquest.

He pleaded eloquently, mainly through his writings and the resolutions of the Congress Working Committee, to the British Government and allied powers to make a declaration of their "war aims" so as to enable Indians to join as equal partners in the common struggle against fascist tyranny. His arguments and entreaties were spurned.

Churchill's arrogant rejection of the Congress demand for a National Government, the Cripps Mission's empty gestures and ultimate failure even when the invasion of India by the Axis Powers was regarded as a certainty, angered and alienated Indian opinion throughout the country. Gandhiji sensed this and his speeches and writings of this period reflected the nation's mood and temper; his celebrated "Do or Die" message to the nation, appeared first in the columns of the Harijan and his hints about the inevitability of an "open rebellion" electrified the political climate of the country.

The passion for action mounted hourly, because it was felt by all patriotic Indians that the time for making a final bid had come and that history might never offer such a favourable opportunity again. The Congress realised that if it did not respond to the burning desire in the hearts of millions for revolutionary action against British rule, the people would discover other channels and form alternative organisations for channelising their determination to fight for liberty. Influential sections of the Congress leadership understood all this and despite their reluctance to come into open conflict with the British, as was usual with them, left it to Gandhiji to find a way out. While Jawaharlal Nehru's hesitation was entirely due to the fact that he was vehemently opposed to Nazism and its allies and did not want its hordes to reap any advantage from India's struggle against British imperialism, a majority of his colleagues on the Congress Working Committee were motivated by varying shades of "pragmatic" considerations.

Gandhiji, however, had made up his mind that to overcome British blindness and obduracy the people would have to go into action for their country's liberation, because softworded admonitions and appeals to the British ruling authorities to mend their ways had met with no response.

But even after he had come to this decision Gandhiji wanted a final opportunity to arrive at an honourable settlement because according to his philosophy of non-violence it was unethical to embarrass one's opponent at a time when he was fighting for his very survival! The British authorities in India had no such inhibitions, they on the contrary were terrified at the possibility of being balked in their designs for suppressing the people. They were afraid that the Gandhian techniques of persuading Whitehall might after all succeed, and a modified version of the Cripps plan result in the formation of a National Government at the Centre. Therefore, without any warning mass arrests were made overnight and the entire organisation of the Indian National Congress was paralysed. Ruthless and ferocious repression being the normal routine of imperialist governments when called to quell a mass rebellion, many acts of barbarity were committed from August 9, 1942 when the Quit India Movement began till almost the eve of British withdrawal from India.

But the Viceroy and his government were obviously not prepared for the manner in which the people took up the challenge. The people, specially the youth, in their blind fury were determined to paralyse, harass, destroy and obstruct the Government's capacity to carry out the administration. Immediately after August 9 in many parts of the country groups of patriotic men and women went "underground"! These developments unnerved the Government and it began to be haunted by the thought that instead tamely going to jail the leaders of this spontaneous movement would organise a regular guerilla form of struggle.

What happend for weeks on end was that the "underground" leadership did without hesitation retaliate by sanctioning sabotage and such other forms of harassment as an unarmed and unprepared people were capable of. Whether it was due to Subas Chandra Bose's broadcasts from Berlin or the literature and propaganda of Partisan Resistance groups in Nazi occupied Europe, the urge to resort to armed insurrectionary action was widespread among patriots of the younger generation.

Satyagraha, the classic weapon in the Gandhian armoury, ceased to be the only form of resistance. There had not been any organised preparation. Nor was there an experienced leadership for the new way of struggle; but a whole generation of brave young Indians fought magnificently. The British Government though taken aback initially unleashed reprisals with all the brutality it was capable of. Such statistics as are available prove that thousands perished and many more were imprisoned and tortured for committing acts of political sabotage, even adopting scorched earth tactics and for distributing treasonous literature.

The 42 "underground" was both a myth and a reality. It was a myth because after the first upsurge subsided it was not able to create a network of active units with adequate resources for carrying on the struggle–according to a well defined insurrectionary programme. It was a reality because despite these limitations it provided a nucleus of persons who by virtue of their earlier record of work in the freedom movements of the thirties and having been declared outlaws (with a handsome price on each of their heads) acquired phenomenal popularity. They inspired the belief that a "centre" however insubstantial had emerged, to which one could turn for guidance and assistance for carrying on the Quit India struggle. And up to a point the "underground" did perform these tasks although whatever it attempted to do would have been impossible were it not for the willing cooperation it received from hundreds of people of all classes. In all surreptitious and insurrectionary movements "the significant few" have to depend on many a silent and self-effacing individual for their personal safety and collective effectiveness.

That this movement gradually wakened and died out was not strange. Apart from lack of capacity to inspire the masses and make it a country-wide expression of the determination to throw the British out physically, there were ideological and political reasons. Even in the first few months of struggle conflicts developed within the underground leadership itself and internal differences became sharp. The Gandhian wing disapproved of what smacked of violence and approached Gandhiji to condemn what the un-Gandhian elements were attempting. The "militant Augusters" evolved their own code of conduct for the struggle and maintained that since they had issued no instructions to kill Englishmen they were not violating the essentials of non-violence!

However, the Gandhians were bent upon dissociating and denouncing these leaders for "deviations". They expressed their conformity to the principles of non-violence by going to jail after "surrendering" to the authorities. As the years dragged on defiance of British authority became purely symbolic but the inner core of the "underground" insisted on carrying on the struggle and was dissuaded by their followers from disbanding themselves voluntarily. India's version of the underground resistance was vastly different from the European because it could not become more than symbolic.

In the absence of a revolutionary tradition on the classical pattern, we were unprepared mentally and ill-equipped for effective action. Unarmed and untrained we failed to seize authority on a wide scale. The territories of Ballia, Satara and Midnapore were isolated instances of parallel rebel administration and even there we could not hold out beyond a few weeks.

Had the underground movement struck roots and emerged as a militant organisation of young cadres trained to carry on armed struggle it could have influenced the course of political events in the country when with the end of the World War II the scene in India changed. But while its leaders enjoyed immense mass popularity the fact that they were not backed by an organised political force made them inadequate.

Otherwise a mighty movement could have been commenced against the partitioning of India and the series of concessions which the British extracted before departing. It is one of the ironies of our situation that those who participated in the '42 struggle had to submit to the leadership of men and women who had only heard of it from behind prison bars.

The bravery and superb courage displayed by at least a million individuals during the long reign of British terror will in all probability never find an adequate place in the history of our freedom struggle, because their deeds of heroism were spontaneous and not meant for recognition and reward. The unknown martyrs whether they perished in the concentration camps of Europe or were flogged and sent to the gallows by the British in India, were the truest of true human beings.

Their martyrdom was meant to freedom from fear, war and want all over the world. In actual reality, however, neither war nor hunger had been outlawed. The inhuman bombing and killing in Vietnam, the suppression of Negroes in America by racial gangsters, the Arab refugees fleeing in fear of Israeli terror and the hungry million of India's workers and peasants—there are the memorials posterity has raised to honour the world's martyrs!

Link, August 15, 1967.

REPUBLIC AND THE PEOPLE

The thoughts and feelings of educated Indians on this 19th anniversary of India's proclamation of a Republican form of

Government vary from class to class, region, village to town. Although they all belong to the educated class they have very little in common. And between this class and the rest of their follow-men are barriers that keep them apart.

The Constitution the people are said to have given themselves had hardly anything to do with the adult millions of our country in 1948. The overwhelming majority were as remote from the proceedings of the Constituent Assembly which hammered out the Indian Constitution as today's man-made satellites are from the whirling stars.

The lawyer-leaders of the Congress of those days from Jawaharlal Nehru and Sardar Patel ownwards were entirely committed to accept the British Parliamentary system in all its essentials as the ideal structure for interpreting democracy. It never occurred to them that its evolution in Britain was conditioned by circumstances—social, economic and political—very different from ours. Nor were they aware of the fact that to the vast sea of Indian humanity, writhing in poverty and living in complete ignorance of the modern age, democracy of the British variety could never mean a living reality.

Although Jawaharlal Nehru often said that while all that belonged to the past should not be worshipped, and that it would not do to develop a contempt for it either, the pattern of democracy enshrined in the Constitution had no roots in any of our traditional political concepts. Despite his assertion that "new patterns must inevitably be adopted but they must be integrated with the old", he yield on all major issues completely to those whose thought-process and values were wholly West European.

Thus political leaders and legal luminaries of every group and party worked zealously under his personal guidance to adopt a Constitution that among other things guaranteed the right of ownership of the means of production and made sacrosanct the privileges and opportunities of those who had acquired feudal and capitalist property under the British. Contrarily, all that the vast body of unlettered, emaciated and disinherited peasants and workers and other wage-earners got was the right to vote, the right to voice their protest. They were expected to be satisfied with the thought of having obtained equality under the laws of the land.

Although, constitutionally, they were the "masters" who had the right to vote representatives in or out of power, economically, socially or culturally, the Constitution had no built-in safeguards for the toiling sons and daughters of our soil. This legal equality which was so magnanimously conferred on the dispossessed millions has caused a great deal of satisfaction to liberals, radicals and all those who swear by formal democracy. The fact that during the last 19 years our people have performed their electoral duties peacefully and intelligently earned them a patronising certificate.

Their maturity and good sense were appreciated so long as they chose to be represented by men who upheld the rights of the property-owning classes and their satellites. But now that they are turning away from traditional leaders and electing such people as want to bring about a socio-economic and cultural revolution, the respectable custodians of law and order are already challenging the Constitution and raising doubts about the sanctity of democratic rights, ridiculing the new entrants to Parliament and State legislatures for their "boorish" and "undignified" behaviour and obstructing their right to form lawfully constituted governments.

The prosperous and educated elite who have functioned as guardians of the social and economic order created by the British had taken it for granted that the dumb millions would remain sub-servient for all time. The post British order made it possible for this new class to capture all the opportunities that a person requires to live fully and they naturally grabbed them as all accidental beneficiaries do. They were fairly confident that despite the loud talk about social justice and Nehru's constant campaign for ushering in an egalitarian order, their own living standards would never be disturbed. Droughts, floods, conflicts, and political upheavals which cause acute shortages and therefore bring distress to the generality of people, they believed, would not affect their creature comforts or prevent them from prospering.

The anti-imperialist national revolution in India was so entirely dependent on the upper-class and upper-caste nationalist leadership that the new ruling class came to dominate the scene with amazing promptness and force. It acquired all the commanding heights earlier held by the British and suppressed the truly revolutionary forces with the aid of its newly won instruments of State power. Highly intelligent, tolerably well-informed and intensely ambitious, the new ruling class achieved a great deal for itself and was justifiably proud of its performance.

It modernised itself rapidly at least in its external trappings. It took to concepts like technology, planning and specialised knowledge and applied them to further its aim of industrial development, patterned naturally on the Anglo-American model. And for some time it succeeded in presenting a picture of advancement, progress, stability and growth.

Why then, with the passing away of Jawaharlal Nehru in 1964, has this confidence given place to a general and widespread feeling of mounting despair, a haunting fear that the process of orderly development has been arrested and that politically India has entered a period of chaotic confusion? All manner of analyses are being attempted and experts and specialists who have the requisite capacity to discover the deep-seated roots of a particular social situation are busily engaged in identifying the cause or a multiplicity of causes.

Long ago, Nehru with characteristic farsightedness wrote : "Our major difficulties in India are due to the fact that we consider our problems—economic, social, industrial, agricultural, communal, Indian States—within the framework of existing conditions. Within that framework, and retaining the privileges and special status that are part of it they become impossible of solution. Even if some patchwork solution is arrived at under stress of circumstances, it does not and cannot last. The old problems continue and new problems, or new aspects of old problems, are added to them. This approach of ours is partly due to tradition and old habit, but essentially it is caused by the steel-frame of the British Government which holds together the ramshackle structure."

True, the steel-framed he referred to is manned by Indians now and the men and women who are governing the country are elected by none other than the Indian people themselves. But a mere replacement of personnel never leads to solutions that can bring true liberation. It is precisely because the leadership has not been able to smash the old framework and replace it with one that could solve the people's problems by satisfying their new social needs, that there is no unity of purpose and action, at the administrative level.

If we have lost the sense of wholeness, in recent years, if we are unable to assume collective responsibility for the well-being of every stratum, every section of our people, it is because the leadership in post-independent India was split on practically every issue of national importance and social significance.

Having realised that India's new rulers were not serious about implementing their promises of upsetting the old acquisitive society based essentially on the principle of exploitation of man by man, a new mood has come upon the masses; they are not prepared to trust those who have broken their pledges. Individual freedom, civil liberties, etc., have little meaning for them because the parliamentary system of democracy has bred a new class of exploiters who have all the advantages while the toiling sons of the soil have to struggle for their right to work, for a proper wage, and are denied even the minimum necessities to satisfy their basic needs. In every calamity, natural or engineered by profiteers and back-marketeers it is the working population that has to bear the brunt.

Dissatisfied and sullen, the working class of this country, demand equality not merely in law but in fact because they want to live as dignified self-reliant people. They want opportunities for releasing their creative energies and talent. In short they went to be masters of their destiny and not slaves of vested interests. The monopoly of right, they believe, can be broken because this has happened in countries where a revolutionary class has assumed power. A new awareness is dawning on the suppressed and oppressed sections of our people as the economic crisis escalates. Specially in our urban centres, their longing for the good things of life is a healthy spur to action. They are being goaded into doing something to avart the curse of poverty.

When our young men after graduating find it difficult to obtain gainful employment and go knocking at every door, only to be turned away, their anguish and humiliations knows no limit. Why should they be expected to be conformist and behave like the rich who enjoy vastly superior resources for the satisfaction of their needs? The affluent youth who entertain one another lavishly can afford to be model citizens with lofty ideas about truth, beauty and goodness. But the youth who has nothing but his famished body to lose, joins every demonstration of protest and anger because whatever he was taught at school and college has been consumed by the fires of hunger and longing. He cannot afford the luxury of having pride in his culture or traditions or even in the land of his birth. The country is seething with thousands of young men in search of sustenance and when they are unable to obtain it their thoughts turn to violence and anger becomes the guiding force of their existence.

Twenty years of freedom have failed to provide an answer to the problems of the generation that was born into it. They will have to discover a way out and end their degradation. Leaderless, cynical and unorganised, they are unable as yet to be a part of the revolutionary forces. And yet it is this generation that will probably be driven to assume the leadership of the revolution of tomorrow. They will, I believe, fill the vacuum in the parties of the Left and provide answers to the baffling question. "Where are the future leaders of the inevitable and ultimate revolution?" Out of their agitated minds will flow fresh thoughts rejecting worn-out phrases, cliches and formulations, moulding new ideas, evolving new forms of the struggle for power. The search for new leaders cannot be mechanically organised. They will emerge as a result of movements against everything that is unjust, against every institution that seeks to fetter the mind and reduce human beings to bestial levels.

Will the coming struggle for power in this vast country be fought around the Ballot Box? If the adherents of multi party parliamentary democracy play the game honestly, the Ballot Box can replace the insurrectionary's barricade. The means never are the decisive factors in struggles between social groups with clashing interests. If the electoral method yields results and those who are worsted accept their defeat gracefully, the victors will not indulge in meaningless bloodbaths. But history has yet to prove that peaceful transitions are lasting and capable of bringing about qualitative changes in human relationships. India's million-fold people are determined to use the Ballot Box to win social freedom. But will those who are likely to be dislodged from their ruling positions accept the verdict?

We who live amidst the shadows of the past are sometimes overwhelmed by a feeling that we are already strangers, unable to understand the emotional urges that are dominant at the moment. At times this brings a sense of desolation. But the future cannot ever reflect all the values of yesterday. The India of tomorrow will be different as it must be. Let our generation live in hope that it will uproot whatever is evil, whatever causes men and women to weep in despair, whatever destroys happiness and brings sorrow. In the endless struggle of good against evil, peace against war, progress against reaction, the people of this land must ever be in the vanguard. Is this a pious hope? To me it is as testament of faith.

Link, January 26, 1968

JAWAHARLAL REMEMBERED

Recollecting the past provides an occupation therapy for those of us who are depressed by the events of today and our inability to overcome what is wrong with these times. This is specially so in the case of people whose adult years began when Jawaharlalji was still under fifty, when Gandhiji was calling upon us to join his army of non-violent civil resisters and when nothing mattered so much as the exciting task of getting rid of our alien rulers. The slime and mud of those years were not as apparent or oppressive as they are now, the future though misty, had all the fascination of the unknown and the fatal shadow of disillusionment had not darkened our hearts and minds.

What concerned us most in those days and years gone by was not how to satisfy our personal aims and ambitions but what needed to be done for strengthening our patriotism, for enlightening our understanding, and how best we could serve the freedom struggle. We were aware of our shortcomings because Gandhiji was unsparing in his criticisms. Not only did we not mind his rebukes but we welcomed them since the reforms be insisted upon helped us to break down the barriers of class and upbringing and made us acceptable to the masses of our people. We never succeeded in drawing near enough to them as we ought to have because our class habits clung to us tenaciously and yet we did undertake periodic efforts to give them up. Even so, by adopting certain austerities for however temporary a period, we felt a little better and imagined quite conceitedly of course that we were made of sterner stuff than those outside the pale. A feeling of exhilaration at having partially experimented with Gandhian ideals of simple living swept us off our feet at times.

How mistaken we were in imagining that the discipline undergone in the Gandhi-Nehru period of the years prior to 1947 has steeled us out of our class instincts for all time!

After the death of Gandhiji with every passing year individuals and groups of nearly every shade, whether revolutionaries, intellectuals, socialists, Gandhians, or even religious-minded missionaries, have slipped into fairly comfortable berths, away from those who need them most—the dispossessed. Men and women of my generation who worked in the struggle for freedom have escaped into activities which can be only remotely related to the things we wanted to do after liberation. Our class compulsions have prevailed upon the compulsions born of the conviction that we must be of the people if we want to work of them and with them. Today at this moment of time, in Jawaharlal Nehru's words uttered so prophetically "We stand on this perilous edge of the present and past and the future to be, and we face all manner of perils and the greatest peril is the lack of faith which comes to us, the sense of frustration that comes to us, the sinking of the heart and of the spirit comes to us, when we see ideas go overboard. When we see the great things that we talked about somehow pass into empty words and life taking a different course".

Quite possibly those who are ten or twenty years younger to us do not share this sense of defeat. But if this younger generation is full of hope and optimism about our nation and its tremendous potentialities, it has yet to assert itself and to prove its capacity to reject what is false as also its ability to create the sanctions necessary for refashioning the entire structure of present day India. May be India's new leaders are going through the process of moulding their thoughts and as and when the social unrest becomes intense and widespread a dynamic leadership will emerge and fling away those who belong to the past and stand in their way. To them, I am convinced freedom's perennial message can become irresistible if only they would read and think what Jawaharlal Nehru has written and said when he was young and rebellious, when he full of courage and idealism, a great crusader against every form of injustice. They should not judge Nehru by what he could not achieve as the head of the Government of India. The Nehru who declared in "the pursuit itself of a mighty purpose there is joy and happiness", should be their source of inspiration.

Had circumstances and his party not failed him when he assumed authority as free India's Prime Minister, had he not brushed aside the very people who shared his convictions, could he but have offered firm resistance to conservatives and reactionaries and their allies, Jawaharlal Nehru would have lived to see the materialisation of his dream of socialist and planned society in India. He need not then have been haunted by the thought that he might not be able to keep the promises he had made to his people.

Why was he unable to exercise the enormous and matchless power given to him by his adoring compatriots and resurrect their dormant energies? Was it because his aesthetic and refined instincts prevented him from using such weapons as were necessary to destroy all that was regressive and oppressive in Indian society? He was too good a student of history not to know that genuine revolutions are not stage performances, that they have to be brought about sometimes by ruthless action often involving bloodshed and cruelty. Why then did he recoil at the thought of continuing the struggle by all means against exploitation in all its forms and not mind the inevitable mass suffering that might have followed?

I believe that his abhorrence of revolutionary means to achieve his goal, become a matter of faith with him only after Gandhiji's assassination. It shock to the depth of his being and he asked in anguished tones "what kind of triumph did Gandhiji wish for us? Not the triumph for which most people and countries strive through violence, fraud, treachery and evil means". He was so overwhelmed by the tragedy that he forgot for the moment the fact that all these reprehensible means are more often than not utilised by those who oppress and exploit innocent men and women and not by revolutionaries who seek to rescue and liberate humanity. Nevertheless as he grew older he never failed to state that he preferred to adhere to the Gandhian method of struggle and political warfare because he had come to believe that "the foundations of lasting victory can only be laid on the rock of truth."

And yet the realist in him saw that there come moments in the history of every people when it is necessary to take painful decisions, of restoring to what is known as armed or military action, be it in self-defence or in order to liberate territory occupied by an aggressor. By implication such a decision means the abanding of the strictly non-violent approach and Nehru realised that when all other methods fail not to take up arms means surrendering to one's foes. Where it not so he need not have agreed to the liberation of Goa, Daman and Diu in 1961. I will never forget the sad, far away look in his eyes, as I sat before him explaining the need for swift and urgent action.

He was given gruesome details of what would happen in Goa if Indian troops went in by those who saw little sense of reason in challenging Portugal, of how blood would flow and thousands butchered by the greatly superior Portuguese army of occupation. I remember beseeching him not to believe such rumours, deliberately manufactured so that he might weaken his resolve at the thought of provoking bloodshed.

I am firmly of the view that had Jawaharlalji yielded to the persuasive powers of "certain friends" of India, the Goan people would have been the victims of an un-imaginably cruel orgy of violence and brutality. By sending India's armed forces into this part of our enslaved soil, Nehru achieved precisely what we of the National Campaign Committee had predicted. There was much less loss of human life in Goa, Daman and Diu when India's armed forces walked into the territories under Portuguese rule than there have been in the numerous firing incidents in India in one single year during peaceful demonstrations and agitations. Despite the growls and howls of the imperialists, Jawaharlal Nehru knew full well that at least one of the many pledges he had taken had been fulfilled. When he visited Goa many months later some of us happened to be there. We heard Jawaharlal Nehru speak at a public meeting. What his unspoken thoughts were when he gazed upwards and saw the national flag sway in the breeze we can well imagine—a tremendous sense of relief that the humiliation of India's subjection to foreign and colonial role had come to an end.

In the long year between January 1929 when I first had a glimpse of him at the Lahore session of the Congress, 39 years ago and the quiet chat on a March evening in the year he left us. I have seen him ever so many moods. Whether he reacted angrily or tenderly—whether irritated or sympathetic, my meetings with

Jawaharlalji used to be the most rewarding experience of a day usually full of frusting difficulties. I wonder if anyone else anywhere in the world who was as big and important as the immeasurably was, could be so easily accessible to ordinary people. He had perhaps acquired this characteristic from Gandhiji whose doors were ever open to all who needed him. Now that those portals are closed to us for all time what we can do is to commune with Nehru, the revolutionary, through his writings. We can also try to understand Nehru, the State builder of free India, by studying its institutions and where necessary changing them. The burden of revitalising our people is upon now upon us. Let us discharge it adequately and thus pay our homage to one who did so much for this people.

Link, November 17, 1968.

SOCIALIST-COMMUNIST UNITY

The main issue confronting socialists and communists whose roots were nourished by Indian nationalism and radicalism during the earlier years of 20th century, is the problem of unity, or, to be more realistic, the problem of disunity. Their ideological positions are so full of complexities that their reflexes to current events do not give a clear indication of their role in the social situation of today. Does the Left realise that it has a function to discharge, an overriding obligation to guide and shape events? Analysing the behaviour of men, especially the intellectuals, is indeed not an easy task. S.A. Dange speaking on a non-political occasion said recently, "You can experiment with water, air, gases, metals, atoms and all that . . . . but you cannot put man in a test tube" to find out why his thought and action patterns should not conform to the objective needs of society. This is indeed correct. Rabical nationalists, social reformers, scientific socialists and even Marxists do not seem to be able to agree as to what should be done immediately to start a process of concrete reconstruction of our society.

The existence of serious differences in political movements of the Left on matters of theory and practice, ideology and organisation are not peculiar to our times or our country. They have been an inevitable feature in other countries ever since the Left as we understand it took shape in the 19th century. This is probably the fate of movements led by individuals who are essentially intellectual and who tend characteristically to be over subjective. Our national movement from the earliest years of 20th century has carried within it a variety of trends, ranging from extreme conservatism to extreme forms of radicalism. Imperialism and its advocates in India took full advantage of these diversities even as capitalism and its apologists do so in present times. Whether it is in the national or the international situation, the leadership of the Left movement tends always to over-react in the first instance, i.e., before it can arrive at a rationally balanced conclusion about the need of the hour in terms of a commonly acceptable policy and programme. During this interregnum the affiliations of different trends within the same broad ideological framework get separately identified and become groups attached to prominent personalities and groups whose "lines" begin to determine the thought and action of the rank and file.

Application of theoretical fundamentals to the objective situation (be it Marxism-Leninism or any other socialist philosophy) rouses passions and fervours that at times negate the very purpose of a collective effort at correct evaluation of the social-political forces at work. Thus the task of devising ways and means of reaching a given goal remain undefined and neglected for long periods because the conflict of ideas get crystallised around the exponents of this or that line, associated with one or the other "leader personality" and distorted political formulations follow. Precious time, critical in the life of a growing nation, is lost in what seems to the layman academic exercises in determining the character and role of classes, the role of the parties and their response in a given situation, and in arguments and counter-arguments which only increase confusion. Set on this course these trends find it difficult to grasp the realities, the basic requirements for effective action; instead, prolonged and bitter controversies emerge which cloud the essential issues facing socialists and communists. This hair-splitting tendency leads to ideological barriers and the tasks of constructing revolutionary "barricades" is relegated to the background.

It is not my intention to suggest that painstaking efforts to reach ideological clarity and formulae are redundant. Far from it, because we who came to the national movement impelled by vague urgings of partriotism have suffered for want of such clarity. We realised rather late in the day that in understanding of politics devoid of its deeper implications, bereft of all scientific explanation of social phenomena, is not only inadequate but acts as a tremendous obstacle for the growth of truly revolutionary forces. Mere awareness that some sort of a social change is all that the victims of an unjust society want, does not help professional revolutionary in his work.

We who did not belong to the Communist or Socialist Parties and groups in the earlier years of 20th century, but were a part and parcel of the Indian National Congress, were so immersed in the daily chores of the struggle against British rule, that it never occurred to us to examine carefully the ideological quality of the work we were doing. Our intellectual queries were stiffled (by the overwhelming need to act) except of course during the long periods of incarceration when serious but haphazard reading helped us to look beyond the immediate needs of the hour.

But what did we read? The literature of the French and American revolutions, and this appeared terribly revolutionary to us till of course we came across books like Reed's 'Ten Days That Shook the world' or very battered copies of the Communist Manifesto and Gorky's 'Mother', etc. In those days Congress prisoners had no possibility of obtaining anything other than "sober and respectable" literature. Marx or Lenin or other classes on communism and socialism were out of bounds. Thus, the bulk of the radical cadre of those days had a very superficial understanding of either socialist or communist theory, notwithstanding the efforts of the Congress Socialist Party and later the Communist Party of India.

Our national leaders, as we all know, were men whose ideas were by and large utopian and liberal although Jawaharlal Nehru did his best to give a scientific explanation of social forces in India and the world. Although Lenin and Gandhiji were contemporaries, the latter had real Tolstoy and not Lenin's or Marx's writings of the French or British socialists of the 18th century such as Fourier and Robert Owen were unknown to them.

But for Nehru we would have been ignorant about what had happened in Russia—about Lenin and the first world war developments and other exciting events at the international level between and after the two World Wars. Politics of the Congress led anti-imperialist struggles in the thirties and forties in India was thus divorced from the Marxist or even pre-Marxist socialist theories. Therefore, a series, of spontaneously oriented rather than scientifically planned struggles were organized for uprooting imperialism and resisting the onslaught of its allies resulting in needless setbacks which meant long spells of mass demoralisation.

The institutional flabbiness of the Congress as an organisation which was in the forefront of our struggle for emancipation can be traced to this fact of total absence of a coherent ideological framework within which Congressmen could function. It was easy for just anyone to proclaim his or her belief in "socialism" because pragmatically it supplied both to the honest as also the unscrupulous politician a convenient slogan for hypnotising the vast masses of our impoverished citizens. Besides, social revolution and social reform were understood by many a well-meaning veteran of the nationalist movement, to be one and the same thing. Till recently they were quite unable to understand why an employed worker should want to strike and is not content with whatever he receives in lieu of his work, since, is he not better off than those who have no employment!

I have digressed deliberately from the topic of disunity of the Left because it is the product of the larger movement for national freedom. The latter, while blind to the ultimate causes of imperialism and capitalism, of war and peace, was somehow able to bring large numbers of men and women of diverse views on to a common platform. Paradoxically the Left which is led by men of much greater social insight, a higher degree of political erudition and greater moral courage and capacity to suffer for their ideological convictions, is finding it difficult to merge the revolutionary and oppositional forces together. We who in the '30s and '40s claimed to be fervent nationalists, could in moments of crisis, combine our forces and sink our differences. Why then should ardent Socialists and dedicated Communists find it so difficult to resolve the problems that divide them, even though they know they have a common quest and a common goal?

No single factor has caused so much frustration and contributed to a sense of humiliating failure in the minds of the Left intelligentsia as the persistent lack of unity in the two

Socialist and the two Communist parties of our country. What are the mysterious reasons that divide their leaders? The average observer is unable to diagnose the disease that makes them so utterly indifferent and insensitive to the compelling need for unity of thought and action. The people expect the Left leadership to lead them to their destined goals and rescue them from the agony and misery of poverty. Analysis of the causes that keep like-minded revolutionaries miles apart is one of the most imperative tasks of Left intellectual. Can they not realise that the historic moment has arrived in India when under their leadership the masses can strike out a new path towards the Himalayan heights of a socialist society? They need to be led and guided by men and women of integrity who are supremely confident of their ultimate triumph.

The leaders of the two communist parties and such Socialists as have not dispensed with the guidelines of Marxism and its scientific theories, owe an explanation for their fratricidal behaviour. Disciplined by their scientific temper, claiming as they legitimately can their noble role in the task of broadening the social vision of the Indian masses, claiming the right to be regarded as the true champions of the down-trodden, men who have shown a high degree of courage by braving all manner of privations and undergoing enormous sacrifices, these good leaders must furnish an answer to the question "why disunity", because it is their revolutionary and moral responsibility not to shirk the facts of life. The million and multi-million masses for whom they have striven over these many years are yearning for a new lead. Recent events in many parts of India, not only in Bengal and Kerala, are replete with instances when they have forced the Communist and Socialist leadership to discard their outworm enmities and come forward and guide them out of the morass in which they are bogged. Very recently, the mass urge for change has even compelled the Prime Minister of India and her colleagues to challenge the authority of monopoly. Their insistence alone has given to Indira Gandhi the confidence and courage to oppose reaction within and without her party. This is India's golden opportunity for reviving the spirit of unity among all who believe in leading the country and its people on to a future of peace and prosperity.

A new generation of Indians has arrived on the scene since the British Empire vanished in 1947. And yet the young intelligentsia of the post-freedom period has barely understood the meaning of social, cultural and democratic freedoms. With a few exceptional exceptions the bulk of them are a generation of scoffers and bitter cynics who are indifferent to the serious consequences of our failure to establish a socialist society after the end of British rule.

By insisting on the application of non-violence both on the personal and the social and political planes. Gandhiji probably felt that he would by this method convert these disciples into missionaries who would obey the higher and spiritual urges of their being and thus transform the mute millions into militant resisters. He searched incessantly for ways and means of purifying the individual so that those who led his movements could be true to his ideal of a free society.

His ideal social order was one wherein men and women would cease to hate one another, would be a source of comfort and joy to all, would become humane, progressive and peace loving. "For me patriotism is the same as humanity. I am patriotic because I am human and humane. We must have the sin but not the sinner", were thoughts he uttered from the depth of his sincere and sensitive being.

He was passionately convinced that the human spirit could triumph over its animal instincts by a process of discipline, by cultivating habits of deep introspection, by not relying on the intellect only as a means for gaining experience and knowledge. And yet he was emphatically of the view that his was not philosophy of individual salvation To work, lie and dic for the progress of one and all, without any distinction of race or class was his chief aim, his dearest aspiration. He was therefore no believer in the ivory towerism of conventional savants and recluses, or an orthodox stereotyped redeemer of "lost souls".

Gandhi, the greatest among India's numerous social reformers and foremost of its liberators, was not merely a man of faith but a man of action who fought injustice on every plane, a realist who experimented with both ideas as well as men and women. Whether against imperialism or Indian fanaticism his anguished protest and call for action were carried far and wide, rousing a dormant people out of their apathy and indolence, urging them to resist the oppressors even if the price to be paid was life itself.

The powerful mass movements Gandhiji led throughout his life often culminating in imprisonment were instrumental in bringing about a new political awakening in our country, and inculcating in the people a sense of resurgent nationhood. But these upheavals did not last long enough to bring about deeper qualitative changes, in our mental and spiritual attitudes. We lapsed into ordinariness as soon as the struggles subsided. Our enthusiasm for and dedication to the cause of political freedom was not matched by an equally ardent desire to reject outmoded and meaningless values. The social behaviour patterns of the mass of our people remained untouched, despite Gandhiji's tireless effort to renovate and reform individuals rooted in the stagnant past.

The spadework needed to loosen age-old superstition and prejudice required patient, painstaking effort, unhampered by fanatical outbursts and frequent diversions. Gandhiji tried very hard to carry on this activity even when his attention was focussed on the political crisis of the period, but the demands of the freedom struggle did not permit him to devote his attention exclusively to problems of social and individual reform, and hence the basic shortcomings of those who flocked to him for guidance.

As Gandhiji's life neared the fatal hour of his assassination, the realisation that he had not succeeded in instilling in the Indian mind his cherised spiritual values had saddened him greatly. When the tidal waves of inhuman violence, hatred and barbarism engulfed India in the first few weeks after British rule had ended, his desire to live wilted and withered. The agonising experience of these gruesome orgies had seared his heart well before the bullet that killed him. He who wanted human beings to be instruments of universal love and brotherly harmony was horrified to find them behaving like savages. The sculptor in him threw away the chisel in disgust as the hateful events of those days swept across our land like a hurricane revealing our hideousness and the utterly barbarous aspects of our national character.

And now while we and the world are preparing to pay homage to Gandhiji's memory, history has once again with cruel irony enacted on his own soil the horrid scenes that preceded his death. The world may well ask, is it by spilling innocent blood that Indian honours one who gave every fibre of his life for her redemption from slavery and moral degradation?

Must carnage and arson be our offering to him who loved his people, suffered and died for them? Or can we learn afresh the lessons that Gandhiji taught and address overselves to the task of cleaning and disinfecting diseased minds? Can these ugly manifestations underlying our "progress" at the top bring all who share the ideal of peace and equality together? Can we work unitedly for the total eradication and liquidation of poisonous growths, nourished by the dark forces of reaction?

The truest way to commemorate Gandhiji's birth centenary is to launch a nation-wide struggle against religious intolerance, dogmatic fanaticism and irrational beliefs. Let us therefore rouse our masses in the spirit of purposeful militancy against their social disabilities, against their squalor and their ignorance. Let us go to people who have no means of earning a livelihood, no hope of leading a decent way of life and organise them, to make them the builders of a new order, Indians who will disdain all that is bestial and mean in our haritage. Let it be clearly understood that only if we struggle for the vindication of the social and economic rights of the millions can be defeat the evil designs of the people's enemies. The legacy of Gandhiji cannot be preserved in monuments of stone or steel, it has to be founded in men's hearts and minds.

Link, October 5, 1969.

OPPORTUNITY FOR PROGRESS

The pernicious legacies of colonialism have not been liquidated even though it ceased to oppress us politically twenty-three years ago, on the 15th of August, 1947. The task of demolishing the feucial superstructures we inherited from our pre-colonial period (or those that evolved after British power established itself) has not been completed because the effort to do so could not be unified on the basis of a commonly accepted national programme of reconstruction. "The politics of competition" substituted the "politics of consensus" with the advent of political independence and every and everyone who was anyone in the political field became engrossed in the struggle for power.

An analysis of the institutional changes on the political and social level in India after British rule came to end reveals that although power had been transferred, the old vehicles of power remained, whether in the from of the Constituent Assembly, Parliament, the Legislatures or the administrative and military apparatus. They were all modelled on the British pattern of institutions of Government; no serious or systematic effort was made to adapt them to suit Indian conditions and where necessary bring about changes.

Thus the British bequeathed not only their language but all the codes and conventions they had evolved during their century-and-a-half stay in India. A political system based on adult suffrage, it was taken for granted by those who took over from the British, would result in an Indian reproduction of the two-party pendulum of Britain's Parliament, reflecting by and large conservative and radical opinion in the country.

The dominant political leadership of the early years did not foresee what eventually happened, namely the emergence of several political parties with differing platforms, verbose election manifestoes and demagogic appeals. Hardly anyone of these parties attempted to explain to their followers the relevance of modern ideas and values embodying a new way of life.

With every succeeding general election a variety of regional and even sub-regional political parties have come into existence, whereas the parties at the national level have splintered into two or more groups. The issues on which all these parties claim leadership of the vast population of this country range from concrete economic demands to dark obscurantist urges. The national upsurge of the days when the imperialist dictatorship held Indian in its grip vanished soon after foreign rule ended. With the partition of India and the carnage that followed it, Gandhii's and Jawaharlal Nehru's charismatic influence dwindled, their cherished dreams clothed in garments of the noblest of ethical ideals receded, patriotism a acquired strait-jacketed and sectarian interpretations, and slowly but surely the old battle-cry of national unity lost its *raison d'etre*.

The concept of Indian nationhood which was essily accepted during the struggle against imperialism changed drastically, primarily due to the acceptance by a section of people of the false two-nation theory with its disastrous political consequences. After independence the compulsion for joint effort weakened steadily because for a long time there was no "national emergency" which could bring them together, except for brief moments during the Chinese and Pakistani attacks.

The failure of the progressive and Left forces lay in the fact that they did not meet this challenge to the secular concept of nationhood by immediately going to the people and telling them that a nation divided against itself cannot either gain economic strength or raise its unison and defeat counter-revolution and its hordes, solidating their forces, parties that believe in socialism and share the conviction that an egalitarian order must be based on secularism, a multi-social and a multi-religious community, have been drifting away from one another. Their disunity is helping the reactionary and conservative elements to suck the masses into their fold and poison their minds with irrational prejudices. As things are with the erstwhile united leadership divided and sub-divided the masses are bewildered and confused and unable to determine their line of action, their way out of a state of gnawing poverty, prolonged unemployment and nagging deprivation. The unfortunate conflict in the Left, if it becomes more and more tense is sure to lead to further disintegration of the sense of unity among the people. It will create a situation in which communal, parochial and obscurantist forces will make common cause, because the year 1970 is drawing to its close and the shadow of the general election has already fallen across the land.

The contenders for political power inevitably are engaging themselves in activities that according to their calculations will strengthen their parties and enable them to win the electoral battle that lies ahead. Obviously, the massive unrest among the landless peasantry and urban working classes, the growing discontent of the average citizen because of the devastating impact of high prices and unemployment cannot be ignored by any party of the left.

They have no option but to come forward and identify themselves with the harassed sections of our people. Simultaneously all the parties opposed to an basic institutional changes in the present social and political order are bound to react perversely and create conditions for thwarting the Left and progressive parties in their bid to win the people's confidence. The reactionary forces are therefore exploiting every possible occasion to convert the struggle for popular demands of their masses into religious and caste conflicts.

The pre-election period is thus likely to be a period in which attempts will be made to intensify all divisive movements by raising contradictory and conflicting slogans and engineering violent clashes so that efforts to build a movement for solidarity against social oppression and economic exploitation may fail.

The forces that hope to gain by greater disruption are on the alert and are trying hard to unify their own leadership. They are also raising false and absurd slogans to mislead and divert the people's minds into parochial and revivalist ways of thinking.

The prevailing situations in the country should cause grave concern among the enlightened intelligentsia and its political representatives because it fraught with dangerous potentialities. Politics cannot be an end in itself, the problems facing the country are numerous, complicated and pressing and cannot be solved except on the basis of a united national effort. The forthcoming elections provide, through the mechanism of democratic choice, an occasion for changing the composition of the new legislatures.

A concerted nationwide effort can result in the success at the polls of genuine believers in socialism, who can bring about a qualitative change in the parlimentary system in India. This is possible if the progressive parties give up the temption to compete with one another, devise ways and means of removing all misunderstandings and act among themselves in a spirit of patriotic co-operation. The events of the past need not necessarily dog their footsteps; as representatives of the millions who are denied prosperity and enlightenment, they should be able to a advance in unison and defeat counter-revolution and its hordes.

Link, August 15, 1970.

VIGILANT LEADERSHIP FOR A VIGILANT PEOPLE

August has always been a significant month in our political calendar. It has become, ever since the unleashing of our people's passionate urge for freedom from foreign domination in 1942, a historic month. It witnesses every year the ritualised observance of India's independence when on the 15th of the month men and women in hundreds of thousands assemble near the Red Fort to hear the Prime Minister's survey of the scene at home and abroad.

The collective response of urban masses as they sit listening to important leaders delivering oratorical exhortations, specially of those belonging to the establishment, is one of spontaneous approval. Their patriotic fervour however does not last very long, because no sooner do they return to the privacy of their homes, they begin to wonder if the promises and pledges of change for a better future, are realisable. Collectively, as part of a large mass, people's reactions are usually in sharp contrast to what they think and feel as individuals. When under the influence of spellbinding speeches, the generality of men and women forget the harsher realities of life. As part of a crowd they are able to share a commonly felt optimism, but as soon as they return to their individual words, they relapse into cynicism.

As the sound of lofty proclamation recedes, they begin to think and feel differently, telling themselves that perhaps in the far away future a brave new world of social equality and golden opportunities for one and all well materialise—but not so today or tomorrow or even the day after. The immediate present, however, is what matters to most adults since as far as they are concerned the future is not for them, it is for others of another generation.

Although the politically conscious elements do not normally take this entirely negative view of life. They are in any event in a minority. It is the silent majority which is prone to suffer pangs of frustration, and when it participates in events such as the Independence Day rally or the Republic Day parade, it allows itself to be lulled into a sense of well being. Besides our national celebrations, their are the innumerable festivals associated with primitive cults and religious rituals when periodically men and women manage to escape the drudgery of daily living and indulge in collective wishful thinking.

This is as it should be, because otherwise life would become intolerably burdensome and even if such respites are brief the change helps to break the monotony of routine. But these are essentially a subjective and superficial reading of the way masses have thought and felt immediately after Independence and till very recently. Gradually, over the years the mass mood has been undergoing a change, specially after the death of Jawaharlal Nehru. From the 1967 general election onwards, to the midterm poll this year, the political thinking of the people has taken rapid strides. The fact that Congress was unable to retain its customary hold on the masses when it pleaded vehemently for another term of office in 1967 proved that they had attained greater maturity.

Their refusal to accept the *bona fides* of an organisation, however venerated in the past, because it permitted its fossilised, old and exhausted leaders to block all avenues of progress, clearly showed that the earlier attitude of acquiescene and docility was undergoing a change.

The death of Jawaharlal Nehru in 1964 marked the beginning of the end of blind faith in the Indian National Congress. Thereafter, the progressively inclined people in general began to drift away, and during the 1967 poll shifted their allegiance to the Communist and Socialist parties. Ironically, large sections in certain regions, in their search for alternatives to the Congress (wherever the Left was weak or practically non-existent) voted in favour of parties of the extreme Right, their reactionary and sectarian outlook notwithstanding.

Observers of the pre-poll scene in 1967 had nevertheless predicted that despite its vested interest orientation, and inner-party dissensions, the Congress would manage to retain its majorities in the legislatures, would continue to rule the States and remain in power at the Centre.

The election results, however, upset all such calculations, causing jubilation among the non-Congress parties, specially of the Left. A new phase of power-relationship began in India with the experiment of governments led by a United Front of Left parties in several States. However, strangely enough, even the United Front Governments much to the disappointment of progressive sections of public opinion did not last long.

This dismal collapse was due mainly to incompatibility of ideas and lack of mutual trust among the coalescing partners—a sad admission that the Left leadership had not kept pace with the growing maturity of the masses.

The disintegration of the Left at a time when social forces, dormant for centuries, were becoming conscious of their potential capacities, could have been arrested had serious attempts to restore the United Front Governments succeeded. But unfortunately with every passing month the cleavages increased, with the result that the forward thrust of the progressive forces and mass pressures lost their earlier vitality.

The collapse of non-Congress regimes in Bengal and Kerala and the growing disunity in the Left, disillusioned large numbers of people all over the country. Since every basic problem affecting the masses remained unsolved, the processes necessary for co-ordinated national advance were thwarted. Wave after wave of communal riots, and increasing anti-social and misguided political violence created a generally felt crisis of confidence in the country which inevitably encouraged the Right to assert itself.

As factionalism became a common malady in both the Leftist and the Congress camps, the peoples' faith in the integrity of political parties and its leaders dwindled. The Congress, in particular, was a house divided against itself, mouthing slogans and empty phrases, unable to offer constructive solutions for reducing the common peoples' burdens.

When a state of near-chaos began to prevail, and realising that the situation could become disastrous mainly due to the peoples' mounting dissatisfaction and acutely felt irritation, Indira Gandhi decided to intervene. By bringing about the removal of Morarji Desai from office and initiating a series of radical measures which eventually bed to the split in the Congress she was able to achieve what had seemed impossible. Almost overnight she started cleansing the Augean stables of the old Congress and restored to it the vitality it had lost.

In politics, charisma by itself does not invest an individual with the extraordinary ability to rouse a nation. Awakened human beings demand action, some immediate proof that those who aspire to lead them believe in putting an end to social and economic stagnation.

Indira Gandhi's success the polls in at the 1971 general election was not merely due to the many advantages she had inherited, but because of her timely realisation that it is not enough to hold on to office even if it be the highest in the land. The desperation of the masses, the revival of terrorism by many groups of angry young people, and indications that fascist minded organizations were exploiting the situation, led Indira Gandhi to the conclusion that some major obstacles to progress had to go.

True, the people of India gave the Congress party their massive electoral sanction to proceed but essentially in this case it was not the organisations but the individual leading it who won their wholehearted support. They rejected not only the forces representing backwardness in all its forms, but by and large even parties committed to a revolutionary change in the social order.

There are many who are apprehensive that the promises and pledges made by the political leadership of the Congress may continue to remain on paper only. The mass awakening we have witnessed in recent months is not a superficial and temporary phase of excitement. It can and should lead to greater organised strength in the people. The progressive forces within and outside the Congress can help to organise and lead movements for the implementation of radical reforms.

There are never any permanent means of guaranteeing progress towards desired goals. A vigilant leadership of a vigilant people can defend their right to life, liberty and happiness. The Independence Day rally this year will be qualitatively different from previous years, because there are some neighbours who are threatening our freedom and want of humble us. We have no option other than to resolve that we shall never again permit hostile forces to destroy this precious heritage.

Link, August 15, 1971.

END OF THE TWO-NATION MYTH

Memories of 1971 will cling to every adult mind in India for a very long period of time. Ruminating about the past, Jawaharlal Nehru wrote that "there is a stillness and everlastingness about the past . . . . it has a touch of eternity."

When future generations turn over the pages of history and read about the story of the martyrdom of millions of Bangla Desh and their liberation, he are sure to be filled with similar awe and admiration because this luminous chapter in the history of India and Bangla Desh will impart confidence and courage to nationals of both the countries.

The impact of the struggle of an entire people, of their heroic endurance against the programmes practised by military barbarians, of their bestial and lustful behaviour towards women will haunt for a very long time people who are sensitive to human suffering.

The storms and upheavals that have devastated and ravaged Bangla Desh, the anguished experience undergone by men and women, bereaved and bereft of life's most precious possessions reminded one of the Nazi terror in Germany. But with the passage of time, these grim happenings and the subsequent triumph, will appear to be the prelude to very significant changes in this part of the globe.

The thinking and way of life of people in India and its neighbour Bangla Desh, will inevitably be very different hereafter because both have suffered together for the commonly shared conviction that religion need not be a barrier to freedom and friendly fraternal relations. As the years go by, the bounds forged in the crucial fight against tyranny will be strengthened, and embittered memories of a quarter century of hatred, fear and suspicion will give place to a sincere relationship of comradeship. Never again can the teachings of medieval and religious fanatics poison the understanding of two sovereign neigbours, each determined to defend its independence, each convinced that its primary task is to wage a war against poverty. The need to overcome the obstacles to a prosperous future, inherited from their long colonial past, will unite them against their enemies old and new. Both the nations will emerge as champions of the oppressed : always vigilant, wary and determined not to lose sight of the fundamentals of socialism, secularism and democracy. Shared values are always a cementing force, and with so much in common, this people of India and Bangla Desh need never fear or be suspicious of one another as they were previously. Moreover, they can complement their resources and energies to further the attainment of new goals and objectives enabling their people to participate in the scientific and technological revolution that is forging ahead elsewhere in the world.

The popular belief that history never repeats itself may or may not be historically valid. Only a research scholar can unearth the origins of this dictum. But that it is men who make history and that whenever necessary they correct whatever needs correction has been proved by the facts of current developments in this part of Asia. A full quarter of a century had to elapse before the people of erstwhile. East Pakistan, ruthlessly exploited by their fellow-countrymen in the West, could release that religion alone cannot be the basis for defining a nation. The imperialists misled and misguided these people by planting the obnoxious and false two-nation theory in their hearts. However, the brave millions of Bangla Desh have had the courage to acknowledge their mistake and declared from the house-tops that the foundations of a nation cannot be built on fanaticism and religious bigotry or unscientific and obscurantist and therefore untenable social theories.

The freedom movement in undivided India was founded on two principals of fundamental importance, namely national unity and democracy. All the political parties that emerged during the British regime were governed by their own constitutions which based themselves on democratic rules and principles. The Congress, specially after Gandhiji and Nehru assumed its leadership, insisted that decision-making must be left to local committees at every level, in rural and urban areas. Besides, anti-imperialism was the key objective of all democratic and left political parties and their membership was open to every one, irrespective of religion, caste, community or language.

The Congress and other secular parties prior to independence, knew that the British Government although it paid lip-service to unity and democracy "encouraged all manner of civil discord and strife between different religions groups so as to destroy the growing cohesion among freedom-loving forces.

Therefore, the religious-communal organisations in India under British rule, as is well known, were the creations of a foreign power whose sole role was to confuse the masses and prevent them from joining the struggle for independence. Unfortunately, demagogic politicians with extreme narrowness of outlook and with hardly any commitment to radical programmes or any truly liberal school of thought succeeded in during the Muslims and a section of depressed Hindu masses in India away from the Indian revolutionary mainstream. Thus, during a crucial phase of the anti-imperialist movement in our country the Muslim League was able to win over some sections of the masses by claiming special protection and privileges for them which it insisted were being denied to Muslims by the essentially upper caste based Hindu Congress.

This was the backdrop of the political scene in the country when in 1947 the British were forced to concede that their away over India had to come to an end. But the policy-makers in England realised that the consequences of their loss of power over this vast and populous sub-continent could be mitigated considerably, provided puppet organizations such as the Muslim League were made to insist on the country's division prior to British "withdrawal". The leaders of the Muslim League thus became their willing tool and blackmailed the leaders of the Congress, who alone were in a position to persuade the militant and radical masses into acquiescing with the partition of India. The threat of a long-drawn civil war resulting in the massive killing of innocent men and women unnerved Gandhiji. He could not bring himself to be a party to the fanatical orgy of death and destruction of thousands, and therefore much against his will and very reluctantly, he called upon the nation to pay the price. The Mountbatten plan for a peaceful transfer of power, provided the partitioning of India was agreed to by the Congress, was eventually accepted. Everyone who mattered in the Congress concurred that although this meant the abandoning of a vital principle its acceptance would prevent fratricide and terrible suffering on a mass scale.

Gandhiji's agony of mind and spirit knew no bounds when communal forces unleashed a reign of terror and carnage, as soon as the British left India. He felt humiliated because he knew he had failed in his mission of peace and harmony. His gentle heart, so full of true love for the lowliest of the low, whatever their caste, creed or colour, was already broken when a dastardly murder fired that fatal shot. Seldom have a people paid such a heavy price for their freedom as did the people of India before partition.

However, a chapter full of calamities and disasters came to an end it was believed that this would be the beginning of the end of communical holocausts. India and Pakistan living in harmony would be free to refashion their future. Jawaharlal Nehru earnestly believed that our two countries which had so much in common could live in amity and corporation and work together for a new social order in which the poverty-sticken masses could at last breath the air of freedom. But the shrewd imperialists (to being with British and later American) had other plans.

Pakistan's servile leaders were prevented from responding to India's proffered hand of friendship. Obviously enmity between India and Pakistan was essential for the success of their aim to make Asians fight Asians. And subsequently hatred and hostility towards India became the key policy of a series of military and dictatorial regimes foisted on the people of Pakistan by American imperialists. Their democratic urges were crushed, their cry for civil liberty suppressed over and over again till the freedom loving sons and daughters of the Eastern wing rose in rebellion. Successive massive resistance struggles against the authoritarian dictatorship were carried on under the indomitable leadership of Shaikh Mujibur Rahman, culminating in the historic events of March 1971. Throughout these months, the freedom struggle of the Bangla Desh people, peasant, worker and intelligentsia, went on gathering momentum while the American Government did everything it could to encourage their oppressors, whereas the Socialist countries led by the Soviet Union extended their sympathy and support to the valiant fighters.

At long past Bangla Desh's hour of destiny arrived when intoxicated by the lust for power the insane rulers of Pakistan turned their wrath against India. Indira Gandhi's superb and competent leadership has succeeded in closing a said chapter of Asian history by seizing the opportunity not only to repel aggression but by responding to the appeal of the tortured millions in Bangla Desh.

By deciding to defend by every means at our disposal the right of the 75 million people of Bangla Desh to live freely and fearlessly, our people and their Government removed a threat to freedom in Asia but helped to preserve world peace.

Gandhiji and Nehru were greatly saddened when the former masters of India out-manoeuvred them by splitting the country bribing the leaders of a powerful religious minority to play their game. Had they lived to witness the day when the banner of freedom fluttered in Bangla Desh and heard Mujibur Rahman proclaiming that a state would rise on the foundations of secularism, socialism and democracy, they would have exulted in the thought that posterity had upheld their cherished values. Therefore year's Republic Day should be an occasion for thanksgiving, and a day of dedication to the ideals for which so many have perished.

Link, January 26, 1972.

THE UNFULFILLED TASK

Before independence those of us who were not mere observers of the political scene were motivated by ideological urges and inspired by the ideal of liberty in our thinking and functioning. This was not surprising because whatever is trivial, mean and selfish in human nature recedes into the background under the impact of extraordinary circumstances.

We were fortunate indeed that we attained adulthood in times when the social and political mileu in India was staturated with the fiery spirit of militant nationalism. This is not to suggest that all of us were paragons of virtue or free from the usual human failings and shortcomings. But the rarefied climate of the quarter century that preceded the advent of political freedom compelled even ordinary men and women to rid themselves of their mundane and petty ambitions. They risked the good life, they suffered and the very brave among them even walked upto the gallows with glowing eyes and smiling lips. With minds constantly enriched by the writings, speeches and talks of the Tagore-Gandhi-Nehru triad, the youth of those times were curious, eager to assimilate the experience of India's renaisance and anxious to learn about the events that had led to its enslavement. They longed to acquaint themselves with the experience of revolutionary movements elsewhere in the world, specially in the Soviet Union, so as to absorb whatever was applicable to India.

Every young person who belonged to the educated classes whether in metropolitan cities or small towns, was intensely conscious of the fact that we were a subject people, ruled by a handful of Englishmen far below us in the scale of civilisation. When Edmund Burke speaking about Indians said, nearly two hundred years ago, "God forbid that we should pass judgement upon a people who framed their laws and institutions prior to our insect origin of yesterday", he was expressing (with commendable magnanimity) the Indian nationalist intelligentsia's feelings of indignation and anger against the British rulers.

Therefore, half a century before independence and more particularly in the latter part of it, Indians of outstanding ability, talent and remarkable strength of character came forward to spread the massage of freedom, propagated the gospel of a new thinking, calling upon every son and daughter of India to rise and snap their chains. Great pioneers of the freedom movement, even before Gandhiji and his eminent contemporaries started their work, organised public opinion by asking the educated classes to give up the slave mentality and take a vow to liberate the motherland.

They taught them the difference between right and wrong, between honour and dishonour, the meaning of a principled way of life and a life that is purposeless and therefore barren.

Gandhiji in particular felt that these ancient and basic values had to be revived because during India's long years of slavery and social decay we had lost the essentials of our spiritual moorings and faith in our capacity to free ourselves. He more than any one else became our constant and daily mentor, from the early twenties of 20th century, flaying us for our stupid narrowness of outlook, our rigid caste taboos and our cowardly acceptance of the white man's claim to intellectual and moral superiority.

The historical process that enabled the people of India to developed the will to resist the "mighty" imperialist who ruled over them began in 1857 and ended on the 30th of January, 1948, when Gandhiji, it's finest flower, was killed by a cowardly, reactionary imperialist agent.

The heart has stopped beating on that catastrophic day was big and warm it had room in it for men and moment of many beliefs—or even unbelief—the so-called terrorist, the Communist, the socialist, the humble and the arrogant, everyone who desired to draw near it was free to do so. Though a firm believer in his own concept of truth and non-violence, Gandhiji's was not a dogma-ridden mind.

His catholicity was as profound as his faith in the unseen power he called God. And today on the 25th anniversary of our freedom we owe it to ourselves to acknowledge once again our gratitude to this unique human being of our times, who taught up to fear no man, but to be true to this inner voice of one's conscience, which alone can be the sole arbiter of our actions.

After him came Jawaharlal Nehru, the heir to the legacy of the Gandhian age, who did his best to retain the essence of his master's political and social outlook by setting them in the framework of modern thought, during the seventeen years of his stewardship of free India. Nehru, the founder and builder of our newly freed nation enshrined his idealism in the nobly worded Directive Principles of the Constitution, but even while he lived, the earlier climate had changed. The market place politician began to push away people belonging to the earlier era; opportunism and not patriotism was what counted.

This was perhaps inevitable in a situation where almost overnight the management of a vast country and its vaster aggregation of human beings was taken over by people whose primary experience lay in smashing the administration and not running it. The assumption of authority by the Indian people 25 years ago unlooked all the gates that had barred their way hitherto, providing new opportunities to the richer classes, and the intelligentsia for wielding political and economic power.

Those who had participated in the freedom struggle except for the elite, were unable to seize the new opportunities because the bulk of them were not intellectually equipped for the new tasks. They slipped into oblivion, although some half-hearted efforts were made from time to time to recognise their "services". Inevitably, the simple and unassuming types who had dedicated themselves to freedom's cause were forgotten and only the ones who had the capacity to struggle through or swim with the tide continued to be in the limelight.

The dream of a free India dreamt by many for almost a century, from decade to decade, has come true. There is no foreign master now who can thwart our desire to transform the country, to provide its millions with what they need for a culturally harmonious and economically satisfying way of life. And yet while freedom is now with us the general happiness that was to follow is still far behind. By and large the old economic structure continues, and the capacity of the privileged classes to exploit has not sufficiently been curbed.

True, the masses have not been inactive and have thrown up agitational challenges over the years but the energetic social action involving vast numbers of people essential for weakening the grip of the possessing classes on our political and economic levers has not materialised.

In theory, the State belongs to the people and is managed by its chosen representatives; even so, the actual masters are suffering incredible hardships and their most elementary requirements are not available to them. The conclusion therefore becomes inescapable that something is amiss with the present leadership. The masses have never failed them nor refused to pay their part if led and organised by men of faith vision and integrity.

When in the past they were called upon to resist the authority of the British Government in India they always came forward, sacrificing all they possessed, undergoing long terms of imprisonment during which they used to be beaten, flogged and subjected to other forms of torture. Fear of punishment never held them back. Today the tasks are much simpler, they have only to be taught to mobilise their energies involved in bringing about institutional changes, to build a new society of truly free men and women.

A nation-wide movement to create a new world for themselves and their children would enthuse them and galvanise them into action if they could be convinced about the genuineness of their leaders. The only explanation for their apathy and luck of enthusiasm can be traced to their want of faith in a leadership which consists of individuals who belong to a class afraid of change and content with *status quo*.

The revolutionary intelligentsia of the freedom movement was able to inspire because they put into practice what they preached, suffering all manner or hardships and did not just theorise about revolution from a safe distance, away from the scene of action. The present system of government is based on the consent of the sons of the soil but this consent has become mechanical. Though they know that it is the wealthier classes who are its main beneficiaries, who can obtain whatever they need, who wield power and authority and are very conscious of their superior status, they do not appear to be capable of effective protest. Occasionally, under popular pressure, some laws are enacted to curb the avaricious tendencies of the ruling cliques; but when they are manipulated and sabotaged, the masses and those who claim to work for them seem helpless. During elections to Parliament and Assemblies there is always loud talk of abolishing a system that exploits the working masses both rural and urban, of bringing about social equality and of refashioning the structure that has led to their impoverishment and unhappiness.

But, once the elections are over, the struggle for existence continues to be as grimly unrewarding and as bitter as before. Unfulfilled pledges and promises made by ambitious politicians over the years have made our people apathetic, without hope. Nonetheless, a courageous band of leaders that can still forge an organic bond with the people, can restore their faith and harness their energies for creating wealth for themselves, out of our vast natural resources. The "Left" in India, whether "old" or "now", could have provided this leadership had it been less confused. Tragically its confusion appears to have increased after imperialism retreated from our shores. Ideological hair splitting or learned formulations about the causes of the present economic predicament and its consequences do not impress the people in the rural and urban areas of the country. Some among the friends of the people belonging to the "left" who honestly believe an bringing about an egalitarian social system and the organisations to which they belong, do make efforts to espouse their cause by organising mass demonstrations and protests.

But most of these have the appearance of moves on a chess board. These struggles may be for land or higher wages and therefore have in them potentialities for involving the greatest part of the nation; but usually they whimper into silence, accepting petty solaces.

Gandhiji could mobilise the millions in a remarkably short span of time because his approach was very different. His technique of identifying himself with them completely was so successful that people believed in him, trusted him and followed him. They knew that he had given up all that the affluent want, that he therefore had not personal axe to grind and above all that it was an article of faith with him to never accept any office of power and pomp. Obviously, it was humanly impossible, even in those years of national upsurge for more than a handful to follow in his foot steps, but his magnetic and compelling personality succeeded in influencing may illustrious individuals from the leisured and will to do classes.

They had to accept the logic of his argument that if they were serious about joining the liberation struggle, they would have to give up ostentation, mingle with the humblest of the humble, look upon the very poorest of the poor and down-trodden as their comrades in arms. Surprisingly, these sophisticated people who came to join the ranks of freedom struggle accepted his leadership with a remarkable degree of discipline for as long as it lasted. It was only when they became the leaders of the new establishment that they forgot whatever he had taught them.

Gandhiji used to insist that the practice of austerity was not meant to be end in itself, but as a form of penance and also personal discipline, to enable the upper class nationalist leaders to forge a link with people who were without work and hungry, but who had to be organised and mobilised in the non-violent war of independence.

The arm chair cynics of those years, belonging to the Left generally, looked upon all this superciliously as nothing more than utopian fads. But the simple minded ardent youth, students, men and women went to the masses, accepted his advice because they know what Gandhiji was aiming at. When the villager saw city-bread folks wearing home spun cloth was prohibited by Gandhiji he was stirred and drew nearer to the followers of the "Mahatma", the friend of Daridranarayan.

The leadership of the national struggle was of course drawn from the well-to-do middle class intelligentsia and therefore had all the failings of this class it vacillated and often deserted the battle-field. But the stalwarts among them had earned the admiration of the common man, because these successful and affluent men sacrificed their flourishing professions, courted hardships, endured long terms of imprisonment, permitted confiscation of their property and took all manner risks, some of them even to the point of endangering their lives.

The times have changed. Politics is looked upon as a means of personal enrichment and influence. Election to legislatures is an investment which brings good dividends to the successful politician, his family and friends. The fearless dedicated qualities needed of a political being 25 years ago are considered redundant and unnecessary. The hard and selfish worker is not wanted because in parliamentary politics the manipulator and buyer of votes is the most important person. The new comes on the national political stage are shrewd, clever and calculating persons, who ridicule and ignore those preach austerity. They assume it is their right to be compensated in terms of material comforts for such services as they render. The establishment of the day has sucked in even such of us into its vortex who during the earlier period had volunteered to be with the disinherited millions; we also along with the new elite are drifting away from the people.

Inevitably, the generation that was born after independence or even the one that was its teens before it has responded to the present environment in which values that the permeated the atmosphere then appear to be irrelevant. Any attempt at orienting their minds in terms of revolutionary ideologies is scoffed at because even Marxism, according to them, has failed to resolve the problems that confront us.

The educational and cultural norms in our universities have not helped the student generation to think of themselves as instruments of change. This education minority, the youth of a country which is in a transitional phase, has grown up in a moral vacuum and therefore is unable to play any effective role. There are students and youth movements but they are confined to fashionable factional struggles in colleges and universities.

The deliberate manner in which false values of life have been permitted to penetrate the educational institutions, has deprived the past-freedom generation of its natural birth right—the desire to live and die for a Nehru's words, "the first cause in the world—the liberation of mankind."

The most compelling argument of overthrowing the **imperialist order in India** used to be that otherwise with **impoverishment and emasculation** of its people would continue. **It is twenty five years since** we got rid of the hated imperialist, but can we claim that we are nearer our objectives of a society in which all its citizens are free and equal in terms of food, cloth and shelter?

In recent times, Indira Gandhi has sensed that we have many miles to go before India claim to be near that much desired goal. Her party, the Indian National Congress has been freed of elements which stood in the way of urgently needed progress towards a Socialist State. She has declared that the nation under her leadership will remove the causes that keep the people naked, hungry and homeless. But can a single individual, even with overwhelming mass approval, even though she has the apparatus of the state at her disposal, accomplish this task?

The Quit India resolution of 1942 became a battle cry and rallied thousands of men and women, old and young, who threw themselves in the struggle with just "Do or Die" as their directive. The "Garibi Hatao" directive succeeded in rallying votes for the Congress because those who voted for it believed the Indira Gandhi wanted in all sincerity to redeem the pledge. But does the Congress of today have the faith that their forerunners had? No one is called upon to go to the gallows or to prison or even remain "underground" for launching an assault on the vested interests. Not adventurism but a new adventure in which the masses are involved should be undertaken by the younger generation and their leaders provided they realise (as we did 30 and more years ago) that poverty (whether physical or intellectual) cannot be removed without a struggle.

For this, the young men and women of today have to go once again to the people and lead them in the battle against hunger and ignorance, just as the leaders of the freedom movement battled against the British in years gone by. Every community or social education centre, every health clinic, primary and higher secondary school, every college in a university campus, can become a vital centre for implementing the governmental plans provided they work under the guidance or a nucleus of selfless and enlightened non-governmental social workers. Discovering new way and means of stimulating social vigilance can expose corruption, thus utilising the nation's resources for public weal and not individual gain.

Where are the leaders who have the patience and energy to devote themselves to such silent and unpublicised activities? Indira Gandhi, the new symbol of economic independence of the millions, must tell her colleagues and the youth again and again that they cannot win it without identifying themselves with their fellow citizens in thought, word and deed.

The Army, Navy and Air Force could throw out the aggressor and help the freedom fighters of Bangla Desh to liberate their country because they were an organised, trained and disciplined force. Similarly the struggle against the powerful entrenched forces that exploit the labour of millions requires a people's force functioning in every village and in the big and small towns. Once again, the battle has to be led by committed men and women who should know that mere patriotism is not enough, that the task of eliminating hunger, unemployment, ignorance, and disease, is a patriot's primary responsibility.

We, a handful of English educated citizens of free India are unable to establish a common wavelength with the bulk of our fellow countrymen because our life style is very different from theirs. This inhibition of communication makes ineffective efforts at national and social integration as have been attempted hitherto.

Link, August 15, 1972.

8

The Republic in Retrospect

Republic days have come and gone every since the day in January 1950 when, at the final session of the Constituent Assembly Jawaharlal Nehru and the other members signed the Constitution of India. For us in the capital city of India the day has been identified with the annual parades which are both spectacular and dazzling, and in which thousands of men, women and children participate.

The smart men of the Armed Forces, the gorgeous pageants from all the States, our enthusiastic youth brigades and last but not the least, our wonderful folk dancers from the hills and plains of our vast motherland stream across the avenues, roads and lanes of the city of New and Old Delhi on the 26th of January every years. Thousands upon thousands of people from the surrounding villages, towns and, of course, from every corner of this city of many millions come to see the nation at its glittering best.

The fact that India's chosen representatives would one day declare it to be a Republic was well know, especially to the learned pundits of those times. The younger elements were not very concerned with the problem, because for them what mattered most was the driving away of the British although none of us could imagine any reordering of India after freedom on authoritarian lines.

We all knew that once we had ceased to be subservient to the British Crown, India would form a government in which supreme power would reside with elected representatives. The demand for a Constituent Assembly, deriving its authority from the people, without any external interference, was the crux numerous resolutions, passed at conventions and conferences of the enlightened and awakened middle class intelligentsia. The history of the Congress before Independence and other militant organizations is strewn with references to Nehru's repeated declarations that Britain must surrender its sovereignty to the people's representatives who would devise their own constitution according to the inner dynamics of revolutionary democracy.

These issues appeared to some of us somewhat academic and hypothetical because the main problem was, first and foremost, one of forging sanctions for wresting political power and combating the remnants of feudalism, the princes, and their sycophants who were the main pillars of British rule in India.

Therefore, the militant Left within the Congress and outside would very often sneer at the liberal elements in it for talking of Dominion Status and the various reforms which the British condescended to bestow on India during fits of simulated generosity, so that they could split the all class unity of the people against their stranglehold. Keeping Indians quarrelling, dividing them by pitting Hindus against Muslims, the upper castes against the lower, was a weapon which they used with considerable success.

The ultimate tragedy of the Indian people as a whole lay in our inability to see through this game despite the efforts mainly of Gandhiji and Nehru, because it eventually led to the division of the country, with consequences of a disastrous nature. The after-effects of the poison they fed us persist even to this day.

Many of us had on the eve of Independence in 1946 became a "hostile" force within the Congress because we could not agree with its top leadership in permitting the British to divide the country instead of spurning their magnanimous offer to quit the country on the condition that "Muslim India" would be allowed to have its own State and the feudal princes the "right" to choose to be with one or the other part of the country. At first the stunning news that partitions had been agreed to was unbelievable. I remember going to Maulana Abul Kalam Azad to demand an explanation for this decision only to be told. "Aur koi chara nahi tha" (there was no alternative). Khan Abdul Ghaffar

Khan was then living in the old Constitution House and I was his neighbour. He wept and said, "Hamare sath dhoka hua"—we have been betrayed! Gandhiji at first was pained and shocked but when Jawaharlal Nehru explained to him that in the interest of saving the people from mass butchery, it had to be agreed to he also finally had to yield and called on us, the socialists in the Congress, to accept the verdict of the leaders as a lesser evil. We were in a minority and had to satisfy ourselves with making angry speeches all over the country but since the Left within and beyond the Congress was hopelessly divided in its understanding of vital national and ideological issues, we could do no more than fume and fret and subside into helplessness.

The Left intelligentsia was powerless and was unable to prevent the drawing up of a constitution which in spite of its liberal accents contained all the essentials for safeguarding the interests of the rich and thus paved the way for the growth of monopolies and hegemony of the landlords in rural society. We failed to prepare the people to organise themselves for the purpose of defending their interests and educating the working class politically.

Gandhiji was not at all interested in what was being said and done in the Constituent Assembly because he was horrified and overwhelmed by the blood-letting just before and after the division of the country. His despair knew no bounds, he was organized at the thought that his life-long experiments with non-violence as a weapon for winning just cause had failed at the very moment of victory, that his message of ahimsa had failed to prevent men from turning into cruel beats, who spared neither the young nor old, men, women or children frenzied by communal passions and refealing all that is mean and cowardly. His confessional speeches during the remaining weeks of his life be arwitness to his agony–no less than the agony of the man who was crucified on the cross for daring of reinterpret the scriptures of the Old Testament.

Jawaharlal Nehru and a few who believed in socialism in all sincerity did their best to make some of the provisions of our Constitution flexible, so that the millions when awakened could assert their will and purge it of whatever stood in the way of their social liberation. He was quite positive even after he became the Prime Minister of India that democracy would be an empty slogan unless the masses were given the opportunity of leading lives free of want and misery. He said : "We want our people to have greater opportunities, not only from an economic or material points of view but at other levels also. We have seen in other countries that economic growth by itself does not necessarily mean human growth or even national growth. We have to keep this in mind and also remember that the growth of a nation has little to do with the shouting to be heard in the market places and the stock exchanges of the country. So, an integrated plan for the economic growth of the country, for the growth of the individual, for greater opportunities for every individual and for the greater freedom of the country has to be drawn up and drawn up within the framework of political democracy. Political democracy will only justify itself it is ultimately succeeds in producing these results."

Ever since 1928 and with greater emphasis in later years he declared that a socialist democracy would be established in India. He earnestly hoped that the dominant middle class and its intelligentsia would be conscious of the advantage of industrialisation. But he was sadly mistaken in imagining that this class would also be able to rise above its petit-bourgeois traits and therefore avoid and see the pitfalls of a capitalist order in a vast country of people writhing in poverty.

With Gandhiji's release in 1944 from his place of detention in Poona the political scene had come to life once again. The mighty mass upsurge of 1942 had subsided under the severe repression of the dying but no dead British imperialism. His magnificent words of courage and comfort soon after were beginning to dispel the depression and gloom of frustration and as World War II saw the defeat of fascism, the anti-imperialist wave rose gradually but slowly. The sagas of the Indian National Army of Subhas Chandra Bose was rousing afresh our patriotic fervour, the uprising in the Indian Navy was energising the working class and its leaders into action but, above all, after the release of Jawaharlal Nehru and his comrades from prison, India sensed that freedom at last need no longer be an unattainable dream. Churchill's defeat in the elections to the British Parliament raised hopes among the political leaders of India, specially the Congress, that the new Government of the British

Labour Party would be compelled to liquidate the Empire England had built for itself in India, leading to its ultimate withdrawal from Asia and Africa.

The visionary that Nehru was saw in all this the fulfilment of his ambition of an awakened continent and began to make preparations for an Asian Relations conference, despite the communalists' efforts to distort the concept of a free and united India. His remarkable optimism, in the face of the communal trouble brewing all over the country, emboldened him to invite (in his capacity as the Prime Minister of India's Interim Government) representatives from all the Asian countries.

The conference which was held in March 1947 and was attended by 250 delegates from all the Asian and Arab countries including representatives from Mongolia, the Soviet Asian Republics, China, Indonesia, Burma and others. The scenes of that glittering gathering assembled in his historic Purana Qila—our "old fort"—are unforgettable, specially the moment when these invitees rose in ovation after the Father of the Nation had spoken to them : "I would not like to live in this world if it is not to one world. I would certainly like to see that dream realized in my life time. If you work with a fixed determination there is no doubt that in our own generation we will realise this dream". But Gandhiji did not gloss over what was ugly on his own soil.

The big cities are not the real India. The carnage which you see going on in various parts of India is certainly a shameful thing. But you are greatly mistaken and you will only mislead others if you go away with the impression that you have seen real India when you have visited a few big cities of India. If you really want to see India, it is to be found not in her dozen or so big cities but in the 70,000 villages where dwell thirty-eight crores of India's population—miserable specimens of humanity with lustreless eyes.

In the months that followed Gandhiji's loud thinking on the Asian Relations Conference about his and his comrades' uncertainties of the manner in which India would attain freedom were becoming clearer. The conspiracy to undermine the firmly-held conviction by every section of patriotic Indians that the British and their camp-followers would never be permitted to compartmentalise India on the absurdly illogical basis of two separate Hindu and Muslim states resulted in the notorious Direct Action Movement of mob violence, arson and terror leading to civil strif in all the vulnerable regions. Undaunted, those who could not contemplate the very thought of a partitioned country, carried on their campaign against the acceptance of the British offer to "Divide and Quit". Gandhiji soon discovered that the 'realist' friends in the "Interim Government" had no alternative but to submit to the circumstances created by our benevolent "liberators"—the charming Mountbattens.

They were not prepared to go back again to the "wilderness" under the Gandhian leadership because they genuinely believed that the opportunity of getting rid of the British had to be seized here and now. It might be the last one for a transition from slavery to freedom without bloodshed because the war had shaken the very foundations of the Raj and its hour of weakness may not last very long. Gandhiji tried his best, on the one hand, to argue the leadership of the Congress out of this understanding and on the other persuade Mountbatten that the "noblest act of the British nation" should be performed irrespective of our internal differences.

Gandhiji's magnanimity lay in his capacity to understand and persuade those who did not pay lip-service to his ideal of non-violence. In those crucial weeks before he finally submitted to the creation of Pakistan as a pre-condition to Independence he gave them an opportunity to state their case.

I remember clearly the talks my colleagues in the Quit India struggle and I had with him on this question, because it was agitating us greatly. He expressed frankly his helplessness to prevent the division of the country. He said he did not agree to the Congress being a party to the demand for partition of the country, that he was prepared for a situation in which the British could even hand ever power to the Muslim League because its wrong policies could easily be resisted "non-violently". We pleaded with him to stop the trend towards 'collaboration' with the British because only he could do so, that "we" were with him on this vital issue, that "the whole country" would support him, etc. But he replied, "I would love to have you with me if you agree with my analyses. You and those over whom you have influence should join me in preparing the atmosphere for non-violence in the country". He, however, candidly confessed that he had doubts whether the "40 group" would "abjure the doctrine that the end justifies the means" and since the Congress was also not prepared to agree with him. "I am left to plough my lonely furrow".

He thought well of us, he had openly said so on many an occasion and paid what I think were undeserving tributes to us "for playing with our lives" but he had also said that "you will have to cultivate the higher courage of dying without killing . . . If you cast in your lot with me. I shall call every one of you top-rankers to defy death with me . . . I own no party. But you will be my party. Long before you were born I was a Socialist. You are armchair socialists . . . . I have therefore only one thing to say to you : carry to its ultimate conclusion the fearlessness which characterised you in 1942. Now is the time and the hour. If you let it slip away it may never return . . . ."

Intoxicated the new-found "glory" of '42 and the exuberance of our spirits, Gandhiji's solemn appeal fell on fallow ground, and we trailed off either into the armchair variety of socialists or began a quest for a scientific socialist path which turned out to be a no more than an escape into smugness and futile sloganizing verbosity, a wandering away from the men and women of the soil.

Therefore, the thoughts that are uppermost in the mind of individuals like me cannot be other than regretful. We failed to rise to the need of the hour and became helpless witnesses to tragic happenings both before and after the Union Jack ceased to fly over India on the 15th August, twenty-six years ago.

Patriot, August 16, 1973.

TOWARDS AN ERA OF PEACE, A NEW ORDER

Fifteen years constitute no more than a speak in the spectrum of history, but for those who belong to the fraternity of men and women sharing a common vision of social change on the universal plane, this decade and a half our history has been significant for several reasons.

To them the post-freedom decade from 1947 to 1957 was a period of intense mind and heart-searching, because none was prepared for the backlash of reaction that overtook free India immediately after its independence. The comprehension that we were no longer colonial slaves had hardly taken root when the nation was subjected to successive onslaughts leading to the division of the country and agonising misery to millions, culminating in the martyrdom of Gandhiji, the liberator. The aftermath of freedom, therefore, was not the rosy dawn of our imagination but a grim nightmare, overwhelming us with baffling problems, creating confusion rather than clarity regarding our objectives and the means to achieve them.

Our lack of preparedness immediately after independence for resisting the evils embedded in the long era of subjugation caught us totally unprepared and incapable of understanding the forces that breed reaction. Nor were we immediately aware of the emergence of neocolonialist conspiracies in the ruling circles of Western Europe and a new phenomenon in the post-war world, namely, that the driving force of imperialism had shifted and crossed the Atlantic, to make the U.S.A. its centre.

The "Left" core of the freedom struggle therefore was quite confused and bewildered with the result that it lacked the ideological cohesion necessary for organising the masses afresh for meeting the challenge of local and international reaction, adequately. Socialist Congressmen of these years did attempt to provide a theoretical base to our thinking processes but their programme and understanding were essentially "social democratic," a carbon copy of the British Labour Party's outlook and therefore they adopted fiercely anti-Soviet and anti-Communist attitude. Sponsoring the cold war logic of monopoly capitalism, our socialist friends could not convince the as yet un-contaminated Congress "Left" that the Soviet Union was a "totalitarian" military power menacing the flowering of national social democracies in countries which, according to them, were liberated by the Western allies from the grip of Nazi fascism. They either tried to ignore the role of the Soviet Union in the anti-fascist war, or developed the theory that its emergence as a strong military power was full of dangers for the free democracies of Europe, America and elsewhere.

Had the learned Acharya Narendra Deva remained free of this interpretation of Communist movements in the world and resisted attempts to raise the bogey that world peace would be threatened once again by Soviet totalitarian dictatorship he could have given the radical forces of the post '42 years a correct lead. More so, had Jawaharlal Nehru enough time to personally guide and organise the Left, specially the younger elements, he could have prevented it from drifting into the arms of cold war enthusiasts. He alone could have persuaded the younger elements of those times to remain in the Congress framework and provide it with a disciplined socialist cadre. Equally, if the radical Congress elements who had led and organised the mass upheavals of '42 and later, had been less impatient and better acquainted with Jawaharlal Nehru's realistic understanding of the world beyond India, they need not have wandered away from his moorings. His realistic and farsighted understanding that in the struggle against imperialism the Communist movement led by the Soviet Union was an ally of progressive forces in their struggle for independence and social justice in Asia and other countries, would have prevented us from remaining rudderless. Thus the progressive elements in India could have become a powerful factor by now in stemming the tide of reaction at home and elsewhere.

Further, Nehru's hands would then have been strengthened as against those of his colleagues who saw in him a dreamy-eyed socialist visionary who, if not restrained sufficiently, might give the new Indian State and its economy a Communist orientation. Nehru never concealed his intense dislike for the manifestations of the capitalist way of life and his frank approval of Lenin's interpretation of Communist theory ad practised in post-Czarist Russia, hence the apprehensions of his senior comrades and colleagues that he would accommodate in India's parliamentary form of democracy a Marxist view of the ideal society. These "ifs" and "buts" of history will always haunt us because we have missed a historic opportunity to grow into a source of strength for our impoverished peasants and workers by failing to organise and discipline the truly revolutionary classes, after the defeat of British imperialism in 1947.

For many of us the decade after independence was a period of quest and a search for a new theoretical base rooted in the facts of Indian history and social tradition. We knew almost instinctively that to be an effective force that could overcome the hidden forces of reaction and its ugly consequences, a socio-political movement must have a scientifically sound frame of reference, and therefore made honest efforts to secure the leadership necessary for inspiring us to think afresh and act in terms of existing realities. However it was quite obvious that revolutionary changes in a complex society such as ours cannot be brought about by merely annihilating what is harmful.

What is bad has to be replaced with what is beneficial, and serious attempts have to be made to identify the cause that have undermined the fabric of India's economy to facilitate the task of a relentless struggle to bring the new out of the old. It was quite some time before we gave up the mistaken belief that there is virtue in creating conditions of chaos. We realised that if chaos leads to fundamental change then it is good, but if it good, but if it leads to counter-revolutionary upheavals it is not merely harmful but criminal to call upon people to indulge in anarchic acts of destruction. All this and more went into the thoughts and feelings of a fairly large number of people after the first ten years of total independence. We found ourselves at the proverbial cross-roads and had to decide upon the next stop in the journey towards the new society of our dreams. A great deal of fresh thinking had to be undertaken if we were to avoid the earlier pitfalls. To steer clear of the beaten tracks that lead to power after a victorious struggle is a fairly hazardous venture.

Once the upsurge subsides and all appears to be well on the surface and the people who need urgent changes are lulled into apathy born of frustration, it requires mental, moral and intellectual effort to analyse the new situation and shun superficial generalisations, and plan for a fresh effort. To accept a simplified view of life, national and international, is to take the easy way out, but to examine the real reasons that cause national stagnation and moral collapse considerable detachment and total identification with the bulk of the masses living within one's national frontiers.

The glamorous achievements of affluent USA and the Western powers belonging to its orbit succeeded in mesmerising the Indian elite by its lavish riches, the glittering civilisation and (comparatively speaking) the general well-being of even the common working people there. Their tremendous scientific and technological capacities magnetised our young intelligentsia and they saw the realisation of their own private utopias in the models set by U.S.A., West Germany and others under American tutelage. They were completely convinced that only in a world of "free enterprise" can one be freed from the degradation of poverty. A democracy in which an individual could amass the good things of life was for them the only viable remedy for pulling India out of the depths of hunger and squalor, because it gave an equal opportunity to all "rich" and "poor" alike, to get what they could.

The slogan of "saving the world from Communism" appealed to this elite because their understanding of the latter meant a life of drudgery and drabness, dull regimentation of one's faculties and sensibilities, an egalitarian order where the urges of their particular class would be suppressed and sub-ordinated to the ideal of the greatest good of the greatest number. They were prepared to listen to any and every prejudiced argument against every aspect of the new socialist societies in the USSR, Eastern Europe and (until recently) in China.

They were completely convinced that our salvation lay in adopting the American way of life and looked down on anti-imperialist movements and their leaders with contemptuous condescension. Everything that went wrong in the Indian economy was ascribed to Nehru's illusions about the Soviet Union and other socialist countries, his encouragement to those who indulged in unrealistic talk of world peace and socialism, his anger against the monopolists and his deliberate opposition to joining the camp of the USA's vast military bloc. The communists and their fellow-travellers in this period were either objects of fear or ridicule; they were looked upon as traitors, not patriots, mere stooges and agents of the Soviet Union and others belonging to its "totalitarian" camp.

This new elite logic (widely prevalent in our universities and bureaucracy) was based entirely on the thesis that the technological and scientific revolution in the West had made all other modes of economy outdated, the Marxism was no longer a valid basis for revolutionary changes in society and that the millennia for all times and all people had been brought about by the marvels of America's great achievements and its mighty power. When, however, these short-sighted sections of Westernised and Americanised Indians learnt that science and technology was not a monopoly concern of their patrons, that in the Communist country of the USSR the space era had begun, that its nuclear capacity could match that of the USA and its allies, they began to have a second look at the world and doubts began to bother them about their earlier assumptions.

Their understanding about the other half of the globe, i.e., where the Socialist powers and the people of Asia, Africa and Latin America were engaged in struggle for liberation from American domination, became less myopic. This peculiarly aberrant class was taken aback by the thought that the next war could not merely devastate the dreaded Communist world but possibly mankind itself, despite the vast protection that the American umbrella gave to its clients. Their cynicism about the capacity of the Vietnamese people to liberate their country from America's vicious war of aggression gradually disappeared and they did not scoff any more at the poor "ideologues" who insisted that American or any other imperialism can be defeated, provided the peoples of the regions subjected to armed aggression were united and determined to die rather than surrender to the enemy. Assistance from the socialist countries, specially the USSR had been assumed to be negligible in comparison with what the puppet regimes obtained from the aggressors and therefore their stunning discomfiture knew no limits, when Vietnam forced the USA to surrender. The tide however had turned, specially during the last five years. Now, those who refused to see in American and Western civilisation the panacea for backward countries like ours can with modest pride claim that we were not so incorrect in our understanding of the facts of life. The balance of forces, as the world understands this expression, has altered in favour of concepts that previously seemed to be irrelevant.

World peace, coexistence of nations and countries in different stages of social evolution, non-alignment and the fact that if a people are led by a dedicated and principled leadership they can overcome the mightiest combination of forces ranged against them, are accepted as inevitable. The recent truce between aggressive imperialism and peace-loving Communism, the desire for mutual cooperation between peoples, whatever their beliefs, the respcet for national frontiers, the belief that a nuclear war is no longer on the agenda of aggressive imperialism have been justified by recent developments in human history.

The Brezhnev-Nixon agreements, Washington's acceptance of Communist China in the UN, the victory of the Vietnamese people and the people of Bangladesh over their oppressors, the realisation that Socialist Cuba cannot be vanquished, the emergence of the German Democratic Republic as an independent Socialist state have proved beyond doubt that war-mongering circles in USA and the West have learnt a lesson.

These developments have also convinced honest people that wherever the liberation forces are inspired by progressive ideas of socialist revolution they become invincible. A fundamental change has taken place in the world and therefore the soil on which the evil seeds of the colonial era flourished has changed its composition for all time to come, and a new age for the future of those who are determined to preserve their independence in every sense of the term has arrived.

The grim era of domination by the world's affluent powers over the more vulnerable section of humanity in Asia and elsewhere is coming to an end and it should give us all a justifiable sense of satisfaction. Even so it must not lead those, who have still to go a long way, into the stifling corridors of complacency and lethargy. Our goal of the fullest satisfaction of the people's materials and cultural requirements, a social environment that gives the lowliest individual all the facilities he needs for his individual development are as yet distant dreams.

We must not forget that improvements, reforms, and radical institutional changes in our respective regions can be brought about not by mouthing slogans and propagating abstract theories. The lesson of history is that for several reasons people in the so-called underdeveloped areas had in years gone by ceased to be vigilant. To build a society of free human beings, we need to be alert once again and resolve afresh to rededicate ourselves to our social and moral requirements. A new generation of nation-builders must come forward to resist the many temptations that power brings in its wake, shun pride of office and abstain from indulging in extravagant luxuries so that they may evoke the respect and admiration of their fellow countrymen.

These exhortations will sound trite to many and even pontifical. But if we want the masses of our people to respond to those who want to lead them, they cannot escape these compulsions. Human beings in the closing years of the 20th century can no longer be treated as pawns in the power-political game.

As we come to the end of the fifteenth year of this journal's publication, we cannot help repeating that none but the people of India and their chosen leaders can bring about the changes for which former generations struggled and suffered all manner of hardships. They can take full advantage of the new discoveries of scientific knowledge and experience of other countries.

But the pace and momentum of their march towards a just, humane and progressive order will depend on the quality and quantity of their own efforts. History has once again given numerous example of the age-old truth that a people's salvation lies in its own effort, its own conviction that theirs is a just cause. The India of tomorrow has enormous potentialities for redeeming the oft-repeated pledge that we shall remain free and it is only by being true to ourselves, can we as a people emerge victorious.

Link, August 15, 1973

ANGUISH, TRIUMPH AND HOPE

We greet the day annually on which the declaration of our independence was announced. Twenty-seven years ago on the stroke of midnight Jawaharlal Nehru declared that India had severed her bonds of slavery. These was more solemnity than gaiety on the very first day of independence and this tradition continues even to this day. The scenes India witnessed in that momentous period, the birth of a new India, are unforgettable. The transfer of total power from the British to the Indian people was a historic act of abdication by the mightiest imperialist power of those times and an eventful day in the life of our nation. We need to remind ourselves of the past when reacting to events of present day.

Equally important is it to know that freedom was not ushered in smoothly and peacefully even if in the final stages it appeared to be a cold-blooded constitutional change of hands. The post-independent generation is invariably under the impression that we gained our liberty in a uniquely peaceful manner and it was a mere matter of jail-going for the few and that freedom came as a benevolent act on the part of those who held away over India for almost a century and a half. Fierce struggles, armed and unarmed insurrectionary upheavals, the sacrifice and heroism of many generations of Indians, since 1857 finally led the British to surrender their dominant role, on August 15, 1947. Naturally non-violent methods were largely responsible for rousing the millions to action under Gandhiji's supreme command.

It was good that it was so, because the failure of other methods of struggle before his arrival on the scene had lulled India into apathy and despair; nevertheless even after Gandhiji took over the reins there were periods of stormy militancy specially whenever the non-cooperation and civil disobedience movements petered out for want of mass momentum.

Besides, religious and communal conflicts often flared up as the ruling power of those times used every occasion to encourage them, so that our united struggles against its regime could be diverted into negative channels. However, India's freedom was wrested from the British only after we had agreed to pay the price they demanded—pound of flesh they insisted upon was given when literally countless human beings butchered one another after the country was torn asunder. Pakistan was born as a result of that meaningless bargain. Indians whether Muslim, Sikh or Hindu, were seized by uncontrollable frenzy brother killing brother and destroying the age-old fabric of a secular and multi-dimensional society. It is with this background of fratricidal fanaticism in mind that India's independence day is celebrated, unlike in other countries which celebrate their freedom in a spirit of gay abandon. What followed soon after, was to further drown the people in horror, anguish and sorrow. Within a few months, the nation paid the ultimate price for its folly when Gandhiji was assassinated, staining the free flag of India with the blood of the greatest Indian of the age. These traumatic experiences are a part of our memory of a time when instead of jubilation we were depressed and ashamed for what had happened, an inglorious end to what ought to have been a triumphant chapter in our history.

Such, according to me, are the reasons for the lack of feelings of joy and jubilation on an otherwise memorable day connoting the emergence of an oppressed people into freedom.

This year of all years has been for us a year of unusual gloom and as we observe once again the sombre rituals associated with Independence Day our thoughts fly back to the years that have gone by. There appear to be valid reasons why we should feel burdened with anxiety and concern. The hardships and difficulties of the people in times of natural calamity apart, what is quite incomprehensible to one and all is the steady erosion of their means of livelihood.

But such was the compulsion of the powerful classes who stepped into power that Nehru was forced to retain much that was obsolete and which obstructed the development of socialism and a steady growth of economic prosperity of the people. The efforts of his *status quo*-minded colleagues succeeded and he could not prevent them from making the constitution of free India a pale imitation of an exploitative order of society. He repeatedly reminded the Constituent Assembly that India's freedom would be meaningless if it could not bring freedom and opportunity to the common man, to the peasant and workers of India, and give them the sinews to fight and end poverty and ignorance and disease.

He raised his voice often and often, to bring home to the constitution-makers that they must take care to enshrine such principles in the constitution as would "bring fullness of life to every man and woman to ensure that they acquire equal rights, privileges and obligations". Throughout his stewardship he assured his people whose bondless confidence and affection he enjoyed that they must wage a war against poverty (the only sort of war permissible), by working hard and by their labour and sacrifice mould a new life for themselves. He urged upon those invested with responsibility to be vigilant and unswerving in their determination to give of their best to the service of their people, to lift the lowly to their rightful place in society.

His abhorrence for all that goes under the lable of an acquisitive society is well known and his repeated warning that wealth should not be concentrated in the hands of the few, his ardent pleadings that it was only in a socialism-oriented society that the world could make progress, fell on deaf ears. Men and women who could shares his lifty aims were wanting or had drifted away from him. He could not thus find it humanly possible to rebuild the Congress into a socialist organisation. The effort to do so is continuing but there is not as yet any sign that it will succeed.

It is obvious now that an economy based on the principles of private profit when mixed with a section only under public ownership leads to the former gaining ground over the latter. All the efforts which have been and are being made by Mrs. Indira Gandhi are well-intentioned and meant to overcome the obstacles. But, functioning as it does, the present state structure even after twenty-seven long years is totally unsuited to further the purposes of a planned welfare state, much less a state in which the working people have the right to claim their legitimate share of the products of their labour.

Brooding by itself or mere regrets cannot yield solutions. Let us confess that the values of the earlier era of national fervour and the spirit of effacing oneself in the larger cause of freedom have ceased to be relevant to the new intelligentsia, the youth. They alone can and should provide a dynamic yet constructive leadership at the present stage of our history. Most of us who had acquired certain intellectual, moral and humanitarian values from the late twenties onwards, known as ideological categories, find ourselves outdated.

Some among the old become angry and frustrated but the old remedies they offer is like old wine being poured into new bottles. Such nostrums as they bring forth are regarded as moth-eaten ideas by younger men and women. The latter have never had the opportunity that Nehru and his kind had in their youth. Superficially educated and rootless, even intelligent young men and women (with rare exceptions) are growing cynical about the past. They have no desire to study the facts of life, to apply their minds to the tasks that they alone can perform because their upbringing has been incoherently planned.

Translating a dream, into action to work for a total change, needs men and women of vision and courage and integrity. When such individuals emerge and I am convinced that later if not sooner they will appear, the next phase of Indian renaissance will find its pioneers. If history is any guide a new leadership cannot be long in evolving out of the present state of confusion and chaos. The older generation of men in politics should ponder on their failures and try not to impose their ineffectual strivings on fresh and turbulent minds.

August 15, 1974

1975—A NEW TRYST?

Quite obviously Independence Day of 1975 will be qualitatively different from the one that we observed last year. The "tryst" with destiny in 1947 had indeed been accomplished but trysts, as we know are merely the beginning of a new world of relationships, a fulfilment that is never an end in itself.

The nation was not in a mood of elation on last year's Independence Day because it was experiencing difficulties which had made life for the average man and woman extremely burdensome. Why, therefore, it may well be asked should they, only one year later not be more depressed? Are there any valid reasons for throwing off the near despair that overtook them last year?

Have unemployment, the high cost of living, problems of housing and health and other essential facilities become matters of a bitter past? We are well aware that these minimum conditions for a life free of anxieties have yet to be realised and nor are they realisable in the span of a mere one year. However, it is a fact that today the sense of uncertainty and hardships has been replaced by a feeling of optimistic expectation. Everyone knows that something has changed, there is something new that has emerged on the national scene.

It was with a long sigh of relief that the people of India heard Indira when she spoke of the many concrete steps the Government and administration was determined to take. And although there was nothing startlingly new in the present programme of action the fact that stern pre-emptive measures were taken instantly convinced them that these assurances were not vote-catching gimmicks but seriously meant statements representing an earnest effort to redeem old pledges.

The reaction of the masses has also not been just an exhibition of wordy demonstration and frothy enthusiasm. A heartening feature of the present Emergency is that our people have matured and are beginning to give up the attitude of irresponsibility. Organized sections of the people in towns and villages all those who work and administer, have realised that they also must contribute their quota of extra effort in terms of efficient and disciplined functioning and resolve never to miss this opportunity to share national tasks in a spirit of patriotism and high endeavour.

They are slowly understanding that changes in the social order cannot be brought about by the old pre-independence attitude of dependence on a "ma-baap" sarkar. Leaders of public opinion should carry the message that popularly elected governments and the people have to co-operate all along the line in the task of eradicating poverty and inequality.

One does not need to recapitulate the events from 1973 to June 26, 1975 that have inevitably led to the present totally new and invigorating developments. For months together, an atmosphere of chaotic disorder was created by mobilising all the tools used by reactionary elements everywhere to challenge duly elected organs of power in the States and at the Centre. A situation of confrontation was deliberately built up in the belief that a weakened administration would aid and abet anarchic disturbances.

But the plans and machinations to seize power through violence, assassinations and upheavals did not succeed beyond a point. The disgruntled leadership of a combination of defeated men should have known better than to imagine that acute as the people's economic distress was, they would refuse to be drawn into a counter-revolutionary game of power politics. The majority of the people of India may be illiterate but they are imbued with that most essential human trait, common sense.

The handful of tried old men who thought they were resurrecting the 1942 Quit India struggle against the British had been tested, tried and found out. Not one of them, individually or collectively, had coherent plans for initiating drastic changes in our social structure nor were they known to be symbols of incorruptibility and lofty idealism. Living in glass houses themselves, casting stones and hurling abuses at their opponents was unbecoming and therefore no one was truly impressed. Traditional India-baiters were the only beneficiaries of their fulminations.

A pseudo-Gandhian stalwart belonging to this motely group of counter-revolutionaries made himself more than ridiculous when he called upon the Indian army and police to disobey the orders of a constitutionally legal Government. A friend has rightly recalled how Gandhiji did not espouse the cause of the Garhwali soldiers at Peshawar—in the pre-freedom days in NWFP. Gandhiji had no hesitation in declaring (despite the criticism from radicals) that, "A soldier who disobeys an order to fire breaks the oath which he has taken and renders himself guilty of criminal disobedience. I cannot ask officials and soldiers to disobey; for when I am in power, I shall in all likelihood make use of those same officials and those same soldiers. If I taught them to disobey I should be afraid that they might do the same when I am in power". These are some of the major causes that have alerted and awakened some of those at the highest levels of decision-making. In fact they have been jolted after months and months of political drift, casualness, and lethargy in performing the tasks they had pledged to accomplish after their massive successes in 1971 and later.

The collective known as the Congress thought that Indira Gandhi was solely responsible for fulfilling the solemn pledges. Perhaps they felt that since she alone could command the truest affection and respect of the people, the duty to implement the promises made to them in 1971-72 was hers alone. The onerous burden of the State, in its entirety may have been shared by Indira Gandhi's colleagues, but this did not produce results to match the hard work, mental and physical, she had to undertake without respite.

Every crisis internal and external, had to be faced ultimately by her in spite of the fact that the Congress as a political organisation has its roots far and wide. Discussions and differences among different sections of Congressmen are inevitable in a situation calling for dynamic action.

But they need not have reached the dimensions they did and thus facilitated the birth of a peculiar type of gangster opposition to the Congress which did everything to exploit its weaknesses and shortcomings. But for this fact, the economic and social conditions after 1972 could have improved in spite of all that had taken place on the West European and international plane and which had led to inflation and its disastrous consequences here in India. But these are matters that need no longer disturb us. Fortunately, the Congress is today led by a man of farsighted understanding of the emerging situation.

In the climate created by the "Emergency"—I would rather redefine the term as Normalcy—we can now take a fresh look at everything from scratch. Gone are the inhibitions that made the law-makers falter at every step while thinking of radicalising the economy and of freeing themselves from the stranglehold of outdated constitutional straitjackets and from conventions born in Anglo-Saxon legislatures and other relics of out-of-date political norms that hamper parliamentary democracy.

Those who can think for themselves can now re-examine every aspect of present day realities and ask themselves frank questions about the validity of a purely capitalist economy when the national goal of socialism has been endorsed by the nation, again and again, over these 27 years and discussed even in earlier times.

The new order we have been dreaming of has yet to materialise. The hostile forces have not been uprooted. They were given too long a rope. Active cadres have to be vigilant about their plans to sabotage and undermine our peoples will even in its rudimentary forms. The masses in the country alone can ultimately bring about a permanent transformation of rural and urban society and not those who exploit them in one way or another. For all this and more the recent decisions of our Parliament have laid the foundations. None of the forces that could freely obstruct the process can any longer do so with impunity. Some enemies of the people are however at large and need to be watched.

Convinced and dedicated believers in a socially just society of men and women have the opportunity now to operate freely from the tehsil upwards to the apex structures of Government and administration. The institutional changes and reforms that have been debated in seminars and symposia by brilliant young men and women can now come down from the heights if they start mobilising and organising the as yet politically inert sections of the people. Inertia can be dispelled easily now because those who live by their convictions can isolate populist demagogues by acting and not talking only.

The world at large has in many ways entered the zone of peace and plenty. India can also throw off all that shackled her will to move forward. Years and years ago Jawaharlal Nehru, the visionary, had said "In India . . . . we find a struggle today between the old nationalist ideology and the new economic ideology. Most of us have grown under the nationalist tradition and it is hard to give up the mental habits of a life-time. And yet we realise that this outlook is inadequate, it does not fit in with the existing conditions in our country or in the world.

There is a hiatus, a lag. We try to bridge this hiatus but the process of crossing over to a new ideology is always a painful one. Many of us are confused and perplexed today because of this. But the crossing has to be made, unless we are to remain in a stagnant water, overwhelmed from time to time by the wash of the boats that move down the river of progress.

This is no time for sceptics or cynics. This is not 1942 when we were deprived of our leaders, suddenly. The young men and women in their thirties today need not "Do or Die". All they have to do is, "To Do."

Thirty-three years ago many thousands had risen in revolt. They were grouping in the dark because of a lack of adequate and well-thought out plans of action, experience and academic education. Today our universities pour out graduates in their thousands. The governments at the Centre and in the States are elected by a vast electorate. The Planning Commission has been at work for nearly to decades.

Link, August 15, 1975.

THIRTY YEARS OF FREEDOM

On this special Anniversary of our Independence, let us first think of the three decades that preceded the final emergence of India as a sovereign nation. Those thirty years were filled with patient struggles (although spasmodic) against a mighty alien power that had held India in bondage for well over a century.

The three decades prior to August 15, 1947 were a very vital period in the long history of our awakening. The realisation that we Indians were not masters of our land had dawned gradually on the new elitist class all over the country from the early years of this century. But as is well known, it represented a microscopic minority confined to westernised affluent families who though intellectually well equipped were concerned only about their narrow interests, and quite unaware of the conditions in which the toiling masses lived. Had Gandhiji not arrived on the scene when he did, the freedom movement could never have reached the heights of militant mass awakening and the struggles that followed against their oppressors.

The magnificent personality of Gandhiji had a magical effect on the rich and the poor. the educated and the illiterate, inspiring them with faith and courage, telling us all in simple and unsophisticated terms that without suffering, scarifice and sincerity of purpose, freedom from foreign rule was an impossibility. What astonished us was the fact that a single individuals pilgrimage—like journeys to every nook and corner of our land brought us together, giving all of us the feeling of oneness, of being Indian and a people who were throbbing with a common desire to become a free nation.

These are reflections on a chapter in our history of times when whatever we did gave value and meaning to our lives. Under the guidance of a rare person who was a unique phenomenon in our part of the world, we who were emasculated by foreign aggression over the centuries, achieved our freedom. And yet again it was in free India that Gandhiji the liberator was assassinated by one of us, a ghastly end to a glorious chapter in Indian history.

However, even before this tragedy a sense of gloom had settled even the country owing to the fratricidal killings prior to the actual date on which the Britishers were to depart. To make things worse the vivisection of our country which seemed an impossibility almost till the day when the nation's leaders set their seal on that fateful decision, bewildered and angered the people and waves of shock engulfed the country.

The leftists in the Congress were forced to realise that since a section of our people misled by communalists could not be rallied under a united leadership, this fatal blow was inevitable. Gandhiji's sorrowful appeal to his countrymen not to reject the Mountbatten Plan at the memorable AICC session held in Delhi could not be spurned because we knew that unless he led us, we would not be able to revive the earlier revolutionary spirit of the masses. His lonely wanderings away from the Capital when the flag of free India was being unfurled on the ramparts of the Red Fort was a touching proof of his agonised soul.

The fury that engulfed the Indian continent for some weeks after the 15th of August, 1947 proved that ours was merely a partial victory and that future generations would condemn us for having failed to rise in revolt against the tottering empire of Great Britain. However, soon after, the climax of disaster was reached on the 30th of January, 1948, the day on which Gandhiji's frail body and lacerated sou ceased to breathe.

Such haunting memories therefore make it difficult to recall the brighter aspect of the 30 years that have elapsed since then. The new State settled down gradually to the hard tasks under dedicated, experienced and talented men with Jawaharlal Nehru at the helm. He roused the people out of the depression that pervaded after the division of India. His stirring speeches and tireless efforts to refashion Asian history raised India's stature in the eyes of the world. More than anyone else Jawaharlal Nehru was aware that after the fascist defeat the world had reached a turning point and that India was destined to shoulder both its global and national responsibilities with vigour and self-confidence. But for his farsightedness and belief in a socialist oriented world order living in peace, our Constitution may not have been given its guiding principle, namely that India must strive so that Indians who are exploited by entrenched interests, shall regain their rights and live as free and equal citizens of a modern progressive country. Nehru's commitments to a world free of military blocs and his passionate disapproval of imperialism in its old and new forms redeemed in some measure our prestige in world forums and the humiliation we had to suffer because of what happened after we attained independence was overcome.

And now, as the country steps into its 31st year since freedom, disturbing questions confront it. The dream of a prosperous people rid of their primitive conditions, the existence of an egalitarian society in which its wealth will belong to those who produce it, a higher quality of life for all who work and a country that will not tolerate external dictation is as yet no more than a mere dream. The orderly progress that the founders of freedom had envisaged seems to have deteriorated into a situation wherein confusion rather than clarity of vision is more apparent. We appear to be grouping for the instruments necessary to bring about social equality and thereby makes our workers and peasants a vital force.

The left intelligentsia is either sulking in silence unable to impart the message of rejuvenation to those who continue to live in penury, or satisfies itself with delivering sermons to parties and individuals working among the masses. The ruling elite in these three decades has failed to respond to the invigorating currents of revolutionary thought and practice in sharp contrast to what is taking palce in Asia and Africa.

Most of them appear to be content with allowing India to drift haplessly instead of calling upon the people to act as their predecessors did. These may be subjective reactions of a defeatist nature and indications that, by and large, the source of intellectual and revolutionary energy of political parties have withered away. Perhaps, below the surface, fresh currents of thoughts and action are germinating. History teaches one that stagnation is a temporary phenomenon, that the human mind knows no rest in its quest for truth and renews itself with ever expanding knowledge.

We in Asia and Africa have to redeem many a pledge before our people can attain their right to live as liberated human beings. The future alone will reveal whether the revolutionary elements in India will come together and organise the inarticulate millions so that their lives may be happier. Their aspirations to live as fully developed human personalities must be realised if our freedom is to be worthwhile.

On the 15th of August, 1947 Jawaharlal Nehru had said, "The future beckons to us. Whether do we go and what shall be our endeavour? To bring freedom and opportunity to the common man, to the peasants and workers of India; to fight and end poverty and ignorance and disease; to built up a prosperous, democratic and progressive nation, and to create social, economic and political institutions which will ensure justice and fullness of life to every man and woman. We have hard work ahead. There is no resting for any one of us till we redeem our pledge in full, till we make all the people of India what destiny intended them to be".

For the generation that is in its full vigour today, this message is as true as it was thirty years back.

Link, August 15, 1977.

REPUBLIC DAY THOUGHTS

While the Congress and the Muslim League representatives were debating, discussing and analysing in the Central Legislative Assembly as to what exactly should be the new Constitution of Free India during 1946-47, I was travelling all over the country for days and weeks together. I was then in search of a new path to social liberation, a path that would end the exploitation of human beings.

Distracted and frustrated I decided to travel from the North to the South and study for myself the conditions in which our people lived. I was unfamiliar with the South, having lived exclusively in the North and was eager to learn and understand the way of life and thought of the southern regions of our country. It was for me a journey which revealed the superb natural beauty and cultural richness, an altoghter unforgettable experience. Age has dimmed those memories but re-reading an account of my travels penned during the trips, I vividly remembered some of those personal reminiscences. Now after three decades I thought of sharing them with the readers of LINK which has entered the 25th year of its publication.

Many readers are sure to look upon these outpourings as that of an emotionally stirred person, devoid of logic, and a political framework. I could not agree more with them because I myself think that I was very confused, almost dazed by the unexpected nature of political developments after the heady years of the 'Quit India' struggle. But whatever their worth, let me look back along with the readers now a mere observer.

If only time would stop, if only there was a breakdown in the time machine! It might then be possible to arrest the swift moving crowded scenes of my non-stop 21-day journey. The roar of the sea and roar of human voices, how similar! Particularly when the latter became muffled and smothered . . . .

Old towns walled and turretted by temple gopurams, tanks filled with sacred waters, field and homesteads full of men, women and children cattle, skies dotted with birds in the day and stars in the night—scenes the eye beheld in between the halts. Each halt had its own individuality while it lasted, its own programme, its local colour—but now with the passage of time one place might be another, every mass gathering like the one that preceded or followed it, one workers' assembly as much like the one that went before or after it! Imaginative integrity and artistic fancy demand a separate recording, a journey that was not meant to be empty of purpose.

The journey began in the afternoon on August 18 from Delhi. In the Nizam's territory a Dornakal, Khammameth and Madira, men and women asked for a message. The new reforms and the recent atrocity campaigns in certain villages have inflammed the state subjects. Bezwada and Tenali and onwards, one plateform meeting after another followed. Everywhere the workers were reporting their 1942 actions and asking for a scheme of work for the future . . . .

Andhradesa is the home of fiery people. The Communists are strongly organised there and busy sowing seeds of doubt in Congress *bona fides*. Nevertheless, the people as elsewhere are not enamoured by their politics. But they have made deep inroads into the labour and kisan field. . . . . A day in Madras town. The Madras Indian is not the phlegmatic he is made out to be. His full-blooded response to 1942 proves otherwise. The rush begins : Villupuram, procession, meeting and then off to Chidambaram, with wayside meetings all the way . . . .

The students of Annamalai University at Chidambaram insisted in spite of official frowns on a meeting. Vociferous shouts of 'Long Live Revolution', brave ideas of willingness to do and die again. Railway workers agitated at strike prospects . . . . French-owned Karaikal, intensely anti-imperialist. One of the most elaborately arranged meetings. When the hour of reckoning comes will we ever be able to make good the loss the people suffered in fighting the White oppressors?

On the run again to Tanjore. Once an emperor reigned here. But people do not remember that now. At Kumbakonam, the seat of South Indian intellectual orthodoxy, fifteen thousand people were jammed into a little park. Here in '42 shooting took place. Nine died including a little boy of ten. Did he know why he died? Will his unlived life increase the value of those who live after him?

In Tanjore the peasantry is in a state of ferment. Anti-Congress agents are busy. Zamindars of Tanjore feel they cannot fight both the Congress and the Communists. They are lining up with the former. In the silent manuscript world of the Tanjore liberary, the past lay docketted and neatly bundled, Tanjore District was one vast sea of turbulent ovation to '42, each garland a piece of exquisite floral artistry, sandalwood, incense and fruit offering. The Hindu mind turns to temple ritual as naturally as the sunflower turns to the rising sun.

Between Tanjore and Erode was another rush . . . Over the great anicut to Trichinopoly where the students and striking railway workers had to be addressed. The workers seemed confused and tense. The strike was a Communist challenge and nothing more. A public meeting. Twenty-five thousand people sat quietly and listened.

Through Mettur and Dharmapuri to Salem. In Salem, Rajaji's area, activity amongst Congressmen is still of the routine hackneyed character. The Netaji Youth League movement is stronger here than the Congress or the RSD movement.

Off through Tiruppur to Coimbatore. Tiruppur is the Khadi capital of Tamilnad. Textile Mazdoors presented a guard of honour. Fifteen thousand come to the meeting. Between Tiruppur and Coimbatore there were meetings at Palladam and Sulur. In '42 the people of Sulur set fire to an aeroplane in a nearby aerodrome. Many were sentenced to life imprisonment, but were released when the Congress became the Government. At Thonda Mathur there was peasants' conference. They came with their womenfolk. Later, the biggest meeting of the whole tour assembled here. A lakh of people. They sat as if they were a military formation, so silently and with such dignity. Tiruppur and Coimbatore were landmarks. Mass and organisational strength intense. Women and men workers and peasants, old any young aflame with the 'eternal fire that never dies'. Union work almost flawless. Coimbatore, a night sky studed with stars— Strong breeze from the west. Working men and women in the entire district devoted to the Congress.

From Coimbatore through Mettupalayam, Pollachi to Udumalpet. A meeting in the bed of a huge tank that is dry. Rapt crowds listening to word images in Hindi translated into Tamil, a language fit for oratory. The Tamilians' response to eloquence very sensitive. Young men eager and anxious to begin work. When will controversies cease to hold the attention of workers and organised work grip our minds? How will we face the enormous tasks of guining men whose faith and trust in the '42 resisters in almost blind.

Palni is a place of pilgrimage. Elements headed the procession with the National Flag held high in their trunks. Through Dindigul, where 5,000 people had patiently waited for two hours, to Madura, In Madura 45,000 people sat and listened. There was tension. The railway strike was on.

From Madura of the Meenakshi Temple through Sivaganga, Devacottah and Karaikudi (where 20,000 people came to the meeting) to Puducottah. This State of the South is ripe for struggle. Its State Congress is looked upon as a moderate body. Its young men and labour workers are intensely active. The Labour Volunteer Corps is almost in military trim. Madura District as a potential Satara area. Puducottah very acutely anti-British and anti-personal value. Devacottah, scene of much repression. Almost on the Ballia scale. From Puducottah south-wards to the Cape.

In the silent hours of the night long past the time of retirement for rest, men and women await one's arrival. The look of mute appeal or glowing resolve in the eyes that gaze out of the assembled heads. The time and space play tricks that almost challenge one's sanity.

As the sun rose out of the sea washing the shores of Kanya Kumari, there was a new feeling in the air, a new tone in the voices around and the clouds poured their rainbow content into the waters of three oceans. The Maiden Goddess guarding this southernmost outpost, so legend has it, awaits the arrival of her groom. The religious mind might liken her vigil to India's impatient waiting.

From the Cape to Trivandrum capital of Travancore. The University Union had to be inaugurated. Five thousand, of whom 500 were women, were present. A visit to the Labour Union office with a girl volunteer's guard of honour. A huge meeting . . .

Though Quilon and Kottayam to Ernakulam, capital of Cochin with about half a dozen crowded meetings in between.

Ernakulam, a town seething with Congress enthusiasm. Less strained in atmosphere than Travancore. Through Alwaye and Trichur, where the S.I. Rly workers again had to be addressed, to Palghat. More meetings on the way. Palghat meeting, one of the most responsive. Speeches in English have such an outlandish effect that it is almost nauseating to continue in it. A night's halt and again on the march. Feroke had a huge meeting. Feroke is famous for its Feroke bridge sabotage of 1942 Calicut . . . .

Travelling in buses and cars over hills and across valleys. Nearly two thousand miles of travelling, what have they brought in their wake? A stock of fresh experiences, images in serried ranks all closing in one upon another, a close-range view of men and women talking Tamil and Malayalam, an impression of intensified hatred of the British and capitalist systems of overlordship. It echoed throughout the journey. Mountain ranges and rivers and provincial disputes are prevalent, But there are really just two nations—of the Have Nots and the Have Gots.

Whether organisational activity will increase in the South after this visit or not I cannot say, I can only repeat that the people are prepared for it. If not we, others will handle them. It may not be a healthy lead. But a vacuum cannot remain unfilled. . . .

And now on the eve of the thirty-fourth Republic Day, we will have to assess the achievements and the failures of the Republic in terms of the aspirations of the people and the conditions prevailing in the country.

Link, January 26, 1983.

LENIN—A TRIBUTE

Panegyrics and eulogies are gushing forth from the hearts and minds of millions of people as they begin to celebrate the day on which Lenin was born, a hundred years ago. Continentwide and countrywide demonstrations of admiration and festivals are being held, where people in their thousands are giving expression to their thoughts and feelings and are paying their homage to the memory of this phenomenal figure of the 20th century.

Lenin's name is familiar to vast numbers of people, young and old, in many lands because even today, although he died over four decades ago, his deeds and achievements continue to give them the inner strength they need to overcome life's trials and tribulations.

Mankind has endeavoured to be free from age to age and century to century. This urge has led human beings from epoch to epoch out or the anarchy and chaos of ignorance to greater awareness of themselves and the universe, to ever-widening horizons of thought, organization and purposeful activity. In the course of this long march they have experienced many defeats and some triumphs, much suffering and great joy.

But humanity's long and exciting search for happiness, its search for spiritual bliss and the good things of life, would not have been so consistently progressive without great leaders and teachers who showed the way by telling people how they should live, what they should never yield to evil. Whether it is a Buddha, a Christ, a Gandhi or a Lenin, although they were individuals who acted and talked differently in their contemporary situations, and were born and brought up in different circumstances their advent charged men's thinking profoundly and made their followers better and nobler human beings.

To take the most recent unlike Gandhiji, Lenin's teachings were not rooted in the religious traditions of Russia, as he was attracted to the revolutionary school of thought founded by Marx and Engels. Nevertheless, his passionate concern for the oppressed, his anxiety to help the victims of tyranny and his desire to liberate those who were suffering helplessly under a vicious social system, invested him with the magnetic appeal of a religious prophet. His legend has grown and not diminished with the passing of years.

As a founder of a party of a new type he stressed the need for dedicated and self-sacrificing cadres prepared to fight for the cause and if necessary perish in the fight. Lenin's leadership lay in his tremendous capacity to know the essential nature of the society he wanted to destroy and his ability to take calculated risks against all odds. His historic decision which gave the signal for the storming of the citadels of Russian power in 1917 changed the course of human history and proved the correctness of his comprehensive understanding of the situation.

Lenin realised quite clearly and had come to the conclusion that a new type of political organization was necessary for mobilising the working classes. He therefore insisted on involving within it the masses who were, according to him, the main levers of revolutionary power. He advised such of his colleagues as were seriously engaged in political activities to devote their energies to the masses because he said "the millions of people will never listen to the advice of parties, if that advice does not fall in with their own experience".

He called upon does entrusted with organisational tasks to "learn to approach the most backward, the most undeveloped members of this class, those who are least influenced by our science and the science of life, so as to be able to speak to them, to draw closer them, to raise them steadily and patiently to the level of Social-Democratic consciousness, without making a dry dogma out of our doctrine—to teach them not only from books, but through participation in the daily struggle for existence of these backward and undeveloped strata of the proletariat".

Lenin carried on a persistent struggle against the opponents of his theory of tightly-knit compact party of ideologically sincere individuals, because without such a party there was bound to be vagueness where inflexible determination was what was necessary. And yet he advocated the necessity to be in tune with the mass mood always and adopt tactics and strategy in conformity with the changing situation. Jawaharlal Nehru noted with admiration the importance Lenin attached to the personal qualities of party members and writes : "Lenin did not care how many people he had with him—he even threatened at one period to stand alone—but he insisted that only those should be taken who were "whole-hoggers", who were prepared to give up every thing for the cause and even do without the applause of the multitude. He wanted to build up a body of experts in revolution who could develop the movement efficiently. He had no use for just sympathisers and fair whether friends."

One could go on enumerating the various aspects of this brilliant intellect and dwell on the marvels of men who quite early in his life made up his mind to live a revolutionary's life and exhaust himself in the process. He faced endless hardships but never faltered and lived with danger as his lifelong companion.

He had the ability to look beyond the horizon and finally led his people out of the prison-house of poverty and suffering. Romain Rolland, the French philosopher, summed up his reading of Lenin's role in history with characteristic clarity when he said that he was "the greatest man of action in our century and at the same time the most selfless".

Gandhi and Lenin : As we in India ponder over the life of this memorable son of Russia who changed the history of his country, who called upon the oppressed of all lands to unite against their oppressors and who dreamt of and worked for world revolution, we are reminded of our own leader Gandhi whose birth centenary almost concedes with Lenin's. Both of them wanted to end the suffering of all who are compelled to starve, they wanted to lighten their burdens and were convinced that wars were a curse and an abomination. Working in very dissimilar circumstances they evolved different techniques for realising their aspirations and both were able to witness the breaking of a new dawn for their people. Men who become enbodiments of noble ideals never die, they live not in monuments of stone and mortar but in fields and factories, in hearts and homes, wherever men and women work and live. They with the passage of time Lenin will not be forgotten because the problems that he dealt with await lasting solutions. Lenin's teachings will live because they are needed by the millions who long for peace, for bread and for freedom. Lenin's memory will endure as long as the citizens of the Soviet Union carry on the struggle against the enemies of the common people, for as long as the citizens of the Soviet Union and their socialist State live up to his glowing ideals.

Link, April 19, 1970.

9

Three Decades of Friendship

My span of life has extended now into three quarters of century. There are therefore large gaps in what I remembered of the years and years that have gone by. And yet certain impression are stamped in my mind as if with some luminous paint. They glow even now with almost the same brilliance as they did when the events occurred. Some of my most vivid memories are those associated with Jawaharlal Nehru and him after Indira. Although I have never claimed or aspired to belong to their inner and intimate circles, I have one of a group of men and women whose minds were attuned to theirs. Jawaharlal Nehru attracted us and evoked our response even though he was considerably order, because he stirred our minds and exited our emotions and gave us a thought-provoking frame of reference which was relevant to our times.

His writings and speeches about what had happened there after 1917, his replies and explanations in response to my innumerable questions regarding the anti-Soviet and anti-communist propaganda raging in certain Indian and Western socialist circles, were utterly frank, unbiased and objective. He used to say that he did not believe in a purely negative attitude. Even his doubts about the ethical implications of the post-Lenin developments in the Soviet Union were free from malice and were qualified with statements which implied that in the given historical and social context in which Marxism and Leninism had to be applied, compromises were perhaps inevitable. One should not dogmatise about anything that has happened in Soviet Russia, he once remarked.

It was therefore natural that, despite his critics, free India under Nehru's leadership established friendly relations with the Soviet Union in 1947. I remember the eloquent speeches in which he unfolded the outlines of his foreign policy. During his visit to the USA in 1949 he realised that its approach to India was not based on acceptance of India as a free and sovereign country which aimed at uprooting all the vestiges of colonial domination and building a self-reliant economy. Jawaharlal Nehru's ideal of friendship among nations was based on mutual cooperation among them in economic, cultural and other spheres on the basis of equality.

He wanted to establish the essential requirements for developing India as an industrial power. Therefore when in 1949 American leaders expressed their reluctance and inability to assist in attaining India's objective, such hopes as Jawaharlal Nehru had about the land of free enterprise and democracy evaporated. In contrast, when the Soviet Union extended its friendship and Jawaharlal Nehru received an affectionate and jubilant welcome during his first visit to the Soviet Union in 1955 as Prime Minister of India, he found a practical confirmation of his faith in Socialism as a liberating force. He grasped the hand of friendship extended by the Soviet Union and commenced the journey to his cherished goal of industrialising and modernising India. At the conclusion of his memorable visit in 1955 with young Indira by his side, he was so moved and overwhelmed by the people's loving ovation that he declared before returning to India that he was leaving a little bit of his heart in Soviet Union.

This happened full 30 years ago. During these three decades India has had no cause for any complaint. It has received generous help from its socialist neighbour. The recently released three hour documentary "Nehru" tells the story of Indo-Soviet friendship and cooperation and its vitalising impact on our economy as well as our mutual concern for each other's well being. Peaceful coexistence as defined by Nehru is not just a platitude. It continues to be the cornerstone of Indian foreign policy. There has never been a turning back on the principle that, notwithstanding our differences with other countries in social and political beliefs and practices, there shall be no attempts to interfere in each other's national way of life.

Why am I dwelling on thoughts such as these? Perhaps for a variety of reasons. First of all, the world is observing the 40th anniversary of the end of a war during which, while it lasted from 1941 to 1945, humanity went through its most agonising years. Years when the human values of civilized living were massacred by blood-thirsty Nazi hordes. Millions upon millions of men, women and children perished as insane hounds lusting for world domination over-ran vast tentorties in Europe. I cannot help recalling Jawaharlal Nehru's intense and burning desire to resist the menance.

His impressioned denunciation of fascism, his impatience with the Western powers because they hesitated to launch an offensive against the enemies of mankind, the anger that welled in him at the Indian people's helplessness and inability to join the crusade—these are for me unforgetable memories.

We as a people shared with Nehru his anguish when we heard that the Nazi armed forces were poised to crush and defeat the U.S.S.R. we also shared his elation when Hitler's army was thrown back by the heroic, death defying Soviet soldiers who rid their soil of the aggressors and liberated their country.

We were fortunate because his only offspring, his beloved Indira, came forward to carry on the tasks he could not complete. And in doing so, Indira as Prime Minister encountered obstacles with often challenged the basics of the Nehru legacy. She withstood most valiantly the pressures from unfriendly directions to take the country back. Had she not realised these pressures with steadfastness and once again, like her father, grapsed the hand of friendship extended by the Soviet leadership, our freedom would have been in peril.

Indira Gandhi knew that the vast gatherings of men and women who greeted her during her numerous visits to the Soviet Union were reaffirming their love for her countrymen and their wish to the prosperity and happiness of India. Their tender sentiments, their affectionate gesture and much else were reminiscent of the scenes she had witnessed when she accompanied her father in 1955. And all though the years when Indira Gandhi functioned as India's Prime Minister the Soviet leadership never faltered, though their friendship for our country was put to test time and again in moments of crisis. And finally after the signing of the treaty of friendship and cooperation the Soviet Union felt it was duty bond to give full support to India at every level and in whatever way India needed such assistance. Throughout Indira Gandhi's momentous carrier as a leader of the Indian people, she was nationally known as an opponent of imperialism and its manifestations and a firm supporter of world piece of the socialist countries, and of leaders of liberation movements in every continent.

It is well to recall all this because even though Indira Gandhi is no longer physically with us, her spirited personality endures. The new leader our people have elected in her place is none other than a person who has the privilege to inherit her whole being both physically and mentally.

Rajiv Gandhi is fully aware of this legacy. The teeming million of India, specially those who are yet to gain their opportunities and privileges, have acknowledged his leadership because they believe that Rajiv Gandhi, the successor of Nehru and Indira, will make their dreams a reality of life. This is an awesome responsibility which history has placed on him.

Rajiv Gandhi will be visiting several world capitals in the coming months. And whenever he goes he will be received with respect. But when he goes to the Soviet Union as India's Prime Minister the leaders and people of that country are sure to welcome him with open arms and with different faiths and ideologies, and belong to different political systems. Yet we all share common anxieties and hopes.

We have been drawn here by our intense concern that a nuclear war should not make this earth, on which we are all fellow passengers, incapable of sustaining human life. We also ches . . . . the desire to create conditions in which women can work with men the terms of complete equality, to build a better and peaceful future for our younger generations.

May this World Congress demonstrate to the vast majority of peace loving humankind, the inherent strength of women, who can no longer be ignored or treated as second class citizens.

May this World Congress serve notice to these who engage in nuclear brinkmanship, that our Mother Earth not perish!

I would like to say, in conclusion, to my young friends here how confident I feel, as I meet and talk to the younger people, that the torch which my generation is passing on to the new generation will be safe in their hands and will be carried forward with a new determination. You have many more miles to go. We stand today at the threshold of a new century.

I am certain that the light of human liberation will burn even brighter, as the world steps into the 21st century. In the end, let me thank the Soviet Women's Committee for their warm hospitality.

Thank you, for your kind attention.

Speech at the World Congress of Women of Moscow, held from 23rd to 27th June, 1987.

GANDHIJI : SOME REMINISCENCES

Memories are like the scent that survives the rose. They remain buried under the debris of time but can always be sought out to revive the past and its images. With every passing year the capacity to feel and learn becomes duller and duller and the desire to linger in the corridors of the past becomes at times an obsession. Every year on the anniversary of Gandhiji's birth and death urge to look back seizes such of us as hand the rare fortune of basking in the sunshine of his affection.

But it is not quite to easy to write as to ruminate about those time. To communicate what was significant in the events that brought insignificant beings into the orbit of Gandhiji's living faith requires a capacity for perserverance, a quality that is alien to my temperament. But the only consoling thought, in the fact that however unimportant and personal the incident the fact that it was woven around 20th-century India's most compelling personality, will be of some interest to the readers. I still cannot help experiencing the teenager's thrill of reading out a welcome address to Gandhiji on behalf of Delhi's citizens in the year 1930 at a time when I had no political existence and my understanding of politics was shockingly elementary. Fortunately for me, the Delhi Congress of those years could not agree upon anyone else because of sharp internal divisions.

The Gandhi Ground was a packed mass of humanity, and as Gandhiji walked up to the khadi-drapped dais deafening cries of

'Mahatma Gandhi ki jai' rent the air. After the garlanding ceremony was over, I read out the printed address. The era of loundspeakers had yet to arrive and I am not very sure if more than a thousand persons could hear me.

Gandhiji spoke for about half an hour and no one in that vast multitude uttered a sound as they sat listening to him. His halting speech, in broken Hindi-Urdu sentences, his gentle mannerisms and quiet exposition of freedom's cause was more a talk than a piece of oratory. It was devoid of all the sophisticated flourishes of polished Persianised Urdu to which Delhi audiences were accustomed in those days. He could not sway them with quotations from Ghalib or Bahadur Shah Zafar and yet he held their attention. Despite the absence of loudspeakers, his soft voice carried the stern message of struggle to that vast assembly of men and women. Their repeated applause in unison was proof enough that the people had understood him. Their subsequent behaviour provide that they were ready to act in accordance with his behest.

I never recovered from the elation and surprise of that first ecounter, because it was an utterly unreal and dreamlike experience. The importance of not being important has its own reward. I realised much later; otherwise could I ever have aspired to get so close to Gandhiji? This purely accidental contact with someone who could only have been worshipped from afar, as far as I was concerned, made me think. I had to be worthy of the opportunity to deserve the honour done to me by our kind though quarrelsome leaders.

By the time I met him later again in Delhi I had grown up a little (politically). This was soon after the Gandhi-Irwin Pact had been signed and the jail gates thrown open as a result. He had to take note of me because there had been some dispute about my release. It had been hold up by a week or more because the Delhi authorities were inclined to classify me as one who had indulged in preaching 'violence'. Since persons convicted for making inflammatory speeches were excluded from the terms of the Pact concerning the release of political prisoners, I was not released along with the others, Gandhiji was, I think, intrigued and wanted to know whether I had really incited people to deviate from the path of non-violent non-coopeation, as he was anxious to know whether the British were honest about implementing the Pact. I had to confess to him that having recently read Savarkar's book on the Indian struggle for Independence in 1857, I could not help being influenced by it and did refer to it quite often in my speeches.

I am not quite sure if he appreciated my point of view. Subsequently, however, many years later, emboldened by a series of events, I had occasion to argue with him about the ethics of means and ends.

We never spared Gandhiji and took every problem to him even though we knew that he could barely snatch a few hours for sleep. On one of his visits to Delhi in the Thirties he had to detrain at Faridabad. This was often done because the milling crowds that gathered at railway stations tried him out and his medical advisers used to caution local Congress organisations against strenuous routine. Acharya Kripalani, the late Farid-ul-Haq Ansari and a few others, including Mr. G.D. Birla, had also gone to Faridabad. We walked on either side of Gandhiji. I remember complaining to him about discrimination against women in the matter of nominations to the PCCs. He was quite emphatically of the view that we must resist injustice and not allow ourselves to be bullied. Acharyaji had his usual humorous but sarcastic dig at our expense but Gandhiji said quite seriously that women must not be overwhelmed by their natural shyness and should put up a stiff fight for their rightful place in the Congress.

The oppressed could always count on his sympathy and support. I believe that we, women, and his Harijans were uppermost in his mind when he spoke against our evil social customs. Such personal anecdotes of thousands of Indians would reveal how in his simple and sincere way he gave everyone who drew near him a feeling of mutual belonging. His catholic mind never rejected off hand a viewpoint he could not accept. The debate about the efficacy of violence fascinated him. But he never insisted on anyone acting against his better judgement. When I wanted to report to him about the happenings in the Quit India struggle of 1942 he invited me to Poona knowing full well that I would 'if discovered' be a British prisoner. He took full note of every aspect of the struggle but disagreed about most of the measures that had led to severe repression. His point was that nothing should be attempted without weighing fully the consequences of such action on the mass morale.

As darkness fell I slipped into his room. Gandhiji's tender concern about my health and safety and his appeal to give up the life of a fugitive lightened my self-imposed burdens. Later he wrote to me.

"You can't hurt me without hurting yourself. I laugh and invite you to share my laughter 'O ye, of little faith!' You lose patience quickly because you misread me. Have I not said 1945 is not 1942? Yet I have not changed because you find that I am covering myself with woollen shawls or even at all. Wait, watch and pray".

Some time after when the British Viceroy and Gandhiji were negotiating a solution I was suddenly summoned by him. He wanted me to accompany him and meet the Mountbattens because he wanted them to hear for themselves the insistence of the 'August' socialists on their demand that the British must withdraw unconditionally. I was quite irritated because I just did not know why I should be picked upon to be the spokesman of the group. My hesitation and irritation hurt him. But all he said was, "I told them that you are in my pocket and that I can always take you with me"! I could not resist this appeal and very solemnly and apprehensively accompanied him.

Lady Mountbatten was a very intelligent conversationalist and I was quite surprised at meeting someone who spoke so forthrightly. Whether Gandhiji's purpose in taking me along with him was served or not I could never know because soon afterwards I had to go to the USA. He wanted me to go, not merely to recoup my health but to bring about austerities in the Indian Embassy in Washington!

Throughout the six months I was there he was in torment because these were the months when fratricidal conflicts had brought out the bestial in us. I was seized by a nameless restlessness by the end of December 1947 and decided to return to India. As I was waiting for my plane in snowbound New York came the news of his end. The man who wanted to "hug all humanity in friendly embrace" was killed by his own kith and kin. The unbelievable had happened. The conscience of a nation was silenced. But his ageless message of peace is heard wherever wars are being waged.

Link, October 2, 1966

How relevant is Gandhiji and his message in 1969, the year that has seen men circling round the moon and walking in and out of spaceships, far away from the earth and its problems? Is he relevant for technologically and industrially backward areas of the world and yet irrelevant for countries where the scientific revolution has brought into existence a new order of men and women? Such questions should rouse our curiosity because it happens to be the hundredth year of his birth. Has a man of faith whose beliefs are not backed by scientific knowledge and the assurance it breeds any place in an age in which every aspect of human conduct is determined by awe-inspiring computer calculations and their mysterious ramifications?

But what was Gandhiji's "faith"? Can it be defined as mere acceptance of "beliefs in spite of evidence", a rejection of the rational or spurning of man's objective knowledge of himself and his environment, mere flabby piety and the blind worship that traditional religion prescribes? If that sums up "faith" and Gandhiji propagated such faith, then quite obviously his life and teaching are utterly valueless and totally meaningless for those who want human beings to respond to all that is challenging in life on this earth and beyond.

His beliefs, however, had nothing to do with a set of dogmas or a static view of man and his social destiny. Otherwise, how could he have cast such a phenomenal spell over his compatriots and become a source of strength for the millions? By daring them to act regardless of consequences, by urging upon them again and again to overcome their intellectual, social and moral lethargy, Gandhiji rejected Indian obscurantism in all its manifestation. As if over-night, "he became a symbolic expression of the confused desires of the people" asking them to "be free", "be slaves no more" trying to tell them that liberation from spiritual thraldom is essential if they are to attain freedom from Imperialist thraldom.

Those who have studied Gandhiji's writings and worked with him are aware that by laying stress on the need to "spiritualise" politics he was in reality laying emphasis on the need for making his people realise that not intellect alone but the moral values of goodness and truth were necessary for strengthening their character, because thus only could human beings be instrumental in winning back their lost heritage. As Nehru has written, Gandhiji was convinced that it was only through "some vital upheaval, to be generated within the soul itself" that we as a people could get back our backbone.

There were occasions when many of the younger generation misunderstood Gandhiji's emphasis on character building, his insistence on work for village and Harijan welfare and such activities as lacked what they considered, any revolutionary "appeal". Oten they scoffed at his vague utopianism, which struck them as nothing more than a colourless version of 18th century humanitarianism. He was misunderstood for his stress on eschewing retaliations and avoiding bitter thoughts even when angered by extreme provocation.

They were suspicious of this "softness" to the opponent and often questioned his determination to liquidate British rule. This superficial view of Gandhian ethics was particularly fashionable among the more westernised of our young people specially those who had come back from European universities with a smattering of revolutionary thought. Their inadequacy in grasping the essentials of the Indian social scene gave them a confused and distorted sense of values. Otherwise they would have plunged into the freedom struggles of the 30s and 40s in overwhelming numbers and helped Gandhiji and Jawaharlal Nehru in organising the vast amorphous masses in fields and factories on a class basis.

Jawaharlal Nehru was an exception. Europeanised intellectual though he was, he could not keep back from any movement initiated by Gandhiji. He has in eloquent language described how exciting it was to live, move and work with the roused masses. As civil disobedience led him and thousands of Indians to prison repeatedly, those who participated in these struggles were unable to accept the theory that these methods were not revolutionary and therefore futile. Nehru, in other words never doubted the revolutionary integrity of Gandhi although he disagreed with him on several momentous occasions.

The criticism that the philosophy and technique of non-violence was essentially counter-revolutionary was rejected by him totally and he said that "in spite of its negative name . . . . it was the very opposite of a meek submission to a tyrant's will". After hearing Gandhiji's explanations and pleadings for the adoption of non-violent non-co-operation as the only form of practicable struggle in India. Nehru wrote : "The way he pointed out was hard and difficult, but it was a brave path, and it seemed to lead to the promised land of freedom. Because of that promise we pledged our faith and marched ahead".

For twenty-two years we the people of India have lived free of external control at least in the sense that we are not ruled by a foreign bureaucracy; nor is there an alien army of occupation on our soil. Gandhiji's voice was silenced twenty-one years ago and with him vanished the moral imperative to remain within the framework of strictly non-violent action. And yet the politically awakened sections of our people have by and large continued to use the forms and methods he used. The new leaders of the people have not so far been able to think of substitutes to the earlier methods of struggle.

India's new young intelligentsia of the post-British period has been unable to make an impact as yet on the minds and hearts of the people of our country. Can this be because they have not been given an opportunity to assimilate the experience and teachings of Gandhi-Nehru and other leaders of the immediate past? It is because they are living in an atmosphere in which trivial things, intrigues and manoeuvres prevail and those who are interested in trying to make this country and the world a better place to live in are disunited and therefore weak? To perform the historic task of our times effectively we need without doubt fresh thinking and new forms of action. But when fashioning their new tools our new leaders have to take care not to discard everything that belongs to the Gandhi-Nehru era.

Their thought and action will continue to be relevant for as long as the existing poverty of thought persists. Without an organic comprehension of social development there can be no meaning in any social action. Gandhiji had acquired an understanding of the conditions that confronted him as he grew into maturity and as a result of keeping constant watch on himself and his social and political environment. A hundred years hence his solutions for civilising human beings may become obsolete but then none would have been happier than he himself because his mission was always to create the self-confident individual who does not need either leaders or even stereotyped system.

Link, January 26, 1969.

MY DISCOVERY OF NEHRU

The last great opportunity of forgoing an alliance of the left with progressive forces in the Congress was thrown away in 1953 when Jaya Prakash Narayan laid down rigid preconditions instead of responding positively to Jawaharlal's invitation to him to join the Government. There was no reason for Jawaharlal making this generous overture, except to hasten the country's progress towards socialism, since the Congress party enjoyed a massive majority in the Lok Sabha.

In an article contributed to Asia magazine of America (June 1936), Jawaharlal Nehru said : "It is curious how one cannot resist the tendency to give an anthropomorphic form to a country. Such is the force of habit and early associations. India becomes Bharat Mata, Mother India, a beautiful lady, very old but very youthful in appearance, sad-eyed and forlorn, cruelly treated by aliens and outsiders, and calling upon her children to protect her".

Adopting this image, one might say that during the two decades from 1869 to 1889 mother India gave birth to a remarkable brood of sons and daughters who would deliver her from foreign thraldom.

Consider the roll of honour (and the list is by no means exhaustive). 1869 : Mohandas Karamchand Gandhi; Vallabhabahai Patel; 1878 : C. Rajagopalachari; 1879 : Sarojini Naidu; 1880 : M.A. Ansari; 1882 : Subramania Bharati and Bidhan Chandra Roy; 1883 : Vinayak Damodar Savarkar; 1884; Rajendra Prasad; 1886 : Rameshwari Nehru and Muthulakshmi Reddi; 1887; S. Satyamurti and Govind Ballabh Pant; 1888 : Maulana Azad, S. Radhakrishnan and M. Asaf Ali; 1889 : Jawaharlal Nehru and Acharya Narendra Deva.

This stellar cluster reminds me of another passage from Jawaharlal Nehru. He wrote in Glimpses of World History about "how, in the lives of nations, periods of brilliant life come and go. For a while they brighten up everything and enable the men and women of that period and country to create things of beauty. People seem to become inspired". The Gandhi-Nehru years were such a period in India's history. I have often remarked to friends that my greatest good fortune was to have been born when I was born .... so that I grew up when the country was aglow with the light radiated by Mahatma Gandhi and Jawaharlal Nehru; and to have married the man whom I married—it was Asaf Saheb who broadened my mental horizons beyond English literature which had been my only enthusiastic interest as a Convent-educated student.

I have been asked many a time, specially by young persons, when it was that I first met Jawaharlal. It will be more accurate to speak of the first occasion when I saw him.

It was early in the winter of 1928, in Delhi. I was nineteen at the time. Asaf and I, who had married a few weeks earlier, in September, were invited to dinner by Brijlal Nehru and his wife, Rameshwari, at their residence on Clive Road (now Tyagaraja Marg). Brijlal, a nephew of Motilal Nehru, wanted us to meet his uncle and his cousin, Jawaharlal, who were on a visit to Delhi and were staying with him.

Though my husband was of the same age as Jawaharlal, he was equally well acquainted with Motilal Nehru, and was a practicising lawyer, unlike Jawaharlal who never developed a serious interest in the profession in which his father had attained high fame and wealth. Asaf often met Motilal Nehru, whom he esteemed as a towering senior both in public life and in the legal profession. This was the background to the Establishment Nehru of Delhi inviting us to meet his seditious clansmen from Allahabad.

As we waited for Jawaharlal's return from a speaking tour of some Punjab towns, the conversation was mainly between Motilal Nehru and my husband, because they were temperamentally akin in their political views, both favouring participation in the legislatures to advance the naitonal cause. Suddenly Motilalji stopped in the middle of the conversation to enquire 'Chote Saab Aagaye'? and instructed the domestics to keep hot water ready for the young master's bath.

At last Jawaharlal burst in, all covered with dust. He barely glanced in our direction as he went quickly in for a wash and change. He must have thought it was the usual evening gathering of some of the Capital's Anglicised elite who were his counsin's colleagues and friends.

Dazzled

I was introduced to Jawaharlal on his joining us for dinner, and was dazzled by the first close view of him. Jawaharlal looked me up and down with amused curiosity. I might well have struct him as a dolled-up slip of a girl, destined to decorate drawing rooms.

It was with very little comprehension that I followed the conversation during and after the dinner.

In spite of acquiring some political knowledge from reading and talks with my husband I was hardly prepared for following the proceedings at the Congress Session in December 1929 at Lahore which I attended. Jawaharlal's election as Congress President earlier that year, when he was only 40, made him one of the youngest to hold the office.

The Lahore Congress was a thrilling spectacle. Jawaharlal, smartly dressed in a black sherwani, rode to the venue of the session on a magnificent white horse at the head of the presidential procession. He looked every inch the knight errant of the freedom movement. Some of us gathered roses and narcissi and presented them to the youthful and winsome Rashtrapati. (That was how the Congress president was referred to till India became a sovereign republic with the head of the State designated as Rashtrapati).

On the last day of the year 1929, at the approach of midnight, Mahatma Gandhi moved a resolution at the Lahore Congress defining the Congress objective as complete independence as opposed to Dominion Status. It was adopted amidst deafening applause. The next morning on New Year's Day 1930, Jawaharlal unfurled the national flag on the bank of River Ravi. As the tricolour fluttered in the breeze, the poet's lines coursed through my mind.

"Bliss was it in that down to be alive,
to be young was very heaven" .

The Independence resolution authorised the Congress leadership to forge the sanctions, through civil disobedience, for realising the objective. Gandhiji decided to base the civil disobedience movement on non-payment of the tax on salt. It was a tax which even the poorest had to pay even through salt was a basic need and a free gift of nature.

I went through my baptism of fire during the Salt Satyagraha, and was imprisoned in 1930 and again in 1932. In 1941 I courted arrest during the Individual Satyagraha which was launched in protest against India being dragged, as a colony, into Britian's war that was claimed to be in defence of democracy. During these years I was a typical desh sevika or a volunteer in the national cause, complying augestingly with the call given by the Congress Working Committee from time to time. It was in 1942, after the All India Congress Committee adopted the Quit India resolution in Bombay and the British authorities rounded up all Congress leaders at one fell swoop in the early hours of 9 August, that I first exercised my own political judgement. I was not sure whether Mahatma Gandhi and Jawaharlal Nehru would approve, but I adopted as my guideline Gandhiji's injunction : 'Do or Die'.

Flag Unfurled

Maulana Azad was to have hoisted the national flag at the Gowalia Tank Maidan in Bombay on the morning of 9 August. Instead, he was under arrest as I found when I accompanied my husband, who was arrested along with other members of the Working Committee, in a police taxi to Victoria Terminus—on his way to an unknown destination. After the train left I decided on an impulse that I would go to the Gowalia Tank Maidan and announce to the people the arrest of the leaders. The police ordered the crowd to disperse. Not wanting the flag to remain unfurled, I rushed up to the dais in a defiant mood, quickly pulled the string to unfurl the flag and told the gathering about the arrest of the national leaders. Few knew my identity.

Some thought that the girl with plaited hair was a college student from Delhi. Hardly has the flag been unfurled when the police lobbed tear-gas shells into the crowd. The assembled men and women ran halter-skelter with tears streaming from their eyes. Among them was Indira Gandhi, though I was not aware of it at the time. "I had my first experience of a tear-gas attack at the flag-hoisting ceremony," she recalls in Remembered Moments.

The experience of that morning made me decide that I would not once again tamely enter jail by offering Satyagraha. The people were indignant and roused at the arrest of the leaders, and indignation should find organised expression in such a forceful manner that the alien rulers would have no option but to Quit India. This was also the feeling of several other delegates who had come to the A.I.C.C. meeting. These comprised Congress socialists mainly but included several Gandhians like RR Diwaker and Sucheta Kripalani.

We all felt that the savage repression let loose by the British occupation forces against the spontaneous protest at the arrest of the national leaders should be canalised into organised resistance, on the lines of the underground movement of the partisans of freedom in Nazi-occupied Europe. I told myself that our action was in consonance with the spirit of the Quit India resolution which called for a "a mass struggle on non-violent lines on the widest possible scale" and which also said : A time may come when it may not be possible to issue instructions or for instructions to reach our people.

When this happens, every man and woman who is participating in this movement must function for himself or herself within the four corners of the general instructions issued. Every Indian who desired freedom and strives for it must be his own guide.

Both on the underground Congress radio and in our illegally circulated literature we were careful to draw a distinction between planned dislocation of Britain's imperialist was effort, on the one hand, and senseless destruction—as by latter-day terrorists—of lives and property. It is remarkable that though some like white Gandhians, more loyal to non-violence than the Mahatma, turned up their noses at us during and after the Quit India movement, neither Gandhiji nor Jawaharlal Nehru disowned us.

Bewildered

When I emerged from underground life early in 1946 following cancellation of the warrant for my arrest, I was bewildered by the spectacle of Congress leaders negotiating with the British rulers to enter the Viceroy's Executive Council in the company of the Muslim League. It seemed to me a betrayal of the cause for which they had given the best years of their lives, and for which we of the younger generation had fought in the Quit India movement. My association with socialist colleagues during the underground years had radicalised my outlook on social and economic problems.

I could not see how the Congress could bring about any fundamental change within the structure of the British colonial establishment. Then came the final blow : acceptance of the subcontinent's partition as the price of independence, because of the Hindu-Muslim riots which swept northern India following the Muslim League's 'direct action' in Calcutta in August 1946. I felt dazed, as Jawaharlal and many others must have felt when Gandhiji terminated the non-cooperation movement of the twenties following an outbreak of mob violence at Chauri Chaura. I would take my doubts and criticism to Jawaharlal. He found time, in the midst of the Political drama in which he was a principal actor, to hear me patiently and to explain the compulsions of the situation as he saw them.

I also gave public expression to my anguish in a series of articles in Janata, the weekly founded and edited by Edatata Narayana. These outpourings of mine, in which I raised many questions without even attempting to answer them, were trenchantly critical of the Congress leadership. Yet, when Achyut Patwardhan arranged for the publication of the articles in book form in 1947, Jawaharlal contributed a foreword which was not only generous to me personally but showed his extraordinary capacity for sympathetic understanding of those who different from him.

It was also a testament of his faith in the capabilities of Indian womanhood. "Among the many strange things that have happened in India during this quarter of a century," he wrote, "perhaps the most notable is the emergence of Indian womanhood. Large numbers of Indian women have played an important role in our struggle for freedom. Many of them have stood out by their ability, capacity for organisation and self-sacrifice for a cause. Some of them can be ranked very high in any assembly of woman all over the world. This fact, more than any other, demonstrates the renaissance of the Indian people and the strong foundations on which we have built our movement for freedom." I would take to Jawaharlal not only my doubts and questions about a transfer of power negotiated with the British rulers on the basis of India's partition but the polarisation in international relations after the Second World War. I could understand Winston Churchill's anti-Sovietism, but why did Indian socialists seem to echo his Iron Curtain speech at Fulton? Was the Soviet Union a vast prison house as its detractors alleged?

Jawaharlal advised me to go to Soviet Russia and see for myself. But before that he said, I would do well to spend some time in London, study the history of the socialist and communist movements at the British Museum Library, and discuss the subject with knowledgeable persons like V.K. Krishna Menon and his friends of the British Left. I did not know at the time that in advising me to visit Russia, Jawaharlal wanted me to go through the same kind of education that he had envisaged for his daughter. It was many years later that I found in the Selected Works of Jawaharlal Nehru his letter of 9 July, 1941 in which he tells Indira : "I had hoped that after your formal education at a university was completed, you might supplement it by some travel in various countries. . . . I wanted you to go to Russia to see things there for yourself . . . . Then with this background of mental training and a wider culture I expected you to return to India and discover the fascinating thing that is India".

Visit to Russia

Early in 1950 I applied for an entry visa for my first visit to the Soviet Union. It took quite some time coming. Jawaharlal, refusing to be provoked by the rude things that were being said about him and Gandhiji at that time by Soviet commentators, had sent Dr. Radhakrishnan to Moscow as India's second ambassador. Krishna Menon was our High Commissioner in London. Both Dr. Radhakrishnan and Krishna Menon tried to help expedite the visa, but what clinched the issue appears to have been Jaya Prakash Narayan's reference, at a socialist party convention in Madras, to my criticism of the socialists for their dilution of Marxism.

I sailed from England to Leningrad in the company of D.N. Pritt, the noted British jurist and Marxist, and his wife, Maria Frances. I was greatly impressed by much of what I saw in the Soviet Union—the eradication of destitution and reduction in disparities, the equal participation of women in all sectors of post-war reconstruction, and the care lavished on children and their education. But I did not hesitate to tell the academicians, A.M. Dyakov and Balabuchevich, who were assigned to act as my intellectual guides, that the Soviets were quite wrong in their negative assessment of Mahatma Gandhi and of Jawaharlal Nehru.

The soundness of Jawaharlal's judgement in sending Dr. Radhakrishnan to Moscow was soon vindicated. The philosopher-statesman's patient and persuasive presentation of India's position, and the Indian Government's peace-oriented initiatives in relation to the Korean war and other issues, convinced the Soviet authorities that our foreign policy was truly independent and non-aligned. A token of the changed perception was Stalin's gesture in receiving Dr. Radhakrishnan for a discussion.

When Stalin died in March 1953, I met Jawaharlal who agreed in the course of our talk that it would be appropriate from him as Prime Minsiter to make a reference in Parliament to the late Soviet leader who was a symbol of his country's heroic resistance to Hitler's aggression Parliament adjourned for the day after Jawaharlal's tribute.

Jawaharlal's kind and friendly attitude to me during these years was in spite of my identifying myself with the Leftist criticism of the Congress and of his Government. I did not realise at the time that if Jawaharlal was a prisoner of conservative forces—a potential Lenin fallen among Kerenskys, as I used to describe him—we of the Left were ourselves substantially to blame. We deserved him instead of strengthening the Congress Left. The Communists, who had alienated themselves from the national mainstream by their People's War policy and opposition to the Quit India struggle, swung to the other extreme and refused for several years to acknowledge that India became politically independent in August 1947.

Even the non-communist Left, unfortunately, chose to be doctrinaire. I remember Jawaharlal telling me that it was not proper for the C.S.P. to have contested the municipal elections in Bombay as a distinct party that could offer a socialist alternative to the Congress. By doing so, the socialists weakened both themselves and Jawaharlal.

Exist of Socialists

How greatly we socialists over-rated our influence was to be demonstrated soon. Following the decision to leave the Congress, Narendra Deva and twelve other members resigned from the United Provinces Assembly to which they had been elected in 1946 on the Congress ticket. The socialists could not win any of these seats in the bye-elections that followed.

The exit of the socialists from the Congress led to such developments as the election of Purshottamdas Tandon as Congress president in September 1950, defeating J.B. Kripalani whom Jawaharlal preferred. Another negative consequence of Rightist dominance was the dropping of the Hindu Code Bill from the Congress manifesto for the first general elections of 1951-52.

It is a different matter that in his own constituency of Allahabad East, when his principal rival, Prabhudutt Bramachari, offered to withdraw from the contest if the Prime Minister would agree to drop the proposed legislation, Jawaharlal spurned the offer and fought the election on the very issue of improving women's status through codification and reform of Hindu law.

The last great opportunity of forging an alliance of the Left with progressive forces in the Congress was thrown away in 1953 when Jaya Prakash Narayan laid down rigid precondition instead of responding positively to Jawaharlal's invitation to him to join the Government. There was no reason for Jawaharlal making this generous overtue except to hasten the country's progress towards socialism, since the Congress party enjoyed a massive majority in the Lok Sabha.

Another example of the broad-mindedness of Jawaharlal and of the Congress of those days was their asking me to stand for election as the first Mayor of Delhi. The party position in the

Municipal Corporation of Delhi was such that the Jana Sangh would have been able to get its nominee elected unless the Congress and the communist members joined hands. I was at that time no longer a member of the Communist Party which I had joined a few years earlier and was engaged in the constructive work of the Bharat Sevak Samaj. As I was acceptable to both the Congress and the Communist groups, Jawaharlal and the then Home Minister, Govind Ballabha Pant, asked me to contest the election. This resulted in my election as Mayor.

In the late fifties, Rightist forces within and outside the Congress became vocal in their criticism of the Nehru Government's policies of naitonalisation and radical land reforms. Several of us who were known as 'Nehru Socialists' now became convinced of the need to strengthen Jawaharlal's hands if the country was not to slide back to the pre-1947 scenario of landlords and capitalists thriving under foreign patronage.

It was in order to explain Jawaharlal's policies and gather support among the intelligentsia that the weekly news magazine Link was established in 1958. The founding editor was Edatata Narayana, whom I had come to know during the Quit India struggle when he gave up his position as assistant editor of the Hindustan Times. He joined the underground resistance. Link was intended to articulate the need to combine patriotism with the imnulse for social justice and to strengthen the bonds of friendship between India and the socialist world.

Vulnerable

Within a couple of years, when the occupation of a considerable extent of Indian territory on the northern border by the forces of communist China was disclosed, Jawaharlal became vulnerable to criticism. And after the humiliating reverses suffered by India in the hostilities that broke out towards the close of 1962, the attack on Jawaharlal became more vicious . . . . He wanted the socialists to function, as they used to, as a group within the Congress.

When objection was raised by some Congress leaders to dual membership, Jawaharlal asked me to advise the socialists to function as part of the Congress. Gandhiji, too wanted the socialists to stay with the Congress. I expressed to him my fear that we would be used like a doormat. He was unimpressed by my objection and reiterated his advice. Maulana Azad was of the same view.

Had we socialists heeded this advice when the Congress imposed a ban on dual membership in its new 1948 constitution, we could have strengthened Jawaharlal's hands within the Congress as against the Rightists. With the senior Congress leaders approaching old age, we socialists could well have acquired decisive influence in the party in few years. But the C.S.P. decided to leave the parent body, imagining that virulent V.K. Krishna Menon serving as a proxy for those who wanted to see the removal of Jawaharlal from power.

The attack now came from two sides. Gunning for him from the Right were those who wanted India to line up with the West. Citing the Chinese invasion as proof of the failure of Nehru's foreign policy, they hoped that if Nehru could be toppled on the sensitive issue of the military reverses, his domestic policies aimed at land redistribution and public ownership of key industries could also be reversed. On the other side, an influential section in the yet undivided Communist Party attacked Nehru for allowing himself to be dragged into hostilities with a socialist neighbour.

Those of us who saw in steadfast adherence to Nehru's policies the only hope for the survival and strengthening of India as a free nation determined to achieve socialism felt the need for a daily newspaper, published from the Capital, which would counter the tendentious campaign lunched against Jawaharlal. The dedicated efforts of Dr. A.V. Baliga, the famed surgeon of Bombay who donated his fabulous earnings to humantitorian and public causes, resulted in the launching of Patriot within six months of the trauma suffered by the country in the autumn of 1962.

It owed not a little to the encouragement and support received from many other friends, including Feroze Gandhi, V.K. Krishna Menon and K.D. Malviya. It was Feroze Gandhi who advised me to make a request to Jawaharlal for the allotment, to the United India Periodicals which had launched Link magazine, of the plot of land on which Link House now stands. Without Link House, the launching of Patriot would have been impossible. Even with the building and the rental income from it, I have often had occasion to recall the warning sounded by Jawaharlal, when I informed him of Patriot Project, about the formidable financial difficulties of running a daily newspaper.

He spoke from his own experience of the National Herald which he founded at Lucknow in 1938. Moreover, there is a difference between the two. Jawaharlal's National Herald was linked to a militant anti-British political movement which the newspaper supported and from which, in turn, it drew support. When Patriot was launched we had hoped to strengthen and in turn to derive strength from a broadbased people's movement to actualise the vision of a free India in which the fruits of development would reach the toiling masses. This expectation has been belied. The cruel hand of death claimed both Dr. Baliga and Nehru soon after a year of our launching the newspaper. Subsequently, owing to the fragmentation of progressive forces, the course of economic and social development has increasingly taken an elitist bent. It has widened economic disparities, making a mockery of Jawaharlal's vision.

I try to derive consolation from the adage that it is darkest before a new dawn. It is for the younger generation to relight the torch of Jawaharlal's vision and to correct the course of development, persons of my generation can but remind today's young people of the India of Gandhiji's and Jawaharlal's dreams. An opportunity to do this came my way when friends connected with the Nehru Memorial Liberary asked me to write about Jawaharlal's contribution to the reawakening of Indian women.

Being no scholar or writer of books, I undertook the task with diffidence. But after I discovered in Shri G.N.S. Raghavan a person who could share the burden and provide the kind of collaboration I needed, the task turned into an intellectually exhilarating discovery of Jawaharlal Nehru—the development of his radiant personality and the maturing of his view of life.

There is a sense in which our discovery of a person become complete only after he or she has passed out of our time and entered history. This has ben true of my comprehension of Jawaharlal's life and work. My understanding of him is now the richer for the re-reading of his speeches and writings and the reliving.

Jawaharlal himself summed up in few sentences his profoundly humanist vision of development in the course of the first Azad Memorial Lecture which he delivered in 1959 (brought out by the Indian Council for Cultural Relations in book form under the title India Today and Tomorrow). He said : "Poverty is a degradation, and the obvious reaction is to get rid of it.

To talk of freedom in poverty is almost a contradiction in terms. But too much wealth and affluence, whether in an individual or a society, has also its attendant evils which are becoming evident. The mere pilling up of material riches may lead to an emptiness in the inner life of man. There is a danger that socialism, while leading to affluence and even equitable distribution, may still miss some of the significant features of life. It is largely for this reason that stress becomes necessary on the individual".

National Herald, special supplement.

KAMALA NEHRU : BRAVE PIONEER

Jawaharlal's participation in the nation's politics began in the very year of his marriage with Kamala. The formation of the Home Rule League in 1916 was followed by material law in the Punjab and the non-cooperation movement launched by Gandhiji. Kamala was strongly attracted by the Mahatma's precept and personal example of simple living and dedicated pubic work. She was a source of encouragement to Jawaharlal in abandoning the affluent life-style to which he had been accustomed, and taking to the hard path of Gandhian satyagraha.

This was not liked by her mother-in-law and some other relatives. Indira Gandhi recalls in an interview (November 1972), that her mother was "a very intense person, and whenever she took up anything she felt very strongly about it. Firstly, when my father came into the political field, there was a certain amount of opposition from the family.

They did not want him to go to that extent, to submerge himself, and I think that was the time when my mother's influence counted and she supported fully . . ." Swarup Rani (Kamala's mother-in-law) "felt that my mother need not have encouraged my father in some of his ideas . . . Even when people were against what my father was doing and saying, they did not blame it on him, but it was taken out on her in a way. . . In our household a lot of people carried tales. She was unhappy . . . . I loved her deeply and when I thought that she was being wronged I fought for her and quarrelled with people . . . . I saw her being hurt and I was determined not to be hurt."

Indira Gandhi also spoke of her mother's lack of interest in a jewellery the acquisition of more and more of which is ruling passion with most women of the middle and upper classes. "She disliked jewellery ever since I can remember. Whether it was because of the influence of Gandhiji or her own I do not know. But she felt jewellery was almost a symbol of slavery and that women were made to wear all this so that they could not function as human beings—something like what the women's Lib say, that they are objects of decoration."

Krishna Hutheesing recalls with grateful appreciation her sister-in-law's helpful role at the time of her marriage : "Though she was far from well that autumn of 1933, Kamala took enormous pains with my trousseau, and saw to all the details of the wedding.

The one thing that upset her was that our family had every little money left. Nearly all her jewellery, and mother's too, had been sold; there was not much left for me. But still she gave me part of what little jewellery she still had; and mother give me a little of hers. Its was Kamala more than anyone else who made my wedding a gay and happy occasion."

Jawaharlal's total involvement in public life from the time of the non-cooperation movement in 1920 ruled out the possibility of his attending personally to the improvement of Kamala's education. A tutor was engaged. In a latter to his father from Lucknow District Jail on 1 September, 1922, Jawaharlal says : "Kamala wanted to know what to pay Chaterji who comes to coach her and Beti. I think Rs. 45 a month should be paid to him.

He used to get Rs. 25 when he came for an hour or more for Beti. Now he comes for two hours and take two pupils." Later in the same month he informs his father that Kamala wished to appear at some examinations of the Prayag Mahila Vidyapith, an institution which sought to promote women's in northern and central India : "She wants to ask your permission but apparently she has not been able to muster enough courage for the purpose. I see no harm in her appearing. In fact I think they will do her good. She will give you particulars."

But life at Anand Bhawan was too unsettled—with Motilal Nehru and more frequently, Jawaharlal leaving Allahabad on political tours, or being in jail—for these educational arrangements to work out satisfactorily. Kamala Nehru's case illustrates the unavoidable sacrifice of same part of the obligations owed to members of one's immediate family when a person dedicates himself or herself to a larger public cause. Both Motilal Nehru and Jawaharlal recognised, and neither was happy about this conflict of duties.

The elder Nehru, who gave up his legal practice and the princely income thereform during the non-cooperation movement, asks his son in a latter (16 September, 1920) : "Have you had any time to attend to the poor cows in Anand Bhavan? Not that they are really cows but have been reduced to the position of cows by nothing short of culpablen egligence on your part and mine—I mean your mother, your wife, your child, your sisters? I do not know with what grace and reason we can claim to be working for the good of the masses—the country at large—when we fail egregiously to minister to the most urgent requirements of our own flesh and blood and those whose flesh and blood we are."

With the maturing of his perception of human worth in terms of character rather than education or other attainments, Jawaharlal become sharply self-critical of his former tendency to take his wife for granted. About the early years of their marriage, he recalls in the Autobiography (in the main body of the work written in 1934-35 when Kamala was still living) : "So great became my concentration in these (public) activities that, all unconsciously, I almost overlooked her and left her to her own resources, just when she required my full cooperation. My affection for her continued and even grew and it was a great comfort to know that she was there to help me with her soothing influence.

She give me strength, but she must have suffered and left a little neglected. An unkindness to her would almost have been better than this semi forgetful, casual attitude". This is the dilemma of those for whom public work becomes an obsession. I faced it from 1942 onwards. Placing public causes above human relationships and duties, I kept travelling round the country even after my emergence from underground life early in 1946.

I would explain my absences jocularly to my husband by remarking–after the title of one of Lenin's works—"You are the State, I am the Revolution." But after Asaf's passing away came punishment in the form of pangs of regret and self-reproach at my neglect of him.

Feeling inadequate and unhappy about her lack of education, Kamala tried to improve her English and to learn Urdu, Sanskrit and French, both in India and while in Europe during 1926-27 for medical treatment. She accompanied Jawaharlal on his first visit to the Soviet Union in 1927, on the occasion of the tenth anniversary of the Bolshevik revolution. The impact made on them by what they saw in the new Russia is described by Jawaharlal in the course of a latter from Moscow (10 November, 1927) to his sister Vijay Lakshmi : "To give an account of our impression and experiences even within the 36 hours or so we have been here would take a long slice off a day and many sheets of notepaper . . . . All one's old values get upset and life wears a strange aspect here. Everybody is tovarish (comrade) . . . . One cannot move or turn in any direction without gazing at Lenin—a statue or picture or photo or painting. Every house and almost every shop window has it. He is the God of the Russians today and a more mention of his name makes them light up.

The shops, though often containing beautiful Russian-made goods, are poor in comparison with shops elsewhere . . . . Finery is not encouraged. The effect of a few hours of Moscow on Kamala was that she wanted to take off the border from a simple sari she was wearing as she felt she was over dressed."

As one who had a special interest in the status and role of women, Kamala was much impressed by the freer position of women in the Soviet Union and by the care lavished by the State on the health and education of children. She also reacted strongly against the racial snobbery and colour consciousness the noticed in England, in contrast to what she had observed in Switzerland and elsewhere in Europe.

Kamala desired not only to overcome her own educational handicap but also to save other young women from it. Her feelings are expressed poignantly in numerous letters (in Hindi and Urdu) to Syed Mahmud, a close friend of the Nehru family and specially of Jawaharlal. She wrote the letters during 1926-27 from Europe where she was being treated at different sanatoria.

Though Syed Mahmud had qualified for the bar in England and obtained a Ph.D. in Germany, the women in his home observed purdah and his daughters were not being sent to school. In a letter of 1 April, 1926 from Montana, Kamala says : "You have not written to me whether your daughters have been put to school. I am impatient to hear the good news. The time has come when women too should work for their country. Only men would not do. Please give up purdah. It has ruined the women and brutalised the men. If you regard Jawahar as your brother and me as your sister, we expect you disown purdah."

In a subsequent letter of 4 November, 1926 from Geneva, she again pleads with doctor Sahib to "arrange to teach English to your daughters, without which they cannot move ahead in this world. And while remaining in purdah they cannot learn anything. Send them to the girls' school at Allahabad, where some Muslim girls are already enrolled. Today only the educated are honoured. People do not want to talk to those who are uneducated, so much so that close relations and even the husbands do not wish to talk to them. . . .

Therefore take pity on them and make them self-reliant." Returning to the subject in yet another letter (15 March, 1927) : "If you love Jawahar, you have to do both these things : abolish purdah and arrange to educate your daughters. Please show this latter to sister (Syed Mahmud's wife) also. Unless you give me the good news that your daughters' education has been arranged, I will not write to you about my health."

On Syed Mahmud attempting to defend the institution of purdah, she replies spiritedly (4 May, 1927 : "I am not convinced about the virtues of purdah that you have suggested . . . I want you men to be put in purdah for some years, and then I should ask you what it is like. Then your answer will be different. Women are intellectually superior to men and given some education they will show it."

These letters of Kamala Nehru demonstrate the growth of consciousness among Indian women, even those who did not receive modern education through English, as early as in the twenties of this country. The ideas and sentiments so boldly affirmed by her should be a source of inspiration for young people now active in the women's movement, many of whom have tended to turn to Western feminist literature rather than the example set by our own pioneers of social restructuring like Kamala Nehru.

Private Face of A Public Person, Radiant Publishers, New Delhi.

MAULANA ABUL KALAM AZAD : PATRIOT, SCHOLAR, STATESMAN

Persons of my generation feel increasingly bereft as with inexorable regularity those who have been our props disappear. Our inner stability gets shaken; every thing grows strangely unfamiliar and a sense of emptiness becomes over-powering.

Every time someone near us reached the end of life's journey, a small part of us withers away. Somewhere within us we register the death of a part of ourselves. This is so when men like Maulana Abul Kalam Azad cease to be. The shock of his sudden end is so immediate that I wonder if I shall be able to say all that I want to, coherently and with objectivity.

In some cases his friends enjoyed privileges denied even to members of his own family, and their member was severely restricted. Although I do not remember him defining precisely the meaning of friendship, I believe I am not misinterpreting him if I say that he was attracted to minds that generally responded as rationalists to the intellectual and social challenge of our age.

Maulana Saheb's associations with my husband began, I believe, when he came to Delhi in 1923 to preside over the special session of the Indian National Congress. But the bond that held them together had many strands. They shared a similarity of political beliefs, an impassioned attachment to the best in the cultural traditions of the Mughal age, both literary and social, and finally a firm conviction that Western liberal values were perfectly compatible with the essence of Islamic teachings.

This perhaps was why Maulana Saheb chose to accept Asaf Saheb as a friend and also his hospitality during his frequent visits to Delhi, right up to the day he joined the Central Cabinet. He felt at home with us, not because we could offer him the amenities of a prosperous home. What drew him perhaps was the opportunity for being with someone to whom he could turn for intellectually stimulating talk, his only relaxation, and which he obviously prized more than physical comforts.

An incident that comes to my mind symbolizes an attitude that was typical of him.

Often during the fateful and evenful years of 1930 to 1941 the Congress Working Committee would be compelled to hold its meetings in the months of May and June. Maulana Saheb was sensitive to the fierce heat of Delhi.

He suffered more than others, and anxious to spare him the discomforts inevitable in the stifling atmosphere of our home in Kucha Chelan, on one occasion I suggested to my husband that Maulana Saheb should be persuaded to stay at the Birla House where some of his other colleagues generally stayed. Asaf Saheb was not quite sure if it was proper on our part to suggest this; but nevertheless agreed. Birla House was also informed that Maulana Saheb would be staying. On my part I was sure that the Maulana would welcome the suggestion as the underable heat would have affected his health, particularly as we were not in a position to lessen its severity for obvious reasons. But I was wrong. Maulana Saheb brushed aside the suggesiton in his own characteristic way.

When he arrived he entered our car and much to my embarrassment, asked to be driven to Kucha Chelan! We were obviously overwhelmed, but I think I am not exaggerating if I say that the meaning of personal values acquired a new significance for me that day.

Much has been said and written and more will undoubtedly follow about Abul Kalam Azad the patriot, scholar and statesman. But I wonder if anyone from amongest his friends and colleagues will be able to write about him as a householder. Some family biographer alone can enlighten us on his childhood, early youth and young manhood, because he was extraordinarily reserved about himself and more so about his family. Very few knew what be meant to his own people. But having come to know some of them of late I have learnt that he was an affectionate and considerate guardian to all those who depended on him. Only he broke their heart when he refused to accept parole during his detention in Ahmednagar Fort when his wife lay dying.

Judged by his personal habits Maulana Azad had a fairly strict code of domestic discipline. His was never the ascetic's approach to the things that make life livable. But equally would he frown upon extraeagance and ostentation. In the early days of our acquaintance I mistook his protest at the elaborateness of our menus as a courteous formality. Then I noticed that having failed to persuade me to give up wastefulness, as far as he was concerned he began restricting his meal to two courses only, ignoring the rest!

Again as a rule in our Indian way of life we are somewhat unaware of the virtues of puntuality. But when Maulana Saheb asked for his tea at 4.30 in the morning and lunch, at 11, he did not mean that it could be 4.35 or 11.15. Once I remembered, something went wrong somewhere and lunch was served half an hour later than usual, and Maulana Saheb went without his meal. That was naturally the very last time such a lapse was permitted. At first it appeared to me that punctuality was perhaps an end in itself with him, a merely meticulous way.

But soon after I knew why he insisted on keeping to his time-table with such strictness. His early hours were precious to him as he spent them in serious reading and writing. And so, he wanted the rest of his day planned in such a way as to make it possible for him to rise refreshed every morning.

A political leader of his eminence has to handle men from all walks of life. Maulana Saheb had to suffer fools as well as cross swords with men of great stature. But he would relax only in the company of those who were more or less conversant with the rich treasures of Urdu and Persian literature, medieval and modern history and theology. It was never very easy therefore to help him to relax. More often than not it was a matter of his host and he sitting and talking for hours together. He naturally wanted an audience of minds capable of talking in what he had to say and if on rare occasions we were able to invite a few such. Maulana

Saheb's conversational brilliance, according to Asaf Saheb would surpass his oratorical skill. As for myself, all I could understand as a very bewildered and ignorant observer from the wings was that for every quotation presented by others he recalled several more to the delight and admiration of those who had assembled.

I was lucky in discovering that he liked taking long drives particularly to the historical sites around Delhi. Besides the known monuments, we would wander admist the ruins surrounding them and he would recount legends that had grown around a particular bridge, mosque or house and his campanions would marvel at his memory, his capacity for detailed observation. Once he expressed a desire to see Suraj Kund near Tughlakabad, and we set forth in search of it before sunrise. We lost our way, but a shepherd boy led us to the spot. He recited a Persian couplet which when translated meant–Knowledge was not the prerogative of the lettered.

Behind that austere expression lay an endless capacity for absorbing natural beauty and human comprehension. How often have those who worked with him and known him closely heard him laugh? I wonder if Jawaharlalji remembers an occasion, sometime in the late thirties, I think, when he was interrupted at a public meeting held in the Gandhi Ground by some communist demonstrators.

As is usual with him he lost his temper and rebuked them and thundered that they shut up. He came to see Maulana Saheb immediately after the meeting and with boyish condour confessed : "Maulana, I have described myself as a shandar admi today". He at once reported : "you have done very well, indeed!" and all three of them, Maulana Saheb, Jawaharlalji and Asaf Saheb roared with laughter. Translation robs the peculiar charm of what was said by the one to the other on that occasion.

Soon after 1939, such occasional patches, free of the tension of insistent public affairs came to an end. After the Ramgarh session of the Congress, the prisons put in their usual claim. Then a brief spell of freedom and then came in 1942, sweeping as it were, all that was before it off the face of India. Some of the old links were broken irreparably but that was the price we paid for freedom.

When I first met him in Calcutta after his release from Ahmednagar I was still legally not free to do so. I expected to be rebuked as we had been told that our work in the 1942 upheaval had not met with the approval of some of the leaders. Instead, he expressed himself in terms which dispelled our fears. But he advised caution and a return to normal conditions.

At the risk of being personal I cannot help recalling the great understanding he gave me in the hour of my personal grief even through politically I had drifted away from the Congress. One day he related a story he said had read somewhere and he wanted me to listen carefully. A poor peasant had an only son. He had worked very hard to enable his son to complete his schooling.

After the boy's success in his examination he was sent to a neighbouring city so that he could start life as an office clerk, his life's ambition. One evening he received a telegram and thought that it must be from his son giving him glad tidings of his success in securing work. But the peasant was illiterate and could not read. So, he hurried to the village school teacher eager to have the telegram rend. The teacher shock his head, looked into his eyes and told him that his son was dead, that he was killed in a road accident.

The peasant's heart stood still and he wept unendingly. After a while he calmed down and left the school teacher's cottage. A little later the teacher thought he heard someone ploughing the fields. He wondered who could have started working his fixed at that time of night. He went out with his lantern to see who it could be and he found the striken peasant busy ploughing. Maulana Saheb said : "You see, he found the remedy for his pain, work".

Tolerance to him did not merely mean religious tolerance. He believed in the absolute right of an individual to differ and hold what opinions he believed to be correct. But he emphasized the need for beliefs. So long as the ends were good and consistent with a rational code of ethics and people who pursued them were also prepared to suffer for them he tried to understand them, even though he did not necessarily agree with them.

Once the Maulana sensed insincerity and sycophancy in any individual he turned away from him and no special pleading could make him alter his opinion. He was intolerant of cant and all that goes with it.

These fragments from a past have flitted back into my consciousness after a decade and a half. But partial amnesia has claimed much that should have remained vivid. In attempting to record them today I have in a very inadequate way only attempted to sketch for our mourning people Maulana Azad's bright and human personality.

From Stout Hearts and Open Minds.

ASAF ALI : PATRIOT AND HUMANIST : THE TRIBUTE

Writing the foreword to a biography of one's spouse is perhaps unusual. Though reluctant initially, I agreed to do so if only because of the opportunity it gives me of placing on record my grateful thanks to Krishna Kripalani, Chairman of the National Book Trust, whose encouragement has made possible the publication of this first account of the life and work of my husband.

A many-sided personality—scholar, lawyer, nationalist, writer and connoisseur of music and the arts—he was a remarkable product of the encounter between, and synthesis of Hindu and Islamic cultures, and of Indian and Western values. He continued his literary and, to a limited extent, his legal pursuits even within jail as a political prisoner. In a letter from an internment camp where he revised his translation of Aeschylus's 'Perse'. Asaf acknowledges the uses of being marooned, but complains : "My trouble is lack of martial. The Introduction to "The Persians' alone demands a whole library. In spite of my life-long study of the connected period. I feel helpless at times trying to recall the correct names in their original, un-Greeked Iranian (Dari) form."

Though an ardent nationalist, he was completely free of chauvinism. Like Rabindranath Tagore whom he greatly admired. Asaf was a humanist first and foremost: "From the egoistic individual to the family, communal, racial and national Ego, each and all follow the same course—each imagining himself or themselves the only chosen people who must be infalibly right". To one with such perception, humility came naturally. "Build your happiness on moderation and contentment, and unostentatious service of mankind, which means those within your humble reach. Attempting too much is to invite disappointment, like expecting too much from life.

And, above all, remember that individuals are very insignificant beings in the sea of humanity, and mankind as a whole is an equally infinitesimal entity in this limitless Universe. Humility of the spirit is the sheet-anchor of contentment. Self-respect is a precious privilege, but it must never be confused with pride or the wrong sort of vanity".

It was but a meagre collection of my husband letters and diaries that I could retrieve and make available to the writer of this biography, Sudhir Pant. Apart from my not being exempt from the national trait of indifference to the chronicling of historical events, which Asaf used to comment on, I was so immersed in my political and trade union activities (which included four years of unsettled underground life) that I could not systematically preserve or record his or my correspondence and conversations with the makers of history with whom we were thrown together. Sudhir Pant has drawn skillfully both on the sparse personal papers and the official records of the three decades prior to independence, which mirror the events of the period as perceived by the against the background of the political events of the time.

I am thankful to G.N.S. Raghavan for going through the manuscript carefully and editing it and amplifying the narrative at some places in consultation with me. I would also like to acknowledge with thanks the help received from the Jawaharlal Nehru Memorial Museum and Library, and my husband's surviving colleagues who shared their memories of working with a valued senior.

I trust that the book will not only be of nostalgic interest to freedom fighters of my generation but will appeal also to the younger generation. I have in mind specially those who were born or grew up after the independence for which Gandhiji, Jawaharlal Nehru, Maulana Azad, Asaf Ali and others. They entertained a vision of free India, united on the basis of social and economic justice, which it is for the post-independence generation to turn into reality.

Foreword to a biography of Asaf Ali, by Sudhir Pant, Published by The National Book Trust in 1984.

ACHARYA NARENDRA DEV : A TRIBUTE

It was my misfortune that I first met this luminous savant, teacher and leader of the Congress Socialist Party only as late as in 1946 and that my acquaintance with him lasted only for a few years.

Looking back, I cannot help rueing the fact that the then circumstances prevented me from acquiring his friendship and guidance. He might have helped me to gain greater clarity of political thought.

Under the spell of the Gandhi-Nehru leadership of the Congress from the 1930s, I was among the radical elements in the Congress attracted by the ideal of socialism, but I was not formally a member of the Congress Socialist Party.

My sister, Purnima Banerjee, who lived and worked in Allahabad, was a close colleague of the leaders of the CSP, in particular of Ram Manohar Lohia and Achyut Patwardhan. Whenever we met, we exchanged notes and shared our experiences, in our respective spheres. Dehi and Allahabad were somewhat different in terms of political environment.

Though Delhi was the capital and the principal centre of the struggle against the British rulers in the legislative arena, Allahabad was the heart of the Congress party not only because it was the home of Pandit Motilal and Jawaharlal Nehru, but the AICC office functioned from that city. Purnima was very close to the Nehru family and specially to Kamala Nehru, I came to learn about the familiar relationships in this unique family and their devotion to Gandhiji and close relationship with many leading lights of the national movement. Among them was Acharya Narendra Dev.

The ties of affection which bound Gandhiji, Jawaharlal Nehru and the Congress socialist leaders will be evident from the following extract from a letter which Jayaprakash Narayan wrote on 7th December, 1941 from the Delhi detention camp to Jawaharlalji: "I cannot but feel extremely happy at your being out when the country needs your guidance most. You must have learnt about Narendra Deva's health. One of his greatest failings is that the cannot take care of himself. What we call sankotch (delicate moral scruple) will prevent him from asking any of his innumerable friends to do anything for him. I am, therefore, writing to you to take a particular interest in this matter and to pack him off to some suitable place. You must not leave this thing to his option. In this matter you must treat him as one treats a child. You may consult Bapu (Gandhiji) also in this connection as he has been taking a keen interest in Narendra Deva's health".

Some eyebrows had been raised when Acharya Narendra Dev also with J.P. and Achyut Patwardhan were included in the Congress Working Committee by Jawaharlal Nehru soon after the historic Lucknow session of the Congress in 1936. Jawaharlalji, who had in his presidential address stressed the need for socialism for an order to solve need the country's problems, wanted to include representatives of the Left-wing of the Congress in the highest decision-making body. He believed that they could influence Congressmen and women with their socialist outlook and help in drawing the masses into the struggle for freedom.

Congress workers at the lower levels of the organisation, like myself, heard that the conservatives among Nehru's colleagues were somewhat perturbed by this development. They felt that it might undermine the organisational structure of the Congress and lead to desunity on ideological grounds.

However, Gandhiji applied the healing touch, as usual, and pacified them. He urged Jawaharlal Nehru to keep in mind the imprerative need for unity. And whatever the CPS leaders ideological reservations about the general line of thinking in the Congress, Acharyaji was too ardent a patriot to encourage any dissidence on the part of his socialist colleagues.

Such was Jawaharlal Nehru's confidence in Narendra Devji that when the National Herald was being planned, he asked him to help in selecting the staff and wanted him to make use that too many individuals known for their conservative views were not appointed.

M. Chalapathi Rau, the veteran journalist and distinguished editor of the National Herald wrote that "Acharyaji was somewhat of a legend and was known for this eloquence in more than one language. Fluency could be fatal to thinking, and it came as a surprise to me, while editing some of his wartime (World War II) contributions to the National Herald, that clarity of thought and expression could go with such power of eloquence.

He was effective in demolishing the case of those who sought to make the war appear first as an imperialist war and then as a people's war. His understanding of events in Europe was as complete as Nehrus and his commentary on the national revolution, though critical, was redeemed by comprehensiveness. He was to me one of the few thinkers in the Congress. His thoroughly modern outlook was wrapped up in old world courtesy and charm. His humility was genuine and not a mask. I was told that a review by me of Socialism and the National Revolution—a compilation of his writings and speeches by Yusuf Meherally—struck him as too generous an assessment which he did not deserve".

In 1942, when the hostilities were at their height, the 'Quit India' struggle united all those Congress socialists as well as other Congressmen who felt that alien regime must be fought from outside prison walls, for as long as possible.

Therefore, when, after 1947, Congress leaders such as Sardar Vallabhbhai Patel and Acharya Kriplani declared that the CSP should either disband itself or quit the Congress, I was in a dilemma. As was usual with me, I sought the advice of Gandhiji, Jawaharlalji and Maulana Azad. All of them asked me to request Achrya Narendra Dev to persuade Ashoka Mehta, Ram Manohar Lohia, etc. to cease to function as a party, but to work within the Congress as a group.

I was asked to approach Acharyaji and I did so. A suffer from chronic asthma, he looked very frail. But he was resolute in saying he could not agree to the proposal. Later, when the socialists left the Congress, such was his adherence to principled politics that the resigned from the United Privince legislature along with his socialist colleagues who had won the elections on the Congress ticket. It is a different matter that, as Socialist Party candidates, they lost in the by-elections which were held to fill the vacancies.

A great admirer of the Chinese revolution of 1949 under Mao Tse-Tung's leadership, Narendra Devji, along with Nehru, campained for the recognition of new China, in spite of opposition from the anti-Communists among his Socialist Party colleagues.

As a member of the first official goodwill mission to China, he spent six weeks in that country studying the approach of the new regime to problems of economic and social transformation. He refused to be brow-beaten by the non-progressive members of the delegation. Acharyaji died early in 1956, when Sino-Indian relations had not yet soured.

M. Chalapathi Rau was a close friend of his alter ego, Edatata Narayanan, who founded the LINK news magazine in 1958, and PATRIOT, the daily, in 1963 to campaign for support to Nehru's foreign and domestic policies in the most crucial period of India's post-independence history.

When the Chinese struck, the reactionary forces shrieked that Communist China had betrayed Nehru's trust and friendship and that he should dismiss Krishna Menon, the Defence Minister, whom they regarded as a crypto Communist. Both Chalapathi Rau and Narayanan were firm supporters of Nehru and did their best through their newspapers to counter the virulent campaign against Nehru and Nehruvians in the columns of what was allied the Jute Press in India.

Had Acharyaji relented on the controversial issue whether the Socialists should work as a group within the Congress, I believe that he would have strengthened Jawaharlal Nehru's hands and thereby contributed to the early fulfilment of the basic needs of our masses and the achievements of self-reliant growth by our country. It was equally distressing that because of narrow considerations of party and individual interests, some of Nehru's colleagues prevented the two noble leaders, so near to one another in their values from working together.

In the preface to The Discovery of India, Jawaharlal Nehru acknowledges in these words his indebtedness to Acharyaji and other fellow-prisoners in the Ahmadnagar Fort prison where the book was written : "Prison is not a pleasant place to live in even for a short period much less for long years. But it was a privilege for me to live in close contact with men of outstanding ability and a wide human-outlook. . . . Though I am grateful to all my companions, I should like to mention especially Maulana Abul Kalam Azad, Govind Ballabh Pant, Narendra Deva and M. Asaf Ali."

When Gandhiji first met Narendra Deva in 1929, he saw in him a jewel of a son of India. And in 1947 Gandhiji wanted him to take up the presidentship of a reorganised post-independence Congress so as to serve the masses at the grass-roots level. Had Gandhiji not been snatched away in 1948, the story of India's march, her long march to make the peasant and worker create their own heaven on earth, might have been quite different from what it is today.

On his death in 1956 after a long period of illness, Jawaharlal Nehru said, "His heath failed him. Otherwise he was a man of rare distinction—distinction in many fields—rare in spirit, rare in mind and intellect, and rare in integrity".

RAMESHWARI NEHRU : GENTLE CRUSADER

Rameshwari Nehru was a woman who along with many a celebrated contemporary of her family, contributed greatly to the awakening of men and women of the intelligentsia, from the early decades of 20th century right up to her death in 1966.

Reading some of her letters to her husband's cousin, Jawaharlal Nehru, in 1906 when he was at Harrow, I was much surprised to know that, despite her social background as daughter of Raja Narendranath of Lahore, and her early marriage of Brijlal Nehru, a senior civil servant, she was thinking of India's political subjection and urging her brother-in-law to serve the country on his return. My amazement was natural. At that point of time the affluent classes were reluctant to identify themselves with the emerging nationality and revolutionary movements in India. And Rameshwari belonged to the aristocratic layers of Indian society. What is more, she was married to a person who was serving in the higher bureaucracy established by the British as the steel frame of their rule.

As such, she was not expected to express views which could be interpreted as being hostile to the British. Except in Bengal where Curzon's politically mischievous partition of the province had outraged the sentiments of the public, high and low alike, the Indian elite at the beginning of the 20th century could not think of openly ranging themselves against the British power and the system established by it. Yet Rameshwari Nehru, barely twenty at that time, had the courage to express her patriotic feelings.

She was acquainted with my husband, through Motilal Nehru, uncle of Brijlal Nehru. The renowned lawyer of Allahabad was invariably the guest of Brijlal and Rameshwari Nehru at their house on Clive Road whenever he came to Delhi. Asaf Saheb knew and looked up to Motilalji as a distinguished senior both in public life and in the profession of law.

My husband and I were invited by the Nehrus one evening, soon after my marriage in September 1928, to meet Motilalji who had come on a visit long with Jawaharlal. I felt lost in what struck me as a sombre gathering of elderly persons talking about problems of the day of which I was utterly ignorant. Till my marriage at the age of nineteen I had been a total stranger to politics. I can never forget how embarrassed and distressed I felt at that evening's informal dinner party. The conversation centred round the seething communal tensions in the country, specially since the assassination of Swami Shradhanand, the Arya Samaj leader, by a fanatical Muslim.

Rameshwari Nehru must have realised, with womanly intuition, how acutely uncomfortable I felt, a newcomer who felt inadequate among person senior by twenty years and more. Otherwise why should she have come over to me, leaving the select circle surrounding the regal Motilal Nehru and discussing momentous matters? Having sensed that I was ill at ease in that serious gathering, and she started asking me about my family and my special interests, and expressed motherly concern about things that are important to a young woman at the very threshold of life. When she thus showed affectionate interest in me, I just rushed into her embracing arms, as it were. I remember how deeply impressed I was by her striking personality, the large and beautiful eyes imbued with sympathy and understanding.

As I came closer to Rameshwariji in the weeks and months that followed, she saw that I was a frightened young thing bewildered by the sharp change in environment from a missionary college in Nainital to life in a Muslim home in the walled city. Rameshwariji and her husband knew of course that Asaf Saheb, a contemporary of Brijlal Nehru during their studies in England, was a Muslim—as they themselves were Hindus—only by the accident of birth, and belonged with them by education and temperament to a small circle of enlightened and liberal Indians.

Realising that I wanted to occupy myself with something in addition to and more significant than domestic chores, Rameshwariji suggested to me that I might join and work for the Delhi Women's League, which she had founded that very year as the local branch of the All India Women's Conference. I was thrilled at the opportunity to work for a cause. This was my first apprenticeship in organisational work, and I gratefully recall the guidance and training which I received from Rameshwariji. She taught me how to organise meetings, prepare minutes of discussions, keep records, and follow up the implementation of decisions. Eventually this training and encouragement led to my being elected as the Secretary of the Delhi Women's League. This assignment gave me an insight into problems faced by the women of India and the need to organise women for their active involvement in movements for social change. It was not enough, I realised, to ask for equality, we had to deserve it and struggle for it.

If my getting to know Asaf Saheb had opened my mind to a world wider than of the limited home of my childhood and my cloistered education, Rameshwariji helped me to enter a wider field of activity. The two were thus my guides in the early years of my life in Delhi. Then came in 1930 the tidal wave of Gandhiji's Salt Satyagraha which carried me into the heart of the struggle for independence.

During 1934-35 Rameshwariji threw herself, as a devoted follow of Gandhiji, into the campaign for eradicating the evil of untouchability from our society. She toured the country extensively in this connection, brining to the cause of Harijan liberation the same zeal she had shown for women's emancipation. I continued to meet her frequently and seek her guidance, responding to her motherly affection with gratitude and devotion. Rameshwariji was completely free of the snobbery and arrogance of the well-to-do. This was what attracted so many of us to her.

Later, at the height of the freedom struggle and after independence, I was drawn into the Left movement, and was delighted when I found Rameshwariji associating herself with the All India Peace Council and subsequently the Afro-Asian Peoples Solidarity Organisation. This came as a considerable surprise because, in the fifties, the peace movement was labelled by conservatives and rightists as Communist-controlled.

The fact was that Rameshwariji was attract to the peace movement because of her Gandhian values, just as these values had led her to espouse the cause of women and of Harijans. She was undeterred by the anti-Communist with-hunt of that period, and by her own leadership proved the broad character of the peace movement. I have referred to my initiation into the women's moment in the late twenties. A quarter century later, when some of us felt the need to widen the base and the objectives of the movement beyond its moorings in the English-educated upper classes and their narrow concerns, Rameshwariji blessed the formation in 1954 of the National Federation of Indian Women which wanted the movement to embrace also women of the peasantry, working class and others in the middle and lower rungs of society.

When Dr. A.V. Baliga, along with my colleagues and myself founded the Indo-Soviet Cultural Society in 1952, Rameshwariji associated herself enthusiastically with its work. Later, as founder president of the Indian Association for Afro-Asian Solidarity, she formed a National Campaign Committee for the liberation of Portuguese occupied territories on Indian soil. I was privileged to be chosen as chairman of this Committee, in whose work Goan patriots were actively involved. During the years that Rameshwariji headed the solidarity movement, freedom fighters of Algeria, Vietnam, Palestine and South Africa began to be invited to India and the Association helped to mobilize moral and material support for these liberation movements.

'Mataji', as she was affectionately called by then, was the personification of humanism, sincerity, simplicity and dignity. These qualities were instantly recognised by those who worked with and came to know her. The reverence with which she was treated by the delegates to the Peace Congress at Stockholm was remarkable. With untiring zeal Rameshwariji travelled to many countries in the fifties to popularise the Stockholm Peace Appeal.

History is sometimes capricious and unfair in the manner in which it awards recognition to individuals who make history. Those of us who knew and worked with Rameshwari Nehru feel sad that her work is virtually unknown to the present generation.

The role she played in the movement for women's emancipation and world peace ought to be known much more widely than it is. Rameshwariji was an early exemplar of the triple cause of peace, equality and development which is now inscribed on the banner of the international women's movement.

She was the embodiment of Indian womanhood at its best, a rare being who never sought any position of power or prestige and who preferred to be true to her beliefs unmindful of criticism. Awareness of her life and work should be an inspiration and spur to young people of today, particularly women.

I am, therefore, very glad that the National Book Trust has sponsored a biography of Rameshwari Nehru this year, on the occasion of her birth centenary. Shri O.P. Paliwal is a happy choice for writing the biography. He had the opportunity of working closely with Rameshwariji for several years, in his capacity as Secretary of the Indian Association for Afro-Asian Solidarity and subsequently as Deputy Secretary-General of the Afro-Asian Peoples' Solidarity Organisation (headquarters at Cairo). He was the first Indian to be chosen for that high office from 1974 to 1978.

For him this has been a labour of love, an opportunity to offer his tribute to one who inspired so many men and women of at least two generations starting with mine. We should be thankful to him for sparing no effort to unearth information from various sources to light up and bring out the significance of Rameshwari Nehru's dedicated life.

New Delhi
May 1, 1986

—Aruna Asaf Ali

Introduction to the biography of Rameshwari Nehru, by Om Prakash Paliwal, published by the National Book Trust in 1986.

SATYAVATI DEVI : ROLE OF DELHI WOMEN IN FREEDOM STRUGGLE

The history of India's struggle for freedom goes back, in my view to the late 18th century when the full implications of our political subservience to British rule dawned in the minds of our forefathers. It gathered momentum thereafter with every passing decade.

Women in India those days, as elsewhere in the world, were confined to their homes and excluded from participating in social or political affairs. This was specially so as far as the middle and upper classes were concerned. Even women who worked as farm-hands were denied by and large their right to function in village Panchayats and other organisations concerned with problems which affected the community. They were as a rule paid lesser wages that men, besides being discriminated against in social and political life.

The movement for social reforms in the 18th century and later were led by men like Raja Ram Mohan Roy, Ishwar Chandra Vidyasagar, Swami Vivekananda, Maharashi Karve and many others in different parts of the country. These great social reformers played a crucial role in focussing attention on the social disabilities of women and the difficult conditions under which they lived. They realised that if women are deprived of opportunities to function as equal participants in all activities that affected the well-being of the community, a country world never be able to rise to the heights of modern enlightenment or achieve freedom and progress.

The Indian National Congress turned to Mahatma Gandhi for leadership from 1920 onwards. He made the struggle for Swaraj a mass movement and called upon women to come forward and join the rank of Satyagrahis. They did so in large numbers over the period from 1930 to 1942, during the several movements of 1930, 1932, 1940 and 1942.

Men had been reluctant to permit women to participate in activities outside their homes. However, Gandhiji civil disobedience movement galvanised the masses, not only men but also women, who suceeded in persuading their menfolk to let them take part in the national struggle. Being the capital of India, Delhi had became in 1911 an administrative unit directly ruled by the Central Government, therefore it attracted Indians from all parts of the country. But in spite of its metropolitan character, the social milieu till the close of the 1920s was very conservative and dominated by the middle and upper classes. From 1930, however, Delhi became the main centre of Congress deliberations and activities. As a result these was an unprecedented awakening among the women of Delhi. From the 1930s to the very end of

British rule in our country, Delhi women joined the struggle in very large numbers. Housewives from urban and rural areas organised themselves for carrying out the Congress programmes of non-violent civil disobedience campaigns. Chandni Chowk and its mohallas in the walled city with its lanes and bylanes were the storm centres.

Smt. Satyavati Devi, grand daughter of Swami Shraddhanand, was the foremost woman leader of Delhi of those years. Her fiery oratory and remarkable capacity for organisation drew women in their hundreds to join the Satyagraha campaigns. It was Delhi's good fortune that this fearless and courageous woman leader emerged to lead the struggle Satyavati electrified the atmosphere with her eloquent speeches. Within a few weeks she set up the Congress Mahila Samaj and the Congress Desh Sevika Dal. Women from all walks of life and all corners of Delhi were attracted by Satyavati's sincerity and her passionate patriotism. Slender and tall, her fascinating personality cast its spell on us.

Had it not been for her, I wonder if I myself would have ever stepped out of my sheltered and comfortable home despite the fact that my husband was popular and respected Congressman who was deeply involved in every phase of the struggle. Having just come to Delhi fresh from an Anglo-Indian college, I was somewhat confused. I lacked elementary knowledge of political conditions in the country and the role of the Congress, I had no understanding of the anti-implerialist struggle that dominated the life of this city. With my westernised habits, I thought I could not adjust my thinking to what was happening. I would remain an outsider. I thought since I could not possibly adopt the way of life that was expected of a Satyagrahi.

But Satyavati with her idomitable courage and burning zeal was irresistible. I was drawn to her and thereafter could not stay away from the fight. My cowardly hesitations were overcome and I plunged into action.

Married to an officer of the Delhi Cloth Mills, Satyavati had a son, Krishan, and two daughters, Kusum and Munna. One of them was a suckling infant whom she had to carry to jail with her at the time of one of her imperisonments. With Satyavati immersed in her political work when not in prison, her mother

Ved Kumari, herself a participant in the movement, used to help in looking after the children.

Satyavati lit in many hearts the torch of burning love for one's country. Women from Delhi's orthodox communities came in large numbers to listen to speeches. Young and old, we marched under her leadership and never fell back even after her frequent arrests, Satyavati became a legend in her brief life-time.

Her political maturity developed with lightning speed. Her work among Delhi's textile workers made them politically conscious and they joined the struggle. Later Satyavati became one of the founder members of Congress Socialist Party.

With frequent jail going and the hard life she led even when free, her frail body fell a victim to the then dreaded disease, tuberculosis. Dispite the serious illness, her spirit was not subdued. Satyavati ignored the advice of the doctors and went on defying every repressive onslaught of the British authorities. I was deeply moved when in 1945, after her release from prison and only a few months before her death, when I was still leading an underground life, she sent a message in the form of a Press statement expressing her happiness that I had kept the flag flying and had successfully evaded arrest. Though Satyavati continued to guide her fellow-workers at Delhi from her sick bed, her physical frame could not stand the stresses and strains for long. Her hectic and incessant activity brought about an untimely end to her life in 1945 when she was only 41. Satyavati had practically stopped leading a domestic life, but the mother in her came out when, realising that her end was near, she wanted that her son should marry at the earliest. A suitable bride was chose by her relations, and though she could not travel of Delhi to attend the marriage, her son and his bride came to her and received her blessings.

News of Satyavati's death shocked Delhi. Those of us who knew her, loved and admired her, were grief-stricken. It is impossible for me and my generation of women (and men) to forget her. Satyavati was a heroic figure of the national liberation movement, of whom the women of Delhi can be justly proud. Were it not for her, the role of Delhi women in the fight for freedom may not have reached the heights it did.

It was in Delhi and Bombay that women came forward in very large numbers, astonishing the country by their matchless capacity to suffer for their beliefs. Police action, however brutal, could not crush our spirit or force us back to domestic existence.

Satyavati's magnetic personality attracted a larger number of students, both boys and girls, specially of the Hindu College and the Indraprastha Girls High School and College. These students helped us to organise groups of housewives who had never before taken part in public demonstrations and the like. Prominent among such women was Memo Bai, a child widow belonging to a very conservative family of Delhi. Though totally unlettered when she came into the movement, she educated herself with the help of some of us and developed qualities of leadership and organisation which made her a close comrade and values lieutenant of Satyavati. Among the prominent women drawn into public life by Satyavati were Sarasvati Gadodia, Parvati Didwania, Damayanti Sahni, Chando Bibi and Chand Kohli.

The Indraprastha School and College for Girls played a significant role in this phase of the freedom struggle in Delhi because its distinguished Australian founder-principal, Miss L. Gminer, was a theosophist and an ardent follower of Annie Besant. The Home Rule League's office worked from this school and soon it began to function in close co-operation with the Indian National Congress. Annie Besant succeeded in attracting men and women of the educated classes for the cause of the Home Rule movement before Gandhiji's arrival on the Indian scene.

It was, therefore, natural for the girls and teachers of the Indraprastha School and College to volunteer for work connected with the Satyagraha struggles. The Chief Commissioner of Delhi threatened to withdraw the official grant to the Indraprastha institution unless Miss Gminer gave up her political activities. However, Babu Jugal Kishore, founder of the School and College, accepted the challenge and appealed to the public for funds to make up the loss resulting from withdrawal of the grant. During the Salt Satyagraha, Satyavati and some of us decided, Delhi being a land-locked city to assemble in a marshy vacant plot in the Shahdara Suburb where the salt content of the sub-soil water was high. I remember how about fifty of us made salt in definance of the salt laws. This went on for about ten days. Packets of salt were prepared and distributed freely. The Seva Dal volunteers of the Congress and the Mahila Samaj, who had organised the Salt Satyagraha, were forcibly dispersed by the Delhi police wielding lathis and hurling tear-gas bombs. This was the beginning in Delhi of the civil disobedience movement for complete independence which culminated in the Quit India struggle and Britain's withdrawal from India.

A noteworthy aspect of the 1930 Satyagraha and subsequent movements was that leading Congressmen encouraged their wives, daughters and even mothers to join the crusade against British rule. Swaroop Rani wife of Motilal Nehru, Mrs. Vijay Lakshmi Pandit, Kamala Nehru and her mother Rajpati Kaul, and many other members of the Nehru family such as Uma Nehru and Mrs. Ladorani Zutshi and Manmohini Saighal are well known. Hansa Mehta, wife of Dr. Jivraj Mehta, Mrs. Nellie Sen Gupta, and several relatives of Subhas Chandra Bose were among members of nationalist families who became comrades-in-arms of their menfolk.

In Delhi, the wives of at least a dozen well-known Congressmen became their panthers in the struggle. Prof. Indra, Deshbandhu Gupta, K.D. Kohli, J.N. Sahni, Dr. Yudhvir Singh, Jugal Kishore Khanna, Gopi Nath Aman, Ganda Mal Sharma, Nand Lal Mehta, Phool Chand Jain, Thakur Hukam Singh and my husband were among the prominent Congressmen whose wives became their colleagues in public life and courted imprisonment in the wake of their husbands' arrest. There were also some women fighters for freedom who were prominent on their own, as Satyavati was in Delhi. Sarojini Naidu was a glowing symbol of Indian womanhood, specially after she joined Gandhiji's historic Dandi March in 1930. Dr. Muthulakshmi Reddi from Tamil Nadu, Durgabai who later married C.D. Deshmukh, and Kamaladevi Chattopadhyaya are among other such women leaders.

Women's participation along with men in India's mass movements is perhaps without a parallel in the world. I am convinced that had we women kept away from this exciting and crucial movement against imperialist rule, we would have remained backward.

With the acceleration of the struggle, under an order of the Viceroy the officials became ruthless in their methods of coercion.

Lathi charges, firing on processions, imprisonment, imposition of Section 144 prohibiting gatherings, collective fines and confiscation of properties became the order of the day. Every act of repression hardened us. The severity with which the authorities tried to crush our spirit only strengthened our will to carry on the fight, whatever the consequence. Organising hartals, boycott of British goods, picketing of liquor shops and violation of Section 144 became daily happenings.

The imprisonment of each volunteer, man or woman, who courted arrest gave everyone a thrill of satisfaction. We felt exhilarated at the thought that we were sharing the burden cast on our leaders. We led a disciplined life during the long weeks, months and years that we spent in prison. We organised the singing of patriotic songs, playing of the charkha, literacy classes, and bi-weekly study circles to promote awareness of the need for freedom from foreign rule in order to build a new India.

Given the opportunity, women, I am convinced, can demonstrate their capacity to break away from domestic captivity. The bulk of our fellow-prisoners had never been to school. Many of them were married when they were adolescents and some were widowed at an early age. They had never known anything other than cooking and looking after their children and their men, washing clothes and utensils, and other domestic chores chores. It was only natural that, unable to read or write, they had no knowledge of national and social problems. As for women of the upper strata, their going out of the home to work, whether for emoluments or for public causes, was unheard of. Therefore, when women who were just house wives stepped out of their homes and unflinchingly faced lathi charges and firings, people everywhere were full of wonder and admiration. The citizens of Delhi in particular were amazed at the courage shown by women who had been known hitherto for their docility. Revolutions, non-violent or otherwise, test the mettle of men and women. As the drums of liberation grew louder, Indian women plunged into the struggle all over the country and thereby earned the right to be free and equal with men. We shock the citadels of orthodoxy and conservatism. No longer could Indian women be regarded as mere goods and chattels, or objects of drawing room decoration. Whatever the handicaps we suffer from even after independence, women have much greater opportunities today to **reshape society** and remove backwardness wherever it exists, as equal partners of men. We cannot expect men alone to smash age-old social shackles. Men and women must together fight to remove all that comes in the way of building a new society.

As the Mayor, she had deep contact with the people whom she met and devised ways and means for the solution of their problems. In this regard, she always sought the assistance of Delhi Administration and the Government of India. People on the whole felt happy on account great help which Arunaji give to the people of various sections of our society.

Being the capital city, Delhi always had its own problems. And these probelms and their solution are always well-understood by Aruna Asaf Ali. Being a secular leader, she always aspires to maintain communal harmony in the city and whenever there is fear of any kind of misunderstanding of disturbance, she always offers her services. People listen to her with much respect and are agreeable to her secular approach in the solution of their socio-political problems.

Aruna Asaf Ali is a forceful speaker and attracts vast number of people on account of her superb knowledge of national and international affairs. She is widely travelled and could propagate India's policy in several countries of the world. Besides she is a very fine writer and has written on several aspects of national and international problems. These articles, contributed from time to time, are read with much interst by the people of India and elsewhere.

I never thought when I came to Delhi at the age of about twenty that I would be able to contribute anything to the great battles that ultimately won us our freedom. The comprehension that I acquired of human nature, during the struggle, has enriched my life immeasurably.

The individual experiences of women who fought for freedom could reveal much that lies buried and hidden in the inner recesses of Indian society at many levels. I often ask myself, had we women lagged behind and kept away from the tidal waves of revolution that swept our country could we have held our heads high?

All over the world, many men and women have throughout history laid down their lives and undergone tremendous sorrow and suffering for freedom from oppression and tyranny. We of my generation in India are indeed fortunate that there came two such leaders as Gandhiji and Jawaharlal Nehru who taught us the lesson of fearlessness and inspired us to rise above our self-centred existence. As the world is about to enter a new century, we women of India must hasten the process of removing the debris of the past.

Article contributed to a volume commemoraitng 100 years of the Congress in Delhi.

10

The Assessment

DYNAMIC INDO-SOVIET PARTNERSHIP

Brezhnev's arrival in India will give our people and our leaders an opportunity once again to express their feelings of friendly comradeship with the people of the Soviet Union. Gone are the years when the very mention of anyone hailing from the country caused eyebrows to be raised in fear or contempt. Even those who used to be benignly indifferent cannot pretend to be so any longer. With every passing year India and the Soviet Union have come nearer each other in several respects. There is not much significance is repeating the many miles we have covered in the common search for peace, cooperation in mutually agreed objectives, and genuine friendship. Now there is a general awareness that ever since the Nehru era took shape before and after our country's independence, our people have tried to understand the people whose distinguished representative, the General Secretary of the Communist Party of the Soviet Union, will once again be with us for a few days.

However, I cannot help reviewing the backdrop of this visit as I believe that it will be meaningful and useful from many points of view. For many of us the immediate present is so utterly different from the past that at times one cannot realise fully the qualitative changes that have taken place in the span of a mere half a century and more.

So much has changed in this brief period that at times it appears as if an entire epoch of historical events has been packed into it. Man has gone through experiences of cataclysmic dimensions and taken long, long strides towards what is new. Obviously it has not been easy to cover the distances because at every step he had to face agonising miseries in terms of human suffering born of want and fear. Two world wars had devastated the growing generation of men, and revolutionary struggles in almost every continent had to be fought to the bitter end. In some places they have triumphed and proved that men and women are not mere worms to be trod under the jackboots of marauders. At others the struggles have been halted knowing full well that there can be no rest or ease for self-respecting people till peace comes to their soil. Despite these turmoilts amazing discoveries in the realm of knowledge and tremendous churnings in man's ethical outlook are gradually leading to a more intelligent understanding of his relationship with fellow human beings inhabiting this earth.

There is, therefore, a new tide in the affairs of men and women in every corner of the globe, a definite uniqueness in the world situation as it exists today because it is so different from the years before the first and second world wars and the years that followed. The most outstanding phenomenon of the post-war age is the emergence for the first time in world history of a viable socialist state, and its further consolidation has provided a focal point from which elemental changes flowed, right across the inhabited continents of this earth. The age of imperialism, it seemed, was doomed from then onwards and its terribly oppressive consequences became intolerable. Its foundations were shaken when the workers and peasants of the territories under Czarist feudal rule in Russia revolted successfully and took over the reins of power and administered that vast piece of land and became from then onwards free as never before. For the first time a new and just social order that idealists had dreamt of was established. Their heroic efforts toward off all the attacks made by the frightened imperialist powers of Europe and their magnificent victory in the civil war instigated by the latter proclaimed to all oppressed humanity that socialism was no longer a remote and unattainable dream. Workers and peasants be sides other oppressed sections all over the world were started out of the pessimism and sense of helplessness of ages past. Gradually all over the erstwhile feudal Russia new organisational formations came into existence which were instrumental in resisting those who had exploited the peasants and workers hitherto and thus they emancipated themselves.

The significance of the October Revolution in the Soviet Union in 1917 cannot and should not be minimised because as the years that followed. Lenin's lucid and brilliant interpretation of Marxism and its scientific application to the complicated problems of social and economic realities in his own country influenced, not only the ordinary worker everywhere, but also the intelligentsia. A new stirring of minds and hearts began and those who had grouped hitherto for the light that was to clear away intellectual cobwebs found in Marxism the meaning and method they had been looking for.

Once again, however imperialists and their allies the fascists, conspired to wage another war not only to divide the world among themselves but to destroy the USSR and its socialist state. Fortunately for the world they got involved in squabbling over loaves and fishes, fought amongst themselves and were compelled to seek the support of socialist Soviet Union. Accidentally as it were, the new fascist empire-builders and the older imperialists could not reach any understanding and thus were not able to defeat their dreaded common enemy. The secret hope that in the war against fascism the Soviets would be shattered and totally demoralised failed to materialise and when instead its strength the hardness of steel, their despair and anger knew no bounds.

Then the Allied Powers of the U.S.A. and Europe woke up to the fact that their world overlordship was once again far from secure as mighty forces and a new consciousness that unity against it was essential to destroy imperialism had come to stay. The most dominant thought in the minds of honest people all over the world was that just as fascism in its most bestial form had been uprooted, imperialism in its new forms must go and to achieve this they must act unitedly. Sensing disaster, the upholders of imperialist power regrouped themselves by entering into all manner of military pacts in distant strategic parts of the world with all those willing to join their unholy crusade against the Soviet Union and its allies. They fashioned anew the theory that democracy was in danger and that Soviet power represented a new menace, that it was a new version of fascism which they called "totalitarian communism."

Initially, in the newly free countries many political simpletons, naive liberals and confused sections of the intelligentsia (specially those nurtured in Anglo-Saxon culture imposed by their former colonial masters) were genuinely convinced and developed Communist-phobia. The extremely well-orchestrated and intelligently devised anti-Communist propaganda machine operating from the USA through numerous organizations, utilising subtle and not so subtle methods, convinced them that Soviet power was no less an enemy of freedom and elementary human rights than the Hitlerian concept of super races and their super powers. The Soviet Union and its postwar leadership was fully aware of the feverish activity of their erstwhile "allies" to reestablish their rule wherever it had collapsed, by fair means or foul. Never for a moment did the leadership of the communist Party of the Soviet Union minimize or underestimate the potentialities of the United States and its friends in Europe to create a mighty military machine capable of devastating the world by unleashing a nuclear war.

Therefore, the Soviet Union had once to take steps to prepare not only to defend its own territories but to neutralise the military preparations of their opponents at every level, by strengthening itself and helping those who needed to defend their countries against imperialist designs. Not only had the ruined territories of war-ravaged socialist countries to be rebuilt but the means to defend world peace had to be evolved. Men and women all over the world responded by accepting the principle of peaceful co-existence and cooperation because they knew there was no other alternative to them but total annihilation of the peoples and their civilisation. Many people were and are somewhat cynical about the organised world peace movement as in their opinion the only guarantee against was is armed preparedness. But the peace movement led by socialist and progressive humanity was not and is not a mere pacifist flourish. It has always underlined the need to struggle against the war-mongers. Quite obviously, in this modern age of science and technology no one in his senses can depend on bows and arrows to fight the enemies of peace, and the plans and programmes of the countries that are wedded to peace do not overlook the need to be prepared to match their strength with the forces that seek to profit by war.

The recent welcome changes in the world situation are due to the realisation by the powers that had calculated on isolating the peoples' movements for peace, independence, social justice and mutual co-operation that they have not succeeded in their designs. For the many millions who live in the Indian subcontinent and in Asia, colonialism has been a scourge which has to be liquidated, whatever the price they have to pay for doing so.

Indira Gandhi has very often voiced this sentiment by pointing out that steps towards detente must be truly international and the non-aligned nations of the world must come closer together to safeguard their security as free and independent countries. Urgent efforts to achieve these ends are called for because for more than a decade in Asia and West Asia peace and progress have been jeopardised. We cannot afford to live in a state of euphoria by assuming that the few bright patches of the political horizon will automatically lead to a cloudless sky all over the earth. The partial successes achieved in very recent times to lessen world tensions must become total before we can relax our vigilance. The forces that believe in plundering others, their territory and labour for selfish ends have not given up all hope of doing so.

We in Asia cannot forget what has happened and what is happening now, and therfore, welcome those who believe in the principle of non-interference in the internal affairs of countries and mutual respect for their sovereignty.

Brezhnev will, therefore, be welcomed here not merely because he is the representative of a very friendly country but as one was shares commonly held values. The Indo-Soviet Treaty of Peace and Cooperation is not an ordinary document. Brezhnev and his distinguished colleagues will undoubtedly see to it that its provisions do not remain static. Dynamism is the very breath of life of all who aspire to change the world and we believe that Leonid Brezhnev is one who belongs to this fraternity.

A characteristic feature of cooperation between India and the Soviet Union is the effort to broaden the industrial base of India by setting up more and more factories in the key industries and by exploring and developing indigenous resources. Trade agreements drawn up on this basis have afforded an element of stability in India's economic relations with the Soviet Union, as with other socialist countries, an advantage in the context of development which has provided its point in the current uncertainties of the international markets.

India's imports have been mainly industrial and power equipment, agricultural and road building machinery, tractors and transport machinery. Recent trade agreements have provided for further cooperation in metallurgy, power, oil and chemical industries.

The Soviet Union has been involved with 70 key projects in this country and with the establishment of the joint commission on economic, scientific and technical cooperation the relationship between the two countries is well on way to be deepened. Reports from LINK correspondents in the States describe the performance of the joint ventures in this country.

In West Bengal the number of Soviet aided projects is not large. There are two major projects at Durgapur : the Mining and Allied Machinery Corporation and the Opthalmic Glass Plant. There are two smaller projects in the private sector : the Empire Watch Company and the Insob Tyre Factory. However the most important Soviet-aided venture to start operation soon is gong to be the underground railway in Calcutta. With the take over of the management of coal mines, the need for an increase in coal production has brought the MAMC into prominence. The MAMC, is the first of its kid in India and the biggest in Asia. It has now completely overcome the teething troubles which it had been in for four years or so. According to its managing director A.C. Chatterjee the average monthly productivity had increased from 30.2 per cent to 45.2 per cent. If the present production trend continued the MAMC would be able to double its present production in 1973-74 and reach break-even point. Chatterjee's optimism was fully shared by P.M. Novikov, chief technical and production adviser, who heads the Soviet team of experts at the plant.

The production range of the plant includes winders, mine fans, battery and diesel locomotives, centrifugal pumps, scraper chain and belt conveyors, friction and hydraulic props and feeders of different types. In 1971 the company had also undertaken production of port equipments like stacker-reclaimer, shiploaders, and material handling equipment for railway wagons. An important task was assigned to the plant in 1971 to manufacture finished equipments and miscellaneous items for the Bokaro Steel Plant. The equipment supplied by the MAMC is successfully working at BSL.

The plant has not only increased production in recent years but is also manufacturing more sophisticated machinery. A better organisation of production as well as the strengthening of discipline were the main principles with have contributed to the recent success. Nervousness and frustration have been replaced by a reasonabie and just policy, imbibing all officers and workers with a feeling of responsibility towards their duties. An incentive system based on work measurement is now yielding good results in raising productivity. This system will be modified to meet any changed requirements. A great contribution has been made by the Soviet specialists at the MAMC who assist with design, improvement of organisation of production, technical preparation of the plant and maintenance of machines and equipments. But the most important task now is to achieve a breakeven point and earn a profit in the next financial year. The yearly production target to be achieved is 18,000 tons or Rs. 18 crores in value. Last but not the least is the fulfilment of orders for Madras. Mormagao and other ports and equipment for the second phase of BSL.

The performance of the MAMC will be an example to other public sector projects in West Bengal where the Central Government has invested Rs. 408 crores in such projects. The figure is impressive compared to that of Maharashtra and Gujarat where the Central investments are Rs. 48 crores and Rs. 49 crores respectively. West Bengal is, therefore, a testing ground for public sector project in India.

The Opthalmic Glass Plant in Durgagur is also a Soviet aided project. Fully equipped with the latest Soviet equipment this Rs. 4 crore plant started production of glass blanks and lenses from October 1969. The plant has now overcome many of its initial difficulties. Labour unrest, which according to the present general manager Taneja, had plagued its progress in the beginning, has been resolved recently. Now the 500 strong work force of the factory is trying hard to eradicate that maladies that had crippled productive effort all these years. Taneja and the chief Soviet expert Reshetniak feel confident that the production target fixed for the ensuring year would be fulfilled with the active cooperation of the workers. The entire process of the complex and highly sophisticated work at the OGP is handled by Indian technicians, 17 of whom were trained in Soviet Union. Soviet experts attached to the plant help with their experience and practical knowledge. Keshetniak holds a very high opinion about his Indian comrades. He told me that the Indian staff of OGP are capable of running the plant independently.

Though the impression I got from a tour of the plant was satisfactory, the commercial performance of the OGP has not been upto expectations. Production is far below the rated capacity. Taneja told me that the plant was not out of woods yet, but with the labour situation having improved, managerial loopholes plugged and productivity enhanced the OGP was now set for a breakthrough in the current year.

The massive economic and technical assistance extended by the Soviet Union has accelerated the pace of industrial development in Madhya Pradesh. Besides Bhilai, the Soviet Union has helped in the construction of a 200 MW power station in Korba. An Aluminium Plant, which will produce 1,00,000 tonnes of aluminium annually and will be the biggest of its kind in India, is being set up also in Korba. The Soviet Union has also provided technical assistance and machinery to the National Coal Development Corporation (NCDC) for the exploration of coal in Korba and Singrauli.

The Madhya Pradesh Government is at present negotiating with the USSR for the purchase of heavy earth-moving equipment and technical know-how for its gigantic project for the reclamation of the ravines of the Chambal valley.

In November 1954 a Soviet Team visited Bhilai, Tanduala and Rajhara. They also flew over the Korba region. The present site of the steel plant was finally chosen in March, 1955, six weeks after the Indo-Soviet Agreement was signed. Although Soviet experts provided technical guidance during the construction and commissioning of the plant, the responsibility for construction and operation of the steel works rested entirely on Indian shoulders. In early 1956, batches of Indian engineers, most of them fresh graduates from colleges and universities, and future operators, were sent to the USSR for training at Soviet plants. In all, 721 specialists, including 338 engineers and 385 operators, were trained in the USSR for periods ranging from 9 to 15 months. In addition, 1500 men received training in India itself. They formed the nucleus of Bhilai's trained personnel, and today many of them occupy important posts.

Certain dates stand out as milestones in the progress of the plant. On January 31, 1959, the first coke oven battery was commissioned and a few days later, on February 4, Dr. Rajendra Prasad, the then President of the India, inaugurated the first Blast Furnace. After the commissioning of the first blast furnace units of the plant were completed in quick succession. On October 2 of the same year, the then Soviet Ambassador, I.A., Benediktov, inaugurated the first open hearth furnace, and Bhilai started producing steel.

Bhilai's fast and impressive progress has won the entire country's admiration. On August 16, 1960 a fresh contract was signed for the preparation of a detailed project report for the preparation of a detailed project report for the expansion of the Bhilai Steel Plant to 2.5 million-tonne capacity. Having established many records, both in production and profitability, nearly 50,000 workers of the plant have set before them a new goal-to expand the plant's capacity to 4.2 million tonnes. According to P.R. Ahuja, general manager of the Bhilai Steel Works, the expansion programme would cost Rs. 264.8 crores. The programme includes also the mechanisation of the Dhalli-Rajhara are mines as well as the setting up to a refractory plant unit which will produce 1,00,000 tonnes of refractories every years.

Although the Soviet Union will give all necessary help, Bhilai's expansion to 4.2 million tonnes will be accomplished with maximum indigenous participation. The expansion of Bhilai's capacity to 4.2 million tonnes of ingot steel by 1976-77 will make Bhilai one of the biggest steel plants in the country, second only to Bokaro.

The Soviet-aided Neiveli Lignite Corporation averted the catastrophe of a total power shutdown during the ten months of serious power shortage till June this year in Tamil Nadu. But for the steady supply-line of nearly 300 mw of power from the NLC, the power cut would have total instead of the around 75 per cent of normal supplies in the State, Neiveli owes its growth, despite some difficulties which persist even now, to Soviet aid. It was the first break from the practice of depending upon Western collaboration that is wholly profit oriented. When West European countries demanded high rates of interest for long term loans, the Soviet Union offered credit at 2.5 per cent interest, total Soviet aid to the project since 1957 has come to over Rs. 7 crores. This is likely to increase when the expansion schemes of the project are taken up in the fifth Plan period.

The Surgical Instruments Plant near Madras is yet another edifice of Indo-Soviet economic cooperation. In this project as many as 166 types of surgical instruments are being produced according to the cold pressing method which has proved its efficacy in the Soviet Union. This plant meets half the country's requirements and lately has started exporting surgical instruments to the Soviet Union itself, among other countries.

In the 1950s, Soviet and was used for expanding the capacity of the Mettur Hydel Station. The Mettur tunnel power house built with Soviet aid meets 10 per cent of the State's hydel power requirements. As many 30 Soviet enterprises supplied 8,000 tonnes of the latest in power equipment to the Mettur tunnel hydro electric station. In Arkonam, about 70 kilometers from Madras, is the House of Steel. This is yet another example of Indo-Soviet collaboration. Here, the Tamil Nadu Industrial Development Corporation, an entirely Government-owned concern, is producing with Soviet technical collaboration steel billets to meet demands of 37 mills in the State.

The Patratu Thermal Power Station, built with Soviet collaboration, which is the biggest power plant of its kind in the Eastern region has since last several years been a sick child of the Bihar State Electricity Board: Because of rampant corruption, bureaucratic bunglings and hurdles created at various stages the Rs. 44 crore-project was delayed by several years. Of its six units, the first one was commissioned in 1966 and the last one of the first stage in 1972. Of the six units, four have generation capacities of 50 mw each and two have generation of 100 mw each. Two other units of . . . . mw capacity each are under construction. In view of the growing demand of power and availability of water in the Nalkari reservoir and abundance of low-grade coal in adjoining coalfield, the Bihar Government is pressing the Centre for further expansion of this project and raising its generating capacity to 1020 mw.

Patratu at present supplies power to most of North and South Bihar including Chotanagpur and besides Heavy Engineering Corporation (HEC) and NCDC, hundreds of medium and small scale industries are served by it. However the power supply has been so erratic that because of interruptions and load-shedding large areas including Patna and Ranchi are frequently plunged into darkness and the HEC has suffered a production loss of nearly 30 per cent during the last several months.

The problems of Patratu Thermal Power Station are mostly man-made. Not even 50 per cent of the recommendations of the Ranchor Prasad Committee on the working of the State Electricity Board, particularly Patratu, have been implemented so far. It is not difficult to locate the guilty persons, but it is difficult to punish them. Two years ago, in mid-1971, things came to a head when because of tug-of war between two top ranking officials and not only Patratu but the Barauni Thermal Power Station was also closed down several times for 24 to 48 hours plunging the whole State into darkness. One of the concerned officials despite serious charges of corruption against him which caused huge losses to the State exchequer, enjoyed the full confidence and patronage of the then Power Minister Kedar Pande. Last year when the viz. Committee started its probe into the affairs of the Board, several skeltons in the cupboard were uncovered.

Out of its installed capacity of 400 mw, Patratu is at present generating only 200 mw daily. According to H.K. Sahay, General Superintendent of Patratu Thermal Power Station, because of bungling in the supply of requisite quality of coal and furnace oil in sufficient quantities and non-availability of spares, it is becoming difficult to maintain even this level of generation. Out of seven boilers only four are under operation. To maintain the present level of generation. Patratu requires about 80,000 to 90,000 tonnes of coal per month. But because of transport bottleneck and other problems, the supply is generally erratic and just around 60,000 tonnes a month. Unless regular coal supply is assured, it is difficult to increase the generation. And this is the situation when Patratu Thermal Power Station is situated in the heart of the coal-belt. While Patratu is starving, coal is moved from its door to far off places in other States.

The lack of coal supply, to Patratu's specifications for which its boilers have been designed, is yet another problem. At present it gets coal from Kathara middlings, Bukbuka seam of Dakra, Bukbuka colliery, Karanpura field, old stock from Kathara colliery and Kathara washery. Coal received from different sources are mixed but the power station has no blending arrangement. If the inflow of coal from the mine is proportionately larger during a month then there are difficulties. The two main factors for proper burning of coal are : calorific value and initial deformation of ash. If initial deformation of ash is low and calorific value is high, fusion of ash takes place resulting in slagging in the boiler and if it takes place one, the whole boiler furnate is filled up with slag within 48 hours. The boiler has to be shutdown then and it takes 10 to 12 days to remove the slag. If coal is received from Karanpura Dewarkhand and Dakra seam of Bukbuka colliery situated at a distance of only about 24 km, the problem can be solved to a great extent.

However the right type of coal for this power plant is located at a distance of only 5 to 6 kilometres at Nadiatoli and Urimari Patanga where over 50 million tonnes of reserve was anticipated. But the mining work could not be started by the NCDC in this and such other mines as some top officials of the State Electricity Board who were interested in buying coal from private collieries failed to make any firm commitment to the Corporation to purchase coal from it in bulk.

Inadequate supply of fuel oil *i.e.*, light diesel oil is another problem plaguing the working of the power plant. Depending upon the load, Patratu needs about 100 kl of light diesel oil per day to run its 4 boilers presently under operation. In case of full loading of the boilers, the consumption is just 30 kl to 64 kl of fuel oil. It has a storage capacity of 2000 kl. and the oil has to come from Barauni Refinery in North Bihar. However, Patratu has been allotted the fourth position in the priority list for despatch of fuel oil and because of non-allotment of wagons often the stock dwindles to as low as 500 to 600 kilo-litres only. In September, 1971, the plant remained closed for 48 hours because there was no light diesel oil in stocks.

Besides the right type of coal and adequate supply of fuel oil, one of the greatest problems facing the Patratu Thermal Power Station is that of the spare parts, nearly 60 to 70 pert cent of which has to be imported from the Soviet Union. In this regard, the Soviet authorities have been extending full co-operation. Besides some half a dozen Soviet experts, a high official of the USSR Trade Commission in Calcutta was recently at Patratu to sort out the problems.

Although the Heavy Engineering Corporation at Ranchi was manufacturing some emergency spares for the power plant, efforts to procure them indigenously have not been successful. The Central Water and Power Commission is reported to have already prepared a list of essential spares and manufacturing designs needed for Patratu and is expected to take up the matter with the aides of the Soviet Communist Party chief Leonid Brezhnev during his forth coming visit to India. This discussion is likely to be followed by the visit of the Indian delegation of Moscow to finalise details.

Besides the Indian Oil Refinery complex in North Bihar and the Patratu Power Station, there are two other giant Soviet-aided projects in the industrial belt of Chotanagpur in South Bihar. They are the Heavy Machine Building Plant (HMBP), the premier plant of the Heavy Engineering Corporation (HEC) complex at Ranchi and the Bokaro Steel Plant. The HMBP is designed to produce steel plant machinery besides excavators oil drilling rigs and press machinery. The annual production programme at full capacity envisages an output of 80,000 tonnes of mechanical equipment, which is sufficient for a steel plant of one million tonne capacity. To meet the demand for structural fabrications work, another plant the Steel Fabrication Workshop (SFW) with 25,000 tonne installed capacity has been set up by the side of HMBP.

However, because of various lapses on the part of the management and frequent changes at the top, the gestation period of the HMBP has been too long. The steel structures shop of HMBP went into production in November 1972. Since then, production both in the HMBP and SFW has been steadily growing. Till the end of 1972-73, the HMBP has turned out 1,28,168 tonnes of mechanical equipment and the SFW 17,411 tonnes of structurals. The capacity utilisation of the HMBP has reached 34.4 per cent whereas for the SFW the figure in 21.4 per cent. The plant is gradually getting over the financial difficulties faced initially. Although the teething troubles are over, a great deal of effort will have to be made to find out what precisely is needed to be done to improve the working in the various areas like production planning and control, material supply, utilisation of labour, improvement of the working level of direct workers etc. The HMBP and the SFW, are expected to reach their full capacity production of 80,000 and 25,000 tonnes respectively by the end of the Fifth Plan (1979-80). But the order book shows a great deal of deficit as against the capacity build up. However with the three new steel plants and expansion of Bhilai and Bokaro Steel Plants to 7 million tonnes and 10 million tonnes capacity, respectively, the order position is sure to improve in the coming years.

After seven years of hopes for obtaining U.S. assistance for setting up the fourth integrated steel plant as Bokaro in the public sector, India was forced to withdraw the proposal because of the conditions put forward by the US Government. However, the Soviet Union immediately stepped in and under an agreement signed on January, 1965, it agreed to extend a credit of 200 million roubles (Rs. 167 crores) to meet the foreign exchange expenditure on import of plant and equipment and the cost of technical assistance.

However, because of various initial troubles, the construction work of the plant could started in full swing only in 1970. Because of delay in supply of structural and mechanical equipments by indigenous firms both in the public and private sectors, the commissioning schedule of the Bokaro Steel Plant had to be revised thrice. Bokaro is called India's first 'swadeshi' steel plant as nearly 90 per cent of building structures, all the technological structures, 65 per cent of mechanical equipment, 48 per cent of electrical equipment, 80 per cent of instruments and 60 per cent of refractories are being procured indigenously. In the context of the protocol signed by the Indo-Soviet Joint Commission on Economic Co-operation in February, 1973, the feasibility of Bokaro's expansion to 10 million tonnes is also under examination. At this level, Bokaro could be one of the largest steel plants in the world.

JAPAN : NEW HORIZONS

Japan, the island kingdom of Asia, floats in the vast blue waters of the Pacific like a brilliantly lit ship. Asians visiting it for the first time are taken aback and overwhelmed by its utter and blaring modernity. It makes them wonder for a while whether modern Japan can really be regarded as a part of the Asian continent. Accustomed as we are to associate the virtues and vices of highly industrialised societies with Europe and America, the urban scene in Japan has a peculiarly incongrous, almost an un-Asian look. Knowledge of Japan's un-Asian history-its leap towards the industrial revolution a century before all other Asian countries, of its wars and empires, its victories and defeats notwithstanding, the visual impact of present-day Japan of fellow Asians, (particularly from countries suppressed for centuries) is irresistably forceful. It stuns them with the sudden realization that tremendous efforts have to be made by an Asian people if they want to live fully in the 20th century and not partially in the fifteenth and even earlier centuries.

Japan's advance should specially thrill the free and forward-looking peoples of Asia and Africa. This feeling of elation however is superficial, in the sense that it does no more than help to lessen the weight of depression and despair over Asian inferiority as against European superiority. Obviously the historic process that led to Japan's rejection of what existed in its pre-modern age was essentially capitalist and imperialist and eventually fascist. Its industrial revolution, therefore, was accompanied by all the restricting and reactionary features of Western Imperialism and a political system that engineered a series of disasters for the people as a whole.

No patriotic and progressive Asian, therefore, can urge that the manner chosen by Japan to enter the industrial age is justifiable and much less be an advocate for a similar way of development for the rest of Asia and Africa. But the fact that despite the absence of any kind of a bourgeois democratic order in pre-war Japan, the working class and its trade union and political organisations could assert themselves and challenge both their own conservative forces and American interventions and machinations so successfully, provides powerful testimony to the innate capacity of the Japanese to imbibe the essentials of the new age of science and industry and political theory relevant to a revolutionary period.

Clearly a remarkable transformation in social attitudes and values has taken place at every level of intellectual leadership in Japan, political, cultural and social because of the Second World War. The new leadership is fully aware of the consequence of material prosperity in a society full of capitalist contradictions. Awareness of the ugly, demoralising and degenerate aspects of the competitive order which influenced Japan in the past and continues in the present is common not only among Japanese communists and socialists but also among liberals like Prof. Okochi Kazuo who told Tokyo University students. "It is better to be a human being dissatisfied than a pig satisfied . . . . The important thing for university graduates is not to set themselves on the road to success, or the route to the executive desk, but to know how to remedy the faults of Japanese society." The faults he had in mind were specifically those of a capitalist society.

This dissatisfaction is not confined merely to the intellectuals. Opposition to the Government and the ruling class for its conservative economics and anti-national social policies is growing, specially when it submits shamelessly to American overlordism. And it is subjected to constant attacks not only by the Socialist and Communist parties and powerful trade unions under the leadership of the Sohyo, but by religious and cultural organisations also. Surprisingly enough, an influential section of the Japanese press (despite its links with big business) in critical of the present Government, again more specifically when it surrenders to American pressure. While the social climate, generally speaking, is not one of total subservience to the West, the vested interest (as in all lands) encourages everything that may protect its privileges whatever the humiliation. However, the bitter memories of imperialist aggression by its own war-mongers and relation by those who have now invaded Japan's fair soil and contaminated seas around it, are as yet fresh in the minds of millions. The resistance to forces which seek to revive militarism and fascism by subtle and devious methods is growing steadily. The vast annual A and H Bomb Conferences, the militant students' movement, and the working class and left wing organisations are unyielding in their determination to usher in a socialist society and free mankind for all time from the menace of nuclear wars. Facing them the conservative elements of Japan are not as powerful as it generally assumed because they cannot pursue their ends without rousing massanger and are very often forced to retreat.

Naturally, reactionary circles are taking full advantage of the Sino-Soviet estrangement and gloating over the fact that it has weakened progressive elements greatly. They are willing to accept the arguments of the present rulers of Communist China in favour of trade relations and are making numerous non-political but friendly gestures by propagating not only theories of racial and cultural kinship with the Chinese people but of even admitting that they owe the Chinese compensation for the wrongs they have suffered at the hands of Japanese war mongers! If Communist China does not object to making deals with a country that has been forced to give full diplomatic recognition to Chiang Kai Shek's regime in Formosa, why should the present Government of Japan and its American advisers mind it! On the countrary, there is every evidence to suggest that the Japanese ruling party's assiduous efforts for a rapprochement with Communist China are viewed with sympathy by the more shrewd among American policy-makers.

It is impossible to gather all the impressions one wants to of a fascinating and stimulating country like Japan and specially its people, in the course of twelve brief days. There are ever so many interesting features that require careful study specially the cultural impact of the West, and its ramifications.

The Japanese are a very aesthetic people. They are sensitive to beauty and, love to make every think about them beautiful. Be it the home, temple, the old world eating house or the modern restaurant, there is always the effort at introducing something that pleases the eye. There is also an air of considerateness about their manners quite different in its quality to the formally polite ways of the Western world. Although they have virtually discarded their national costume in favour of modern European clothes they have proudly held on to their language and made it the vehicle of all learning including the most abstruse scientific subjects.

Our hosts in Japan were convinced socialists and they were full of optimism and hope that a socialist Japan is, if not imminent, a certainty in the foreseable future.

Bibliography

Unpublished and Published Sources

Home Political records, 1920-22, available in the National Archive of India, New Delhi.

Debates, Legislative Assembly, 1920-22.

Debates, House of Commons, 1920-22.

A.I.C.C. Papers, 1920-22.

The Collected Works of Mahatma Gandhi, relevant volumes.

Young India, relevant volumes.

Selected Works of Jawaharlal Nehru, vols. I and II, (edt.)

S. Gopal.

Private Papers

Chelmsford Papers

Gandhi Papers

Jawaharlal Nehru Papers

Motilal Nehru Papers

Reading Papers

Sapru Papers

Oral History Interviews Available in Nehru Memorial Museum and Library, New Delhi

Smt. Vijay Lakshmi Pandit.

Smt. Renuka Ray.

Newspapers

The Hindustan Times

Times of India

Amrita Bazar Patrika

The Hindu

The Tribune

The Searchlight

Indian Journals

Journal of Indian History

India Quarterly

The Indian Journal of Political Science

South Asian Studies

Indian Economic and Social History Review

Bengal : Past and Present

The Quarterly Review of Historical Studies

The Indian Historical Review

Studies in History

The Panjab : Past and Present

Foreign Journals

Bulletin of the School of Oriental and African Studies

The Journal of Asian Studies

Journal of Contemporary History

South Asia.

The Australian Journal of Politics and History

Asian Affairs

The Journal of Modern History

Pacific Historical Review

Modern Asian Studies

Journal of South-East Asian Studies

The Journal of Commonwealth and Comparative Politics

Pacific Affairs

The Journal of Imperial and Commonwealth History

New Zealand Journal of History

Secondary Works

Abbot, G.F., *Turkey in Transition*, London, 1909.

Afzal Iqbal (ed.)., *Selected Writings and Speeches of Maulana Muhammad Ali*, Lahore, 1944.

Aga Khan, *Indian in Transition*, London, 1918.

Agarwal, Amar Narain, *Gandhism : A Socialistic Approach,* Allahabad, 1944.

Agarwala, M.M. *The Hindu-Muslim Riots : Their Causes and Cures,* Lucknow, 1944.

Aiyar, R.P. and Bhandare, L.S., *The Congress Caravan : The History of the Indian National Congress and of India's Struggle for Swaraj, 1885-1945,* Bombay, 1945.

Alexander, Horace, *Social and Political Ideas of Mahatma Gandhi,* Delhi, 1949.

Ali, Ameer Syed, *The Spirit of Islam,* London, 1935.

Ali Brothers, *For India and Islam,* Calcutta, 1922.

Ali, Muhammad, *Freedom of Faith and its Price,* London, 1919.

——, *My Life—A Fragment*, Lahore, 1946.

Ali, Zaki, *Islam in the World,* Lahore, 1947.

Amery, L.S., *India and Freedom,* London, 1942.

Andrews, C.F., *How India Can Be Free,* Madras, 1921.

——, *The Indian Problem,* Madras, 1921.

——, *The Meaning of Non-Cooperation,* Madras, 1923.

——, *Mahatma Gandhi at Work,* New York, 1931.

——, *Mahatma Gandhi's Ideas.* London, 1949.

Anjaria, J.J., *Essays on Gandhian Economics,* Bombay, 1945.

Appadorai, A., *Dyarchy in Practice,* London, 1937.

Arberry, J., and Landau Rom, *Islam Today,* London, 1942.

Agrov Daniel, *Moderates and Extremists in the Indian Nationalist Movement, 1883-1920,* Bombay, 1961.

Arnold, Thomas W., *The Caliphate,* Oxford, 1924.

Asaf Ali M., *Constructive Non-Cooperation,* Madras, 1921.

Asquith, *Memories and Recollections, vols. I and II,* Boston, 1923.

Athalye, D. V., *The Life of Mahatma Gandhi,* Poona, 1923.

Ayengar, A.S., *All Through the Gandhian Era, Indian, 1915-50,* Bombay, 1950.

Azad, Maulana Abul Kalam, *India Wins Freedom,* Delhi, 1959.

Aziz, K.K., *Britain and Muslim India,* London, 1963.

Baksh, S., Khuda, *Caliphate,* Lahore, 1954.

Bakshi, S.R., *British Diplomacy and Administration in India, 1807-13,* Delhi 1971.

——, *Simon Commission and Indian Nationalism,* Delhi, 1977.

——, *Ranjit Singh and Charles Metcalfe,* Delhi, 1980.

——, *Gandhi and Salt Stayagraha,* Delhi, 1981.

——, *Bhagat Singh and His Ideology,* Delhi, 1981.

——, *Jallianwala Bagh Tragedy,* Delhi, 1982.

Bamford, P.C., *Histories of the Non-Cooperation and Khilafat Movements,* Delhi, 1974.

Bandyopadhyaya, J., *Social and Political Thought of Gandhi, Calcutta,* 1969.

Banerji, Nripendra Chandra, *Gandhism in Theory and Practice,* Madras, 1923.

Banerji, R.C., *The Story of the Khilafat,* Jessore, 1922.

Banerjea, S.N., *A Nation in Making : Being the Reminiscences of Fifty Years of Public life,* London, 1925.

Barkatullah, Mohammad, *The Khilafat,* London, 1924.

Barns, Margarite, *India : Today and Tomorrow,* London, 1937.

Basu, Aparna, *The Growth of Education and Political Development in India, 1898-1920,* Delhi, 1974.

Bayly, C.A., *The Local Roots of Indian Politics, Allahabad, 1880-1920,* Oxford, 1975.

Besant, Annie, *How India Wrought For Freedom,* Madras, 1915.

——, *The Birth of New India,* Madras, 1917.

——, *Gandhian Non-Cooperation or Shall India Commit Suicide?* Madras, 1920.

——, *Shall India Live or Die?* Madras, 1925.

——, *India : A Nation,* Madras, 1930.

——, *India : Today and Tomorrow,* London, 1937.

——, *India Bond or Free,* Adyar, 1939.

——, *Speeches and Writing,* Madras, n.d.

Besterman, Theodore, *Mrs. Annie Besant : A Modern Prophet,* London, 1934.

Bevan, Edywn, *Indian Nationalism : An Independent Estimate in India,* Delhi, 1966.

Bhagwan Das, *The Meaning of Swaraj or Self-Government,* Banaras, 1921.

——, *The Philosophy of Non-Cooperation,* Madras, 1922.

Bipan Chandra, *Rise and Growth of Economic Nationalism in India,* Delhi, 1966.

——, *Nationalism and Colonialism in Modern India,* Delhi, 1979.

Birla, G.D., *In the Shadow of the Mahatma : Personal Memoirs,* Bombay, 1968.

Bisheshwar Prasad, *Bondage and Freedom : A History of Modern India, 1707-1947, vol. II, Freedom, 1858-1947,* Delhi, 1979.

Bolitho, Hector, *Jinnah : Creator of Pakistan,* London, 1954.

Bondurant, Joan, V., *Conquest of Violence : The Gandhian Philosophy of Conflict,* London, 1959.

Bose, Nirmal Kumar, *Studies in Gandhism,* Calcutta, 1962.

Bose, Nirmal Kumar, and Patwardhan, P.H., *Gandhi in Indian Politics,* Bombay, 1967.

Bose, Subhas Chandra, *The Indian Struggle, 1920-42,* New York, 1964.

Brailsford, Henry Noel, *Rebel India,* New York, 1931.

——, *Subject India,* New York, 1943.

Brecher, Michael, *Nehru : A Political Biography,* London, 1959.

Bright, J.S., *The Himalayan Blunders of Mahatma Gandhi,* Lahore, 1946.

Brockway, A. Fenner, *Non-Cooperation in Other Lands,* Madras, 1921.

——, *The Indian Crisis,* London, 1930.

Brown, Judith M., *Gandhi's Rise to Power : Indian Politics, 1915-1922,* London, 1972.

Bryant, John Forbes, *Gandhi and Indianisation of the Empire,* London, 1924.

Buch, M.A., *Rise and Growth of Indian Liberalism,* Baroda, 1938.

——, *Rise and Growth of Indian Militant Nationalism,* Bombay, 1940.

Caveeshar, Sardul Singh, *India's Fight for Freedom,* Lahore, 1936.

Chakravarty, Amiya, *Mahatma Gandhi and Modern World,* Calcutta, 1945.

Chatterjee, B.C., *Gandhi and Aurobindo,* Calcutta, 1967.

Chatterjee, Dilip Kumar, *C.R. Das and Indian National Movement,* Calcutta, 1956.

Chatterjee, Jogesh, *The Search of Freedom,* Calcutta, 1967.

Chatterjee, Nandlal, *India's Freedom Struggle,* Allahabad, 1958.

Chesney, George, *Indian Policy : The System of Administration*, Delhi, 1976.

Chintamani, C.Y., *Indian Politics Since the Mutiny*, Allahabad, 1947.

Chirol, Valentine, *Pan-Islamism*, London, 1906.

——, *India : Old and New*, London, 1921.

——, *India*, London, 1926.

Cole, F. Seymour, *India Should Know Turkey*, Bombay, 1943.

Coupland, R., *The Indian Problem, 1833-1935*, London, 1942.

——, *The Goal of British Rule in India*, London, 1948.

Craddock, Reginald Henry, *The Dilemma in India*, London, 1920.

Crozir, Frank Percy, *A Word to Gandhi : The Lesson of Ireland*, London, 1931.

Curtis, L., *Dyarchy*, Oxford, 1920.

Das, C.R., *India for Indians*, Madras, 1921.

Das, M.N., *The Political Philosophy of Jawaharlal Nehru*, London, 1961.

——, *India Under Morley and Minto*, London, 1964.

——, *Indian National Congress Vs. The British, 1885-1918*, Delhi, 1978.

Datta, K.K., *History of the Freedom Movement in Bihar, vol. I, 1857-1928*, Patna, 1957.

Desai, A.R., *Social Background of Indian Nationalism*, Bombay, 1959.

Desai, Mahadev, *The Story of Bardoli*, Ahmedabad, 1957.

Dhawan, Gopinath, *The Political Philosophy of Mahatma Gandhi*, Ahmedabad, 1946.

Digby, William, *Prosperous British India*, London, 1901.

Diwakar, R.R., *Satyagraha : Its Technique and History*, Bombay, 1946.

——, *Satyagraha in Action*, Calcutta, 1949.

——, *Satyagraha : The Power of Truth*, Illinois, 1948.

Doke, Joseph, *M.K. Gandhi : An Indian Patriot in South Africa*, Madras, 1919.

Duncan, Ronald, *Select Writings of Mahatma Gandhi*, London, n.d.

Dutt, K. Iswara, *Congress Cyclopaedia, vol., I*, Delhi, n.d.

Dutt, K.N., *Landmarks of the Freedom Struggle in Assam*, Gauhati, 1958.

Dutt, R. Palme, *India Today*, Bombay, 1949.

Dutt, Ramesh Chandra, *The Economic History of India in the Victorian Age*, vol. II.

Dwarkadas, Kanji, *India's Fight for Freedom, 1913-1937,* Bombay, 1966.

Edib, Halide, *Conflict of East and West in Turkey,* Delhi, 1935.

Elwin, Harry Verrier Holman, *Mahatma Gandhi,* London, 1932.

Fischer, Louis, *The Life of Mahatma Gandhi,* New York, 1950.

——, *The Essential Gandhi,* London, 1963.

Fraser, Andrew, *Among Indian Rajahs and Ryots,* London, 1911.

Fuller, Bampfylde, *The Empire of India,* London, 1913.

Fuller, J.F.C., *Indian in Revolt,* London, 1931.

Gallagher, J., Johnson, G., and Seal, A., (ed.), *Locality, Province and Nation : Essays on Indian Politics, 1870-1940,* Cambridge, 1973.

Gandhi, M.K., *An Autobiography or The Story of My Experiments with Truth,* Ahmedabad, 1958.

——, *Hind Swaraj,* Madras, 1921.

——, *Swaraj in One Year,* Madras, 1921.

——, *Communal Unity,* Ahmedabad, 1948.

——, *Non-Violence in Peace and War,* Ahmedabad, 1942.

——, *Economics of Khadi,* Ahmedabad, 1941.

——, *Constructive Programme : Its Meaning and Place,* Ahmedabad, 1948.

Ghose, P.C., *Mahatma Gandhi As I Saw Him,* Delhi, 1968.

Ghose, Shankar, *Political Ideas and Movements in India,* Calcutta, 1975.

Gokhale, G.K., *Speeches,* Madras, 1916.

Gopal, Ram, *Indian Muslims : A Political History, 1858-1947,* Bombay, 1959.

——, *How India Struggled for Freedom,* Bombay, 1967.

Gopal, S., *British Policy in India, 1858-1905,* London, 1965.

——, *Jawaharlal Nehru : A Biography,* vol. I, London, 1975.

Gordon, Leonard, A., *Bengal : The Nationalist Movement, 1879-1940,* Delhi, 1974.

Gour, H.S., *The British Impact on India,* London, 1965.

Gregg, Richard B., *Psychology and Strategy of Gandhi's Non-violent Resistance,* Madras, 1929.

——, *Economics of Khaddar,* Ahmedabad, 1946.

Griffths, P.J., *The British Impact on India,* London, 1965.

Gupta, Nagendranath, *Indian Nationalism,* Bombay, 1946.

——, *Gandhi and Gandhism*, Bombay, 1948.

Gwyer, Maurice and Appadorai, A., *Speeches and Documents on the Indian Constitution, 1921-47*, vol. I, London, 1957.

Hamper, D.A., *John Morley, Liberal Intellectual in Politics*, London, 1968.

Hasan, Mushirul, *Nationalism and Communal Politics in India, 1916-28*, Delhi, 1974.

Hitti, Phillip K., *Arabs*, London, 1960.

Holmes, John Haynes, *Gandhi Before Pilate : A Sermon on the Indian Revolution*, New York, 1930.

Horne, E.A., *The Political System of British India*, Oxford, 1922.

Horniman, B.G., *Amritsar and Our Duty to India*, London, 1920.

Houghton, Bernard, *The Issue in India*, Madras, 1922.

——, *Realities of Today*, Madras, 1923.

Hoyland, John S., *The Case for India*, London, 1929.

——, *Indian Crisis : The Background*, London, 1943.

Hull, William Issac, *India's Political Crisis*, Baltimore, 1930.

Hunter, W.W., *The Indian Musalmans*, London, 1972.

Husain, Azam, *Fazl-i-Husain : A Political Biography*, Bombay 1946.

Hyde, H. Montgomery, *Lord Reading*, London, 1967.

Hyndman, H.M., *The Awakening of Asia*, London, 1919.

Iyenger, C.S. Ranga, *India in the Crucible*, London, 1927.

——, *How To Lose India*, Lahore, 1935.

Jayakar, M.R., *The Story of My Life, 1873-1922*, vol. I, Bombay, 1958.

Jha, Shiva Nand, *A Critical Study of Gandhian Economic Thought*, Agra, 1961.

Iyer, Raghavan, N., *The Moral and Political Thought of Mahatma Gandhi*, London, 1978.

Kabir, Humayun, *Muslim Politics, 1906-42*, Calcutta, 1943.

Kamath, M.S., *The Home Rule League*, Madras, 1927.

Karmarkar, D.D., *Bal Gangadhar Tilak : A Study*, Bombay, 1956.

Karve, D.G. and Ambedkar, D.V., (ed.) *Speeches and Writings of Gopal Krishna Gokhale*, vol. II, Bombay, 1966.

Kaura, Uma, *Muslim and Indian Nationalism : The Emergence of the Demand for India's Partition, 1928-40*, Delhi, 1977.

Kaushik, P.D., *The Congress Ideology and Programme, 1920-47*, Delhi, 1964.

Keer, Dhananjay, *Lokamanya Tilak : Father of our Freedom Struggle*, Bombay, 1958.

——, *Mahatma Gandhi : Political Saint and Unarmed Prophet*, Bombay, 1973.

Keith, A.B. (ed.), *Speeches and Documents on Indian Policy*, vol. II, London, 1922.

Kenworthy, J.W., *India : A Warning*, London, 1931.

Kidwai, Shaikh Mushir Hasan, *Pan-Islamism*, London, 1908.

Kohli, M.S., *Mahatma Gandhi's Confessions*, Lahore, 1943.

Kohn, Hans, *A History of Nationalism in the East*, New York, 1929.

Koss, Stephen, E., *John Morley at the India Office, 1905-1910.* Yale University Press, 1969.

Kripalani, J.B., *The Gandhian Way*, Bombay, 1946.

——, *Gandhi : His Life and Thought*, Delhi, 1970.

Krishnamurti, Y.G., *Gandhi Era in World Politics*, Bombay, 1943.

Kumarappa, J.C., *Gandhian Economic Thought*, Bombay, 1931.

Kurup, T.C.K., *Gospel of Gandhi*, Madras, 1921.

Lajpat Rai, *The Political Future of India*, New York, 1919.

——, *India's Will To Freedom : Writings and Speeches On The Present Situation*, Madras, 1921.

——, *Ideals of Non-Cooperation and Other Essays*, Madras, 1924.

Lal Bahadur, *The Muslim League : Its History, Activities and Achievements*, Agra, 1954.

Lawton, Lancerton, *Empire of the East, Part II*, London, 1912.

Lovett, Verney, *A History of the Indian Nationalist Movement*, London, 1920.

Lucas, Charles, *The Empire at War*, London, 1921.

Mackenzie, Brown, *Indian Political Thought from Ranaae to Bhave*, Berkeley, 1961.

MacDonald, J. Ramsay, *The Government of India*, London, n.d.

Macnicol, Nicol, *The Making of Modern India*, London, 1924.

Mahmud Ahmad, *Non-Cooperation and Islam*, Lahore, 1921.

——, *Indian Problem and its Solution*, London, 1926.

Mahmud, Syed, *The Khilafat and England*, Patna, 1922.

Majumdar, R.C., *Three Phases of India's Struggle for Freedom,* Bombay, 1961.

——, *History of Freedom Movement in India, vol. III,* Calcutta, 1963.

Malhotra, P.L., *Administration of Lord Elgin in India, 1894-99,* Delhi, 1979.

Mary, Countess of Minto, *India, Minto and Morley, 1906-10,* London, 1934.

Masani, R.P., *Dadabhai Naoroji : The Grand Old Man of India,* London, 1939.

Mathur, J.S., *Essays on Gandhian Economics,* Allahabad, 1960.

Mazumdar, H.T., *Gandhi : The Apostle,* Chicago, 1923.

——, *Mahatma Gandhi : Peaceful Revolutionary,* New York, 1952.

Mehrotra, S.R., *Indian and the Commonwealth, 1885—1929,* London, 1965.

——, *Towards Indian Freedom and Partition,* Delhi, 1979.

Menon, P.K.K., *The History of Freedom Movement in Kerala, 1885-1938, vol. II,* Trivandrum, 1972.

Meston, Lord, *India and the Empire,* London, 1924.

Mishra, D.P. (ed.), *The History of Freedom Movement in Madhya Pradesh,* Nagpur, 1956.

Mitra, S.M., *Indian Problems,* London, 1908.

Mody, H.P., *The Political Future of India,* London, 1908.

Montagu, E.S., *An Indian Diary,* London, 1930.

Moon, P., *Gandhi and Modern India,* London, 1968.

Moore, R.J., *The Crisis of Indian Unity,* Oxford, 1964.

Moraes, Frank, *Jawaharlal Nehru : A Biography,* New York, 1956.

Mukerjee, H., *India Struggles for Freedom,* Bombay 1946.

——, *Gandhiji : A Study,* Calcutta 1958.

Naik, V.N., *Indian Liberalism,* Bombay, 1945.

Nair, C. Sankaran, *Gandhi and Anarchy,* Madras, 1922.

Namboodiripad, E.M.S., *The Mahatma and the Ism,* Delhi, 1958.

Naoroji, Dadabhai, *Poverty and Un-British Rule in India,* Delhi, 1962.

——, *Speeches and Writings of Dadabhai Naoroji,* Madras, n.d.

Narayan, Shriman, *The Gandhian Plan of Economic Development of India,* Bombay, 1944.

Nariman, K.F., *Whither Congress*, Bombay, 1933.

Nehru, Jawaharlal, *An Autobiography*, London, 1936.

——; *Glimpses of World History*, Bombay, 1945.

——; *The Discovery of India*, Calcutta, 1946.

——; *A Bunch of Old Letters*, Bombay, 1960.

Nevinson, Henry W., *The New Spirit in India*, Delhi, 1975.

Nomon, Mohammed, *Rise and Growth of All India Muslim League*, Allahabad, 1941.

——; *Muslim India*, Allahabad, 1942.

Nundy, Alfred; *Indian Unrest, 1919-20*, Dehradun, 1921.

O'Dwyer, Michael, *India As I Knew it, 1885-1925*, London, 1925.

Pal, B.C., *The Spirit of Indian Nationalism*, London, 1910.

——; *Nationality and Empire*, Calcutta, 1916.

——; *Non-Cooperation : Four Lectures*, Calcutta, 1920.

——; *Swaraj : The Goal and Way*, Madras, 1921.

——; *Swadeshi and Swaraj*, Calcutta, 1954.

Pande, B.N., *Nehru*, Delhi, 1977.

Panikkar, K.M., *The New Empire*, London, 1934.

Pardaman Singh, *Lord Minto and Indian Nationalism, 1905-1910*, Allahabad, 1976.

Parmanand, Bhai, *The Story of My Life*, Lahore, 1934.

Pavate T.V., *Bal Gangadhar Tilak*, Ahmedabad, 1958.

Patil, V.T., *Nehru and the Freedom Movement*, Delhi, 1977.

Paul, K.T., *The British Connection with India*, London, 1927.

Payne, Robert, *The Life and Death of Mahatma Gandhi*, London, 1969.

Polak, H.S., and others, *Mahatma Gandhi*, London, 1949.

Pole, D., Graham, *I Refer to India*, London, 1929.

——, *India in Transition*, London, 1932.

Prabodh Chandra, *Sixty Years of Congress*, Lahore, 1946.

Pradhan, R.G., *India's Struggle For Swaraj*, Madras, 1930.

Prasad, Rajendra, *Satyagraha in Champaran*, Ahmedabad, 1949.

——; *Autobiography*, Bombay, 1957.

——; *At the Feet of Mahatma Gandhi*, Bombay, 1961.

Price, Clair, *The Rebirth of Turkey*, New York, 1923.

Pylee, M.V., *Constitutional Government in India*, Bombay, 1965.

Raju, J.B., *A Critical Study of the Non-Cooperation Movement*, Nagpur, 1920.

Ram Rattan, *Gandhi's Concept of Political Obligation*, Calcutta, 1972.

Ramachandran G., *Promotion of Gandhian Philosophy*, Mysore, 1966.

Rao, C.V.H., *Civil Disobedience Movement in India or The Indian Struggle for Freedom*, Lahore, 1946.

Ray, Prithwis Chandra, *Life and Times of C.R. Das*, Calcutta, 1927.

Reading, Marquess of, Rufus Isaacs, *First Marquess of Reading*. vols. I and II, London, 1945.

Reynolds, Reginald, *The White Sahibs in India*, London, 1937.

Rivelt, Kenneth, *Economic Thought of Mahatma Gandhi*, Delhi, 1959.

Ronaldshay, Earl of, *The Life of Lord Curzon*, London, 1928.

Roy M.N., *One Year of Non-Cooperation from Ahmedabad to Gaya*, Calcutta, 1923.

——; *The Future of Indian Politics*, London, 1928.

Rutherford, V.H., *Modern India : Its Problems and Their Solution*, London, 1927.

Ruthnaswamy, M., *The Political Philosophy of Mr. Gandhi*, Madras, 1922.

Santhanam, K., *Gospel of Gandhi*, Bombay, 1967.

Sarkar, Sumit, *The Swadeshi Movement in Bengal, 1903-1908*, Delhi, 1973.

Shakir, Moin, *Khilafat to Pakistan*, Delhi, 1970.

Sharma, Bishan Swarup, *Gandhi As a Political Thinker*, Allahabad, 1956.

Sharp, Gene, *Gandhi Wields the Weapon of Moral Power*, Ahmedabad, 1960.

——, *The Politics of Non-Violent Action*, Boston, 1972.

Shridharani, K., *War Without Violence : A Study of Gandhi's Method and its Accomplishments*, New York, 1939.

Singh, Hira, Lal, *Problems and Politics of the British in India*, Bombay, 1963.

Singh, Sita Ram, *Nationalism and Social Reform in India*, Delhi, 1968.

Sitaramayya, B. Pattabhi, *History of the Indian National Congress, 1885-1935*, vol. I, Delhi, 1969.

Smith, W.C., *Modern Islam in India,* Lahore, 1947.

Smith W.R., *Nationalism and Reform in India*, London, 1973.

Speeches and Writings of Bal Gangadhar Tilak, Madras, n.d.

Spart, P., *Gandhism An Analysis,* Madras, 1932.

Street, C.J.C., *Lord Reading,* London, 1926.

Swinson, Arthur, *Six Minutes to Sunset,* London, 1964.

Sykes, Frederick, *From Many Angles : An Autobiography,* London, 1942.

Tara Chand, *History of Freedom Movement In India, vol. III,* Delhi, 1972.

Tendulkar, D.G., *Mahatma : Life of Mohandas Karamchand Gandhi,* vols. II and III, Delhi, 1961.

Thomson, Edward, *The Reconstruction of India*, London, 1930.

Vaswani, T.L., *Non-Cooperation and National Idealism,* Calcutta, 1921.

——, *India in Chains,* Madras, 1922.

Wasti, Syed Razi, *Lord Minto and the Indian Nationalist Movement, 1905 to 1910,* Oxford University Press, 1964.

Wint, Guy, *The British in Asia,* New York, 1954.

Wolpert, Stanley A., *Tilak and Gokhale,* California, 1962.

Woodruff, Philip, *The Men Who Ruled India,* London, 1974.

Woolacot, J.E., *Britain's Record in India,* London, 1927.

——, *India on Trial,* London, 1929.

——, *India The Truth,* London, 1930.

Yajnik, Indulal K., *Gandhi As I Know Him,* Delhi, 1943.

Zakaria, Rafiq, *Rise of Muslims in Indian Politics,* Bombay, 1970.

Index

S